W9-CCK-129

Stokes, Arch
Equal opportunity handbook
for hotels...

DATE DUE	JUL 28		
MAY 2 1983			
MAY 1990			
APR 28 1992			
FEB 15 1993			
DEC 18 1995			
NOV 4 1996			

The Equal Opportunity Handbook for Hotels, Restaurants, and Institutions

ARCH STOKES

CBI

CBI Publishing Company, Inc.
51 Sleeper Street, Boston, Massachusetts 02210

*For the beleaguered personnel professionals
who understand the true meaning of the phrase
"Too much sanity is madness."*

Library of Congress Cataloging in Publication Data

Stokes, Arch Y
    The equal opportunity handbook for hotels,
restaurants, and institutions.

    (Stokes employee relations series)
    1. Discrimination in employment—Law and
legislation—United States. 2. Hotels, taverns,
etc.—Law and legislation—United States. 3. Restaurants, lunch rooms, etc.—Law and legislation—
United States.
    I. Title. II. Series.
KF3464.S86   344'.73'012   79–859
    ISBN 0-8436-2148-X

Printed in the United States of America

Printing (*last digit*): 9 8 7 6 5 4 3 2 1

81850

Contents

APPENDICES

Foreword

It is a Herculean task to attack the morass of legislation affecting the employee, employer, and the business place.

In the last decade the author and others have attempted to give concise expression and definition to 200 years of legal shadowboxing with a basic tenet of the Constitution and Bill of Rights that "all men are created equal."

It is essentially true that laws are designed by attorneys—for attorneys—and frequently appear to dare understanding by others. It is difficult to distinguish between laws that satisfy a political system and laws that attack a social disease.

The need to understand both the law and human behavior are inextricably intertwined in the satisfaction of equal opportunity.

The laws governing equal opportunity represent a challenge. For the bigot, the challenge is circumvention. For the enlightened and lawful, the challenge is understanding and compliance.

Arch Stokes, attorney, knows the law. His analysis of the Equal Opportunity Law provides a useful guideline for understanding and compliance. Arch Stokes, writer, cares about achieving a result beyond comprehension and compliance with the law.

Rather than cursing the darkness of contradictory laws, overlapping laws, and verbose laws, the author lights one candle in the search for the preservation of human dignity.

Philip J. Lombardi
Vice-President, Industrial Relations
Hyatt Hotels Corporation
Chicago, Illinois

Preface

The author has delivered many entertaining and educational versions of his well-known speech "Too Much Sanity Is Madness" to organizations and meetings all over the United States. While the specifics, illustrations, and emphases may change from group to group and state to state, the theme remains the same—governmental overregulation of the business community.

Thus, Arch Stokes and CBI have collaborated to produce the *Stokes Employee Relations Series* of handbooks for hotels, restaurants, and institutions, which assist in implementing the only rational approach to this overregulated society—the practice of *preventive law.*

THE EQUAL OPPORTUNITY HANDBOOK FOR HOTELS, RESTAURANTS, AND INSTITUTIONS explains in everyday language one of the most expensive and litigious areas of the law.

The subject is extremely dynamic, constantly changing at all levels—federal, state, and local, as well as from the standpoint of regulations and judicial decisions. Therefore, professionals must assist to ensure competent implementation of *preventive law* policies, practices, and procedures.

CAVEAT: Equal Opportunity Laws change constantly, both through legislative action and judicial action. Accordingly, contact your attorney for specific questions, legal problems, and cases.

This HANDBOOK affords managers and personnel specialists the basics with which to create an ongoing program from the standpoint of Equal Opportunity Law.

CBI is privileged to continue this commitment to the industries it serves.

CBI PUBLISHING COMPANY, INC.

Acknowledgments

All handbooks in the *Stokes Employee Relations Series* published by CBI are products of my firm's commitment to the practice of preventive law. Thus, I acknowledge with appreciation the many progressive hospitality and foodservice companies, public assembly facilities, hospitals, and health-care centers, associations, clubs, and corporations in many industries which allow my firm the privilege of representing them.

I acknowledge with special appreciation the attorneys and staff of Stokes, Lazarus & Stokes who support me in all phases of the practice of law while I travel extensively.

I am deeply indebted to my two partners, Wayne H. Lazarus and Marion B. Stokes, III, authors themselves of a practical legal book, THE SELLER'S CREDIT GUIDE. I am also indebted to several of our associate attorneys: John H. "Chuck" Watson, Cynthia FitzGerald, and Terry Lamb. Members of our staff who have been helpful in the preparation of this book are Office Manager Norma Bridges, Barbara Taylor, Shirley LaBarge, Robin Hickam, and Michelle Braun.

Patricia, Jennifer, and Austin deserve special credit for unparalleled support during times of separation required by this project.

I am grateful to my mother and father, Bishop and Mrs. Mack B. Stokes, for fostering in me a desire to pursue excellence in all endeavors.

I acknowledge all my friends at CBI for their highly professional editing, publishing, and marketing of this book.

Norman Stanton, Gary Conger, Rebecca Handler, and Robin Riley have all exhibited the gracious professionalism illustrative of CBI's commitment to the industries it serves.

Arch Stokes
May 1979

I.

INTRODUCTION

"Who knows where madness lies; Perhaps to be too practical is madness; To surrender dreams—this may be madness; To seek treasure where there is only trash . . . ; Too much sanity may be madness; And maddest of all is to see life as it is and not as it should be."

—Miguel de Cervantes
DON QUIXOTE (1605)

1.

Overview

1-1.   Introduction

Throughout history minority groups have usually overcome discrimination and prejudice and upgraded their status by various means—from violence to social and legislative reform. In the last twenty years America has experienced a socio-economic upgrading of minorities not heretofore seen. This movement toward equal opportunity for all has been fostered, supported, and supplemented by social action, legislation, executive decree, and judicial pronouncements.

The most significant impact of this development on the hospitality and foodservice industries has come from governmental regulations. This behemoth called government is permeating the hospitality and foodservice industries to an extent unparalleled in our 200-year history, and, in fact, is reaching a point of infringement that may be inconsistent with free enterprise.

The mere growth of government is astounding. Government payrolls now total almost one-quarter of all payrolls in the United States. Government spending is growing faster than almost any other aspect of our economy. For example, the Gross National Product (GNP) of the federal government is almost 40 percent of the nation's total GNP. This government spending represents many times the combined, after-tax profits of all U.S. corporations.

Spending by major regulatory agencies is also increasing at staggering rates. For instance, in 1970 there were about twelve major federal regulatory agencies which spent approximately $1.4 billion. In 1975 there were seventeen such agencies, spending about $4.3 billion. Thus, spending tripled in only five years.

The mere growth of paper is unbelievable. Dealing with the government—complying with government regulations, etc.— might be referred to as "the great paper exchange." Again, looking at the period from 1970 to 1975, the number of pages in the Code of Federal Regulations jumped over 30 percent, from 54,000 to 72,000 pages.

Most experts estimate that executives now spend 25 percent to 50 percent of their time simply dealing with government. One prominent company quantified its annual costs of excessive government regulation at over $50 million a year.

With increasing government involvement, the acronyms of government have become household words. We are all familiar with the EEOC, NLRB, OSHA, EPA, OFCCP, SEC, FTC, and others.

Governmental agencies regulate more money and people than any other arm of our society. Those of us specializing in labor and employee relations law feel that much of this government regulation is inordinately directed at the personnel and labor relations policies, practices, and procedures of the hospitality, foodservice, convention, and institutional businesses.

Since "too much sanity is madness," it is fitting and proper that the purpose of this book is the study of Equal Opportunity Law as it applies to hotels, restaurants, and institutions.

1-2.   EEOC

The United States Equal Employment Opportunity Commission (EEOC) and the various state and local Equal Opportunity or Fair Employment Practice agencies are obvious examples of this meteoric governmental growth.

In 1966, moreover, the EEOC had an annual budget of about $10 million and received some 9,000 charges of discrimination. In 1977 the budget had increased sevenfold to over

$70 million dollars and approximately 70,000 new charges of discrimination were filed, not including a backlog of more than 130,000 cases. From 1972 to 1979 the size of the EEOC General Counsel's staff rose from about 60 to more than 500.

Worse, the EEOC itself was sued for discrimination—and lost! Several districts of the EEOC have been accused by another agency, the General Accounting Office (GAO), of ineptitude, inefficiency, and waste.

Recently, the EEOC has increased its influence tremendously by becoming *the* responsible agency for the enforcement of the Equal Pay Act of 1963 and the Age Discrimination in Employment Act of 1967, among other new duties. Fortunately, this new jurisdiction has coincided with new, experienced management and updated procedures which may help all parties.

The creation of the EEOC and related state and local administrative agencies seeking to right the wrongs of discrimination have resulted in a new area of the law, often referred to as Equal Opportunity Law, Discrimination Law, Civil Rights Law, Fair Employment Practice Law, and so forth (hereafter sometimes referred to as Equal Opportunity Law).

Equal Opportunity Law is that area of the law which includes all federal, state, and local laws, statutes, ordinances, regulations, and case decisions dealing with fair employment practices and all forms of discrimination in employment and public accommodations. As complicated as many try to make Equal Opportunity Law, it can be described in a nutshell as follows:

Employers must always endeavor to select the best qualified individual for the job based upon job-related qualifications, and regardless of race, color, creed, sex, national origin, age, or handicap.

1-3.   Protected Groups

The list of "protected groups" has expanded dramatically in recent years to approximately *thirty*. They include the following:

Affectional Preference	National Origin
Age	Personal Appearance
Ancestry	Physical Disability
Arrest	Physical Handicap
Color	Place of Birth
Creed	Political Affiliation
Equal Pay	Pregnancy
Family Responsibilities	Public Assistance Status
Faulty Eyesight	Race
Height	Religion
Hemoglobin C Trait	Religious Creed
Medical Condition	Retaliation
Marital Status	Sex
Matriculation	Sexual Orientation
Mental Handicap	Unfavorable Military Discharge
Military Service Liability	Weight
National Guard Service	

Thus, one can see that this area of the law has developed into one of the most fertile grounds for litigation. Equal Opportunity Law cases represent more than 10 percent of all pending civil cases in the federal courts.

Additionally, the law is peculiarly applicable to the hospitality and foodservice industries due to a high degree of turnover, transience, and mobility of the work force. Hotels, motels, restaurants, hospitals, clubs, institutional foodservice establishments, public assembly facilities, and health-care centers, all have a high incidence of employment discrimination cases, both administrative and judicial.

1-4.   Reaction of Employees and Employers

The reaction of employees adversely affected by employment practices has been to file an increasing number of discrimination charges and lawsuits. Some of these actions are legitimate attempts to correct injustices, such as a sex discrimination case for unlawful refusal to hire a waitress at a fine restaurant at night.

On the other hand, the ease with which an employee can "file" discrimination charges and lawsuits coupled with the myriad of "protected groups" have encouraged such frivolous claims of discrimination as Ms. Cooperman's judicial attempt to "neuterize" her name to become "Cooperperson." A female *clarinetist* accused a city of sex discrimination when she was refused a position on the all-male city *drum and bugle* corps.

The reaction of companies attempting to avoid violations of Equal Opportunity Law and to reduce the rising number of administrative charges of discrimination has been similar—from the progressive to the bizarre.

On the one hand, reasonable approaches toward affirmative equal opportunity have been adopted without resulting in discrimination for or against anyone. At the extreme, however, some employers have seen fit to discriminate in favor of one group at the expense of another by establishing quotas. Furthermore, there have been mass attempts at "neuterizing" and "executizing" job titles and classifications, apparently in the hope that more cosmetics will eliminate substantive discrimination. Hence, we have the absurd example of the powder room maid (generally regarded as both a sexist and racist classification) being neuterized to become "washroom attendant," only later to be "executized" to become the "head of the center for pressure relief" or the "director of seating arrangements."

Other employers and unions have gone to the extreme of "neuterizing," "executizing," and "dehumanizing" job titles. For instance, "bellboy" and "pageboy" were subjected to this process to become "bell-packer" and "page combination"— which sounds like either a sandwich or a football play! One should not allow extreme interpretations of the law to produce a dehumanizing of the employee who performs that job.

There are numerous improvements to be made, including reclassificaton of job titles. However, one should not take the "hospitality" out of the hospitality business by allowing a supposedly "legal interpretation" to result in arbitrary destruction of years of nondiscriminatory and hospitable traditions.

2.

History

2-1. Early Development

No law can be read in a vacuum. Laws are interpreted according to their application to the facts in the case at hand. Therefore, while basic legal principles are generally applicable regardless of the industry affected, the "holding" of any case necessarily includes the facts and the result. Thus, one must examine how a particular law affects a particular industry.

Since hoteliers, restaurateurs, caterers, tavern keepers, innkeepers, and the like have been subjected to increasingly high standards of care and duties to guests, patrons, members of the general public, and employees, it is important to appreciate the special way in which any law affects hotels, restaurants, and institutions.

In 1975, for instance, $6.3 million was awarded a plaintiff for personal injuries, including paralysis, incurred after diving off a poorly constructed diving board at a Washington, D.C. hotel.

Because the standards of care in personal injury and negligence cases are high due to the quasi-public nature of innkeeping, Equal Opportunity Law has been applied with increasing scrutiny and breadth to hotels and restaurants.

Inns and taverns have existed for thousands of years. Their development into the modern luxury hotel of today is an essential ingredient in understanding how any law impacts the hospitality business.

The history of inns in Great Britain reflects the traveler's need for food, shelter, and protection, particularly during the fifteenth and sixteenth centuries. The law developed accordingly, requiring innkeepers to protect guests from personal injuries and property losses to a greater degree than most retail businesses. For example, travelers in medieval England were so often subjected to highwaymen, and very literally, to "sandbagging," that the law imposed a duty upon the innkeeper to receive guests and to protect them.

Obviously one of the earliest reported factual situations was the refusal to receive Mary and Joseph because *there was no room at the inn.* While this has always been a defense to an unlawful-refusal-to-receive-a-guest lawsuit, an innkeeper must establish clearly that there actually was no room at his establishment.

2-2.   Public & Quasi-Public Duties—A Foreshadowing

The public and quasi-public duties of hoteliers and restaurateurs clearly established a foreshadowing of legal liabilities and standards of the future.

Innkeepers were prohibited from refusing guests except for specific reasons, such as communicable disease, insufficient funds, boisterous conduct, no room at the inn, the guest's notorious or infamous character, and others. However, cases did not uniformly hold that an innkeeper could refuse someone because of his/her race, color, creed, sex, national origin, age, or handicap for that reason alone.

Even though the public accommodations section of the Civil Rights Act of 1964, Title II, was direly needed, it appears that case law would have supported a plaintiff in an unlawful-refusal-to-receive-a-guest case against an innkeeper who based such refusal upon race alone. *A fortiori,* it is clear such would have been the case today in light of the various actions brought by women not protected by Title II.

Thus, the laws of innkeepers developed to require equality of treatment, as well as a duty not to discriminate in which guests to receive, absent certain exceptional situations. Therefore, hundreds of years ago, hoteliers, and to a great degree restaurateurs, were required by case law to be nondiscriminatory in public accommodations.

While this development did not specifically deal with the employer-employee relationship, the foreshadowing of nondiscrimination in all aspects of public and quasi-public innkeeping was established earlier in this industry than in any other.

In sum, an attitude of nondiscrimination with respect to the receipt of guests is inherent in the very nature of innkeeping and catering.

3.

Public Accommodations

3-1.   Title II, Civil Rights Act of 1964

For centuries hoteliers have been under a common law duty to receive all guests who seek accommodations. However, it was not until the civil rights movement of the 1960s that the need was felt for a specific statute requiring hotels, motels, restaurants, convention centers, theatres, hospitals, and so forth, not to discriminate against those who seek accommodations. Why? *Well, just as an innkeeper's common law duty to receive all guests who seek accommodations was hundreds of years old, so was a pervasive form of racial discrimination.* Recall Rosa Parks' refusal to sit at the rear of the bus—in blatant violation of Alabama's segregation laws—and how that black woman's action in December 1955 prompted the passage of the Civil Rights Act nine years hence.

While hoteliers were required not to discriminate against guests who sought accommodations, nineteenth-century cases did allow them to furnish "separate but equal" accommodations to blacks. However, late in the nineteenth and early twentieth centuries, many states started to enact statutes prohibiting discrimination in places of public accommodation because of race, creed, color, or national origin. Despite these state statutes and a trend toward truly nondiscriminatory treatment of guests, the civil rights movement of the 1960s prompted the enactment of Title II of the Civil Rights Act of 1964, proscribing discrimination in accommodations on account of race, color, religion, or natural origin.

A violation of Title II can result in a private lawsuit or an action instituted by the Attorney General of the United States for an injunction prohibiting such violation, as well as attorney's fees and court costs. The constitutionality of Title II was upheld in the case of *Heart of Atlanta Motel* v. *United States,* where the United States Supreme Court unanimously stated that Congress could statutorily prohibit racial discrimination by hotels and motels.

3-2. Constitutional Right to Travel

Again, in the late sixties and early seventies, the Supreme Court of the United States began to recognize a "constitutional right to travel." The increased travel and mobility of citizens made it obvious that the law should protect transients from discriminatory treatment, e.g., onerous residency eligibility requirements.

In a series of cases involving residency requirements for various licenses, admission to practice law, voting rights, welfare eligibility, and so on, the Supreme Court upheld a constitutional right to travel, as balanced against a state's interest in favorable treatment to those who have made a commitment to the local community. Thus, most residency requirements for various rights and benefits were struck down unless they were of short duration or patently reasonable.

The impact of this development upon the hospitality and foodservice industries is obvious. With a greater recognition of the mobility and transience of the American public has developed an expanded duty to eliminate discriminatory treatment in public accommodations.

3-3. Sex

Title II of the Civil Rights Act of 1964 does not specifically prohibit discrimination in public accommodations on *account of sex.* However, the definite trend of the law is to protect women from refusal to receive or accommodate on account of their sex.

The more recent cases confirm that a woman (or a man) states a claim for relief when she (or he) accuses a hotelier or a restaurateur of discriminating in public accommodations on account of sex.

Example: How many hotels, restaurants, lounges, taverns, nightclubs, bars, etc., have had policies of asking an unaccompanied female who seeks service, "Are you alone?" It is probably grounds for a meritorious lawsuit for an employer in these industries to maintain a policy of refusing service to unaccompanied females. It is this author's strong warning that such a policy is not only economically unproductive, it is legally dangerous—and obviously against the overwhelming weight of social trends.

No state law to date protects individuals from discrimination in public accommodations on account of sexual orientation, homosexuality, bisexuality, transsexuality, transvestitism, etc. There are, however, a few city and local ordinances which do prohibit discrimination against homosexuals in public accommodations.

It appears that the current conservative trend in the courts, and among the public in general, will mitigate against liberalizing state Equal Opportunity Laws in public accommodations from the standpoint of sexual orientation.

On the other hand, as a practical matter, hoteliers and restaurateurs are apolitical from the standpoint of who their guests and patrons are. They generally do not care about a guest's or patron's politics, much less their personal proclivities. While the hospitality and foodservice industries have been confronting the question of discrimination on various grounds in public accommodations for hundreds of years, the development of Equal Employment Opportunity Laws is of very recent vintage. Furthermore, it has become the most expensive aspect of labor and employee relations in these industries.

HOTELS AND RESTAURANTS SHOULD NOT DISCRIMINATE IN PUBLIC ACCOMMODATIONS ON ACCOUNT OF SEX

4.

Equal Employment Opportunity Laws

"A Constitution is made for people of funda-mentally differing views."

—Justice Oliver Wendell Holmes

4-1. Early Laws and Civil Rights Acts

Fifth Amendment to the U.S. Constitution (ratified 1791)
No person shall . . . be deprived of life, liberty or property, without due process of law . . . "

While no federal statute specifically implements the Fifth Amendment, this amendment provides a direct claim for relief against federal deprivation of individual rights, or against joint participation by states with unconstitutional federal activity.

Thirteenth Amendment to the U.S. Constitution (ratified 1865)
Section 1. Neither slavery nor involuntary servitude, except as a punish-ment for crime whereof the parties shall have been duly convicted, shall exist within the United States, or any place subject to their jurisdiction.

Section 2. Congress shall have the power to enforce this Article by appropriate legislation.

Obviously, slavery or involuntary servitude is unconstitu-tional. Employers should note that while actions under the Thirteenth Amendment are rare, they are by no means ex-tinct. Working conditions which have the impact of creating a "servitude status" could be considered violative of the Thirteenth Amendment.

The Civil Rights Act of 1866 (42 U.S.C., § 1981)
All persons within the jurisdiction of the United States shall have the same right in every State and Territory to make and enforce contracts . . . as is employed by white citizens.

The Thirteenth Amendment and Section 1981 generally prohibit racial discrimination only. However, while the Thirteenth Amendment and the Civil Rights Act of 1866 are inapplicable to sex discrimination, they have been held to cover discrimination because of alienage and even national origin.

Generally, Section 1981 is a concurrent remedy with Title VII of the Civil Rights Act for employment discrimination on account of race.

Fourteenth Amendment, U.S. Constitution (ratified 1868)
Section 1. . . . No State shall make or enforce any law which shall abridge the privileges or immunities of citizens of the United States; nor shall any state deprive any person of life, liberty or property, *without due process of law*; nor deny to any person within its jurisdiction *the equal protection of the laws.*

Section. 5. The Congress shall have power to enforce, by appropriate legislation, the provisions of this article. (Emphasis added.)

Obviously, the Fourteenth Amendment can be interpreted to apply to almost any form of discrimination and protected group.

The Equal Protection Clause of the Fourteenth Amendment affords individuals equality of treatment under the law if there is some form of "state action" involved in the case.

Example: Seidenberg v. *McSorley's Old Ale House, Inc.*, 308 F. Supp. 1253 (S.D.N.Y. 1969), found that the National Organization for Women [NOW] stated a valid claim for relief when it accused a bar of discriminating against women by catering only to men for more than a hundred years. Since a state alcoholic beverage license was required to sell and distribute alcoholic beverages at the bar, the policy of excluding women constituted "state action" within the meaning of the Fourteenth Amendment.

Thus, while this case involved public accommodations

rather than employment practices, employers should be advised that discriminatory actions of all kinds may be considered unconstitutional.

The Civil Rights Act of 1871 (42 U.S.C., § 1983)
Every person who, under color of any statute, ordinance, regulation, custom, or usage of any State or Territory, subjects, or causes to be subjected, any citizen . . . to the deprivation of any rights, privileges, or immunities secured by the Constitution and laws, shall be liable to the person . . . .

The Fourteenth Amendment and Section 1983 apply to sex as well as national origin discrimination. Sex-based classifications have been subjected to the same stringent standard of review as race cases under the Fourteenth Amendment.

Hence, not only are there old cases, customs, and prohibitions against discrimination found in the laws of innkeeping, there has been for more than a hundred years ample statutory authority prohibiting discrimination in the United States.

4-2. Categories of Discrimination

Since English common law did not specifically protect individual groups from employment discrimination, almost all specific prohibitions against this form of discrimination are contained in statutes and implementing regulations. The interpretive case law of these statutes and implementing regulations make Equal Opportunity Law more complicated, since judges are prone to decide cases on an *ad hoc* rather than legislative basis. While this is the only proper way to pursue justice in any lawsuit, it does breed inconsistencies and exceptions.

Example: In Regents of the University of California v. *Bakke,* (June 28, 1978), the Supreme Court held that Allan Bakke was unlawfully denied admission to the University of California Medical School at Davis on account of his Caucasian race, since a minority admissions program reserving sixteen places for minorities was held unconstitutional as violative of the Equal Protection Clause of the Fourteenth Amendment; several Supreme Court Justices opined it was violative of Title VI of the Civil Rights Act of 1964. On the other hand, while the majority (5–4) ruled in favor of Bakke's admission, there was ample authority to support the consideration of race as a factor in any admissions program and indirectly for affirmative action programs in employment.

In addition to statutes, the Fourteenth Amendment of the United States Constitution states that "no state shall . . . deny to any person within its jurisdiction the equal protection of the laws." Accordingly, when a state establishes some form of discriminatory treatment, it is possibly violative of the Equal Protection Clause of the Fourteenth Amendment of the Constitution.

Example: State protective laws requiring employers to discriminate in favor of women with respect to wages and hours, have frequently been ruled unconstitutional as violative of the Equal Protection Clause.

While Equal Opportunity Laws were fostered primarily by racial discrimination against blacks, the categories of protected groups generally include the following: race, color, creed, sex, national origin, age, or handicap. However, the list of protected groups, as indicated in the introduction, includes almost any category imaginable and is growing regularly.

To date, moreover, there are approximately *thirty* separate protected groups under various state Equal Opportunity Laws. Section 1–3 lists these groups.

4–3.   Labor Laws

While Chapter 14 of this book covers the subject more specifically, employers should be aware that every federal labor law has been interpreted to prohibit discrimination against individuals on account of union preference or status. The *Railway Labor Act of 1926* covers this subject as it relates to railroads and airlines.

The *National Labor Relations Act,* or *Wagner Act of 1935,* as amended by the *Labor Management Relations Act,* or *Taft-Hartley Act of 1947,* and the *Labor-Management Reporting and Disclosure Act,* or *Landrum-Griffin Act of 1954,* prohibit unequal treatment on account of an employee's union preference or status.

Obviously, *right-to-work laws* prohibiting compulsory unionism also protect employees from being required to join a union in order to maintain their employment. (*See* Chapter 14.)

4-4.   Recent Equal Opportunity Laws and Agencies—
The Age of Acronyms

Since 1963 employers have been deluged with statutes, regulations, ordinances, and judicial decisions proscribing various forms of discrimination. This section summarizes a few of those statutes and agencies implementing the laws.

THE EQUAL PAY ACT OF 1963 (EQUAL PAY PROVISIONS OF THE FAIR LABOR STANDARDS ACT OF 1938, AS AMENDED). One of the first significant Equal Opportunity Laws is the Equal Pay Act of 1963, which requires that employees must receive *equal pay for equal work,* regardless of sex, if the work they perform is equal in skill, effort, and responsibility, and performed under similar working conditions.

The Equal Pay Act was actually an amendment, and, therefore, a provision of the Federal Wage & Hour Law, the Fair Labor Standards Act of 1938, as amended. From 1963 through June 30, 1979, the Equal Pay Act was administered by the Wage & Hour Division, Employment Standards Administration, United States Department of Labor. (*See* Chapter 12, THE WAGE & HOUR HANDBOOK FOR HOTELS, RESTAURANTS, AND INSTITUTIONS.) As of July 1, 1979, the Equal Pay Act is administered by the United States Equal Employment Opportunity Commission (EEOC).

While equal pay problems are often lumped with "sex discrimination," the statute is quite precise, and the jobs must be substantially similar within the meaning of the requirements of the statute.

MILITARY SELECTIVE SERVICE ACT (VETERANS RE-EMPLOYMENT RIGHTS, SECTION 9). This statute is implemented by the Office of Veterans Re-Employment Rights

(OVRR) of the United States Department of Labor and protects returning veterans from being discriminated against because of such service. There are various reemployment rights in terms of seniority, vacations, pensions, promotions, job position, dismissals, and other categories, which a veteran is entitled to under this act.

TITLE VII, CIVIL RIGHTS ACT OF 1964 (42 U.S.C. § 2000e ET SEQ.). This is the most significant Equal Opportunity Law ever enacted by Congress. It prohibits discrimination in employment on the basis of race, color, religion, sex, pregnancy, or national origin. It is implemented by the EEOC which, since 1972, has had the authority to file suit against employers who violate Title VII.

Additionally, the EEOC is empowered under Title VII to promulgate regulations, issue opinions, conduct investigations, process charges of discrimination, and make "determinations" as to whether there is reasonable cause to believe that an employer has discriminated against an employee on account of race, color, religion, sex, pregnancy, or national origin.

There are more employment discrimination cases filed under Title VII of the Civil Rights Act than all others combined.

Almost all hotels, motels, restaurants, foodservice institutions, public assembly facilities, hospitals, health-care centers, etc., are covered by Title VII. Private and public employers must have fifteen or more employees, as well as *affect interstate commerce,* to be subject to Title VII. Obviously, almost all hospitality and foodservice facilities *affect interstate commerce.*

The prohibitions of Title VII against discrimination in employment practices include *all* employment practices, e.g., selection, referral, promotion, transfer, demotions, discipline, dismissal, and separation.

Labor unions and employment agencies are also covered by Title VII.

Generally, if a particular state Equal Opportunity Law prohibits employment discrimination and provides the same remedies as Title VII, the EEOC will defer to the state or local agency until that agency has had an opportunity to process the charge of discrimination. Therefore, it is important to become familiar with state law, as well as the federal Equal Opportunity Law.

AGE DISCRIMINATION IN EMPLOYMENT ACT OF 1967. Pursuant to amendment effective January 1, 1979, the Age Discrimination in Employment Act of 1967 prohibits discrimination in employment against persons between the ages of forty (40) and seventy (70). Please note that various state Equal Opportunity Laws have eliminated a maximum age limitation, e.g., California and Washington.

Between 1967 and June 30, 1979, the Age Discrimination Act was enforced by the Wage & Hour Division of the U.S. Department of Labor. (*See* Chapter 13, THE WAGE & HOUR HANDBOOK FOR HOTELS, RESTAURANTS, AND INSTITUTIONS.) As of July 1, 1979, the Age Discrimination Act is enforced by the EEOC.

VOCATIONAL REHABILITATION ACT OF 1973. If the hospitality or foodservice facility is considered a government contractor or subcontractor, its employees or prospective job applicants are protected from discrimination on account of mental or physical disability under the Vocational Rehabilitation Act of 1973.

This act is enforced by the Office of Federal Contract Compliance Programs (OFCCP) of the United States Department of Labor.

VIETNAM-ERA VETERAN'S READJUSTMENT ASSISTANCE ACT OF 1974. Employers with government contracts and/or subcontracts must engage in affirmative efforts to provide employment for disabled veterans and veterans of the Vietnam era.

This statute is enforced by the OFCCP of the U.S. Department of Labor.

EXECUTIVE ORDER 11246 (32 C.F.R. § 173). This presidential order, implemented by the OFCCP, prohibits employment discrimination by employers with federal contracts or subcontracts of $10,000 or more.

Executive Order 11246 requires equal employment opportunity and affirmative action by contractors and subcontractors with the federal government.

Many hotels, motels, restaurants, foodservice institutions, public assembly facilities, hospitals, health-care facilities, etc., are government contractors or subcontractors according to the OFCCP, regardless of whether there is an actual written contract to this effect. (*See* Chapters 19 and 20.)

4-5. Private Agencies and Organizations

In addition to becoming familiar with various governmental administrative agencies such as the EEOC, NLRB, Wage & Hour Division, OFCCP, OSHA, and OVRR, hospitality and foodservice companies should be aware of numerous private agencies and organizations that have an impact on Equal Opportunity Law and lawsuits.

It is advisable to become familiar with local chapters and offices of various private agencies and organizations active in equal opportunity cases.

Example: The National Association for the Advancement of Colored People (NAACP), The American Civil Liberties Union (ACLU), National Organization for Women (NOW), The Urban League, Common Cause, Coyote, National Right-to-Work Committee, gay liberation organizations, significant committees of the Republican and Democratic parties, Chambers of Commerce, and so forth, all have taken significant positions on various aspects of Equal Opportunity Law, both publicly and in the courts.

Additionally, labor unions consistently take positions on Equal Opportunity Law relevant to employers.

Employers should appreciate that Equal Opportunity Law is not only dynamic but political by its very nature. Since hoteliers and restaurateurs are generally apolitical with respect to guests and patrons, it is generally advisable to be likewise with respect to employees. Hospitality and foodservice facilities are inherently public or quasi-public. Thus, their actions are subject to public scrutiny to a greater degree than other types of employers.

Example: Since 1978 NOW and various other women's organizations in favor of the Equal Rights Amendment have advocated that associations boycott those cities in states which had refused to ratify the Equal Rights Amendment.

Example: Whether an employer is a government contractor or subcontractor, or regards himself/herself as such, that fact is economically irrelevant to the conventioneer who demands a demonstration of equal opportunity in employment practices before agreeing to stay at that particular hotel or motel.

Therefore, hoteliers and restaurateurs and managers of public assembly facilities, in particular, must be acutely appreciative of how Equal Opportunity Law is interlaced—legally, attitudinally, and economically—with the very fabric of hospitality and foodservice to guests and patrons.

II.
JURISDICTION, PROCEDURE, AND ADMINISTRATION

"Jarndyce and Jarndyce drones on. This scarecrow of a suit has, in the course of time, become so complicated, that no man alive knows what it means. The parties to it understand it least; but it has been observed that no two Chancery lawyers can talk about it for five minutes, without coming to a total disagreement as to all the premises. Innumerable children have been borne into the cause; innumerable young people have married into it; innumerable old people have died out of it. Scores of persons have deliriously found themselves made parties in Jarndyce and Jarndyce, without knowing how or why. Whole families have inherited legendary hatreds with the suit. The little plaintiff or defendant, who was promised a new rockinghorse when Jarndyce and Jarndyce should be settled, has grown up, possessed himself of a real horse, and trotted away into the other world. Fair wards of court have faded into mothers and grandmothers; a long procession of Chancellors has come in and gone out; the legion of bills in the suit have been transformed into mere bills of mortality; there are not three Jarndyces left upon the earth perhaps, since old Tom Jarndyce in

*despair blew his brains out at a coffee house
in Chancery Lane; but Jarndyce and Jarndyce
still drags its dreary length before the Court,
perennially hopeless."*

–Charles Dickens
BLEAK HOUSE (1853)

5.

Jurisdiction and Coverage

5-1. Introduction

The typical sex discrimination lawsuit filed in Federal Court takes approximately five (5) years from the date of the allegedly unlawful employment practice, e.g., discharge, refusal to hire, etc., until final adjudication by the United States Court of Appeals reviewing the U.S. District Judge's decision. The total cost in legal fees and expenses, inclusive of the lost management time and productivity, is approximately $50,000.

While in the United States we do not have the delays of justice to the extent of those satirized by Charles Dickens in his account of "Jarndyce and Jarndyce," the time and expense of employers is so great that many cases are settled simply because of short-range economic consideration. This is particularly true of hotels, motels, restaurants, institutions, public assembly facilities, etc., since these facilities are constantly attempting to achieve good gross operating profits (GOP) on a monthly basis. The legal fees alone in defending an employment discrimination case will have a substantial impact on a property's GOP.

However, employers should understand the procedures and administration connected with employment discrimination charges and cases in order to be able to cope with this administrative and judicial onslaught, as well as to formulate successful *preventive law* policies.

While the typical discrimination lawsuit does not compare to the famous *Sontoni* case, which lasted from 1830 to 1975, or to the longest recorded case in Poonca, India, which lasted from 1205 to 1966, it nevertheless involves a Herculean effort to defend competently a discrimination lawsuit. Thus, one must consider jurisdiction and coverage, as well as administration and procedure, in connection with how Equal Opportunity Law affects hospitality, foodservice, and institutional businesses.

Generally, almost every hotel, motel, restaurant, inn, tavern, bar, lounge, foodservice facility, hospital, health-care center, public assembly facility, stadium, auditorium, etc., is covered by some federal or state law, regulation, local ordinance, judicial decision, or ruling—embodied in Equal Opportunity Law.

There are basic jurisdictional and coverage criteria that must be established before an employer has to comply with any particular statute. However, it is a rare case when a hospitality or foodservice facility, or related institutional operation, is not covered by Equal Opportunity Law. Therefore, the material in the next section of this chapter includes a brief summary of general rules concerning jurisdiction and coverage under federal law.

5-2.   Federal Laws

Once it is established that the employer affects *interstate commerce,* generally there is jurisdiction and coverage. However, some statutes specifically require a set number of employees before the employer is subject to the federal law. For example, one must employ fifteen (15) or more employees to be covered by Title VII of the Civil Rights Act of 1964. One must employ twenty-five (25) or more employees to be covered by the Age Discrimination in Employment Act of 1967.

Since the threshold number of employees is normally not a great jurisdictional impediment, it is difficult for a hospitality or foodservice employer to claim it is not covered by Equal Opportunity Law.

Since the question of jurisdiction is whether a particular court has power to rule over the dispute before it, generally federal district courts have jurisdiction over employment discrimination cases involving hotels, motels, restaurants, public assembly facilities, hospitals, health care centers, and so forth.

Note: Title VII specifically exempts "a bona fide membership club which is exempt from taxation" under the Internal Revenue Code. While a private membership club may be exempt from Title VII, a race, color, or national origin lawsuit may be brought against a club under Section 1981. Furthermore, there is increasing authority that private membership clubs may be sued for employment discrimination on account of other protected groups.

Thus, the EEOC generally has jurisdiction to process employment discrimination charges against employers in the hospitality and foodservice industries on the basis of race, color, creed, sex, national origin, and equal-pay-for-equal-work claims.

On the other hand, whether an employer is subject to affirmative action plan requirements of the OFCCP depends upon whether the employer is a government contractor or subcontractor. (*See* Chapters 19 and 20.) Briefly, most luxury, convention hotels do enough business with the federal government and/or government contractors to be subject to the OFCCP and the statutes it implements.

5-3. Selected State Laws

Every state except Mississippi has some form of state Equal Opportunity Law. While the variety of protected groups or categories varies from state to state, again, these state Equal Opportunity Laws generally prohibit discrimination on the basis of race, color, creed, sex, national origin, age, or handicap. One should become familiar with the specific groups protected under the applicable state Equal Opportunity Law. The following discussion merely illustrates the variety of protected groups under state laws. (*See* Section 5-6 for a chart of every state's Equal Opportunity Laws, including protected categories, the required number of employees for jurisdiction, and the name of the responsible state agency; and Appendix B for a summary of each state's Equal Opportunity Laws.)

ARIZONA

The Arizona Civil Rights Division of the Department of Law functions as the state agency enforcing Arizona Equal Opportunity Law prohibiting discrimination in employment because of race, color, religion, sex, or national origin, and discrimination in public accommodations because of race, color, creed, national origin, or ancestry.

CALIFORNIA

California's Equal Opportunity Law is enforced by the Division of Fair Employment Practices of the California Department of Industrial Relations. The Fair Employment Practice Commission functions much the same as the EEOC.

The California Fair Employment Practice Law forbids private and public employers, employment agencies, and unions from discrimination in employment because of race, color, national origin, medical condition, ancestry, sex, pregnancy, age (age 40 and up), religious creed, physical handicap, and marital status.

California, like many states, has promulgated an extensive *Guide to Pre-employment Inquiries,* reproduced opposite for illustrative purposes.

HAWAII

The Hawaii Department of Labor and Industrial Relations enforces the state Equal Opportunity Law which prohibits discrimination in employment on the basis of race, sex, age, religion, color, ancestry, physical handicap, marital status, or arrest and court record (which does not have a substantial relationship to the functions and responsibilities of the prospective or continued employment).

It should be noted that Hawaii Equal Opportunity Law also prohibits employers from requiring an employee to submit to a polygraph or lie detector test as a condition of employment or continued employment. As a matter of fact, the violation of this antipolygraph law is subject to a fine of not more than $1,000 or imprisonment of not more than one year, or both.

State of California
FAIR EMPLOYMENT PRACTICE ACT
Guide to Pre-employment Inquiries

Acceptable Pre-employment Inquiries	Subject	Unacceptable Pre-employment Inquiries
"Have you worked for this company under a different name?" "Have you ever been convicted of a crime under another name?"	NAME	Former name of applicant whose name has been changed by court order or otherwise*
Applicant's place of residence How long applicant has been resident of this State or City	ADDRESS OR DURATION OF RESIDENCE	
"Can you, after employment, submit a birth certificate or other proof of US citizenship or age?"	BIRTHPLACE	Birthplace of applicant Birthplace of applicant's parents, spouse or other relatives Requirement that applicant submit a birth certificate naturalization or baptismal record†
"Can you, after employment, submit a work permit if under eighteen?" "Are you over eighteen years of age?" "If hired, can you furnish proof of age?" /or/ Statement that hire is subject to verification that applicant's age meets legal requirements.	AGE	Questions which tend to identify applicants over 40 years of age.
	RELIGIOUS	Applicant's religious denomination or affiliation, church, parish, pastor, or religious holidays observed "Do you attend religious services /or/ a house of worship?" Applicant may not be told "This is a Catholic/ Protestant/Jewish/atheist organization."

Acceptable Pre-employment Inquiries	Subject	Unacceptable Pre-employment Inquiries
Statement by employer of regular days, hours or shift to be worked	WORK DAYS AND SHIFTS	
	RACE OR COLOR	Complexion, color of skin, or other questions directly or indicating race or color
Statement that photograph may be required after employment	PHOTOGRAPH	Requirement that applicant affix a photograph to his application form Request applicant, at his option, to submit photograph Requirement of photograph after interview but before hiring†
"If you are not a U.S. citizen, have you the legal right to remain permanently in the U.S.? Do you intend to remain permanently in the U.S.?" Statement by employer that if hired, applicant may be required to submit proof of citizenship	CITIZENSHIP	"Are you a U.S. citizen?" Whether applicant or his parents or spouse are naturalized or native-born United States citizens Date when applicant or parents or spouse acquired U.S. citizenship Requirement that applicant produce his naturalization papers or first papers† Whether applicant's parents or spouse are citizens of the U.S.
Languages applicant reads, speaks or writes fluently	NATIONAL ORIGIN OR ANCESTRY	Applicant's nationality, lineage, ancestry, national origin, descent or parentage Date of arrival in United States or port of entry; how long a resident Nationality of applicant's parents or spouse; maiden name of applicant's wife or mother Language commonly used by applicant. "What is your mother tongue?" How applicant acquired ability to read, write or speak a foreign language

Acceptable Pre-employment Inquiries	Subject	Unacceptable Pre-employment inquiries
Applicant's academic, vocational, or professional education; schools attended	EDUCATION	Date last attended high school
Applicant's work experience Applicant's military experience in armed forces of United States, in a state militia (US), or in a particular branch of US armed forces	EXPERIENCE	Applicant's military experience (general) Type of military discharge
"Have you ever been convicted of any crime?" If so, when, where, and disposition of case?	CHARACTER	"Have you ever been arrested?"
Names of applicant's relatives already employed by this company Name and address of parent or guardian if applicant is a minor	RELATIVES	Marital status or number of dependents Name or address of relative, spouse or children of adult applicant "With whom do you reside?" "Do you live with your parents?"
Name and address of person to be notified in case of accident or emergency	NOTICE IN CASE OF EMERGENCY	Name and address of relative to be notified in case of accident or emergency
Organizations, clubs, professional societies, or other associations of which applicant is a member, excluding any names the character of which indicate the race, religious creed, color, national origin, or ancestry of its members	ORGANIZATIONS	"List all organizations, clubs, societies, and lodges to which you belong."
"By whom were you referred for a position here?"	REFERENCES	Requirement of submission of a religious reference
"Do you have any physical condition which may limit your ability to perform the job applied for?" Statement by employer that offer may be made contingent on passing examination	PHYSICAL CONDITION	"Do you have any physical disabilities?" Questions on general medical condition Inquiries as to receipt of Workers' Compensation
Notice to applicant that any misstatements or omissions of material facts in his application may be cause for dismissal	MISCELLANEOUS	Any inquiry that is not job-related or necessary for determining an applicant's eligibility for employment

KENTUCKY

The Kentucky Civil Rights Act, implemented by the Kentucky Commission on Human Rights, prohibits employment discrimination because of race, color, religion, national origin, sex, or age. Discrimination on the basis of handicap is prohibited by another law.

The Kentucky Civil Rights Act also prohibits denying "an individual, *because of sex*, the full and equal enjoyment of the goods, services, facilities, privileges, advantages, and accommodations of a restaurant, hotel, or motel." (Emphasis added.) It naturally prohibits denial of public accommodations on the basis of race, color, religion, and national origin as well.

MASSACHUSETTS

The Massachusetts Fair Practice Law prohibits discrimination on the basis of race, color, religious creed, national origin, sex, age, ancestry, criminal record, or mental illness. It prohibits discrimination in public accommodations on the basis of race, color, religious creed, national origin, sex, pregnancy, blindness, or deafness.

MICHIGAN

The Michigan Civil Rights Commission enforces the Michigan Civil Rights Act which prohibits discrimination because of race, religion, color, national origin, age, sex, pregnancy, marital status, handicap, height, weight, or arrest record.

Michigan has a "preventive services division," a very interesting unit of administrative authority dealing with compliance with the state Equal Opportunity Law. This division processes information complaints, and the enforcement division of the Michigan Department of Civil Rights processes formal complaints. This organizational structure appears to be very desirable, because it is one of the few states with a preventive section. The prevention of employment discrimination is a more progressive form of administrative implementation of legislative intent than is the imposition of judicial sanction.

MINNESOTA

The Minnesota Human Rights Act protects all persons from discrimination in employment because of race, color, creed, religion, age, national origin, sex, pregnancy, marital status, disability, and status in regard to public assistance.

It prohibits discrimination in public accommodations because of race, color, creed, religion, national origin, sex, and disability.

The Minnesota Department of Human Rights is one of the most efficient and objective of all state equal opportunity agencies. It has conducted informal hearings for the early resolution of discrimination complaints for several years.

NEW HAMPSHIRE

The New Hampshire Commission for Human Rights enforces the Law Against Discrimination which declares that "no person shall be denied the work because of race, color, religious creed, national origin, ancestry, sex, age, marital status, or physical or mental handicap."

NEW JERSEY

The Division of Civil Rights of the New Jersey Department of Law & Public Safety implements the New Jersey Law Against Discrimination which states:

All persons shall have the opportunity to obtain employment without discrimination because of race, creed, color, national origin, ancestry, age, sex, marital status, or physical handicap, subject only to the conditions and limitations applicable alike to all persons.

New Jersey law also prohibits discrimination on account of "liability for military service."

While all state agencies generally produce literature interpreting the applicable state Equal Opportunity Law, New Jersey's *A Guide for Employers to the New Jersey Law Against Discrimination* is one of the best publications at the state level. It includes common questions and answers, a guide on pre-employment inquiries, a sample application form, and even a brief summary of the legislative history of the New Jersey Law Against Discrimination.

New Jersey Equal Opportunity Laws have been in existence since 1945.

NEW YORK

The New York Human Rights Law prohibits discrimination in employment on account of race, creed, color, national origin, sex, age, disability, marital status, or arrest record.

It further prohibits discrimination in public accommodations on account of race, color, creed, national origin, sex, disability, or marital status.

New York protects individuals between the ages of eighteen (18) and sixty-five (65) from age discrimination in employment. The New York Law Against Discrimination was passed in 1945 and prohibited discrimination in employment on account of race, creed, color, or national origin. Thus, there is a long legislative history of nondiscrimination in New York.

NEVADA

The Nevada Equal Rights Commission is charged with the responsibility of prohibiting discrimination in employment on account of race, color, religion, sex, age, physical or visual handicap, or national origin. It also enforces those provisions of the law prohibiting discrimination in public accommodations on account of race, color, religion, national origin, or physical or visual handicap.

WASHINGTON

The Washington State Human Rights Commission enforces the Law Against Discrimination which prohibits discrimination because of race; creed; color; national origin; sex; marital status; age; the presence of any sensory, mental, or physical handicap; as well as prohibiting by regulation employment discrimination on the basis of arrest.

It also prohibits discrimination in public accommodations on the basis of race, creed, color, or national origin.

WYOMING

The Wyoming Fair Employment Practices Act prohibits discrimination in employment because of race, color, sex, national origin, creed, and ancestry.

The Wyoming Fair Employment Practices Commission, like other state agencies, has a list of terms considered to be discriminatory and nondiscriminatory with regard to employment advertising.

5-4.   Selected Municipal and Local Laws

While it is beyond the scope of this book to either summarize or discuss in detail city, county, or other local laws on equal opportunity, one should be aware that they do exist in many municipalities and countries.

Example: East Chicago, Ind.; Gary, Ind.; New York, N.Y.; Philadelphia, Pa.; Seattle, Wash.; Tacoma, Wash.; Baltimore, Md.; Bloomington, Ind.; Dade County, Fla.; Minneapolis, Minn.; and Omaha, Neb. are just a very few examples of localities with Equal Opportunity Laws.

SEATTLE

Seattle, Washington, created a Department of Human Rights and a Human Rights Commission. The Equal Opportunity Ordinance applies primarily to city contractors and prohibits discrimination on the basis of race, creed, color, sex, age, or national origin, unless based upon bona fide occupational qualifications.

NEW YORK CITY

New York City's "Law on Human Rights" created the Commission on Human Rights and prohibits an employer from discriminating on the basis of age, race, creed, color, national origin, marital status, or sex. The administration of the United States Equal Employment Opportunity Commission is patterned after New York City's.

DADE COUNTY

Dade County, Fla., has created the Dade County Fair Housing and Employment Commission with authority to enforce a county ordinance prohibiting discrimination in public accommodations, housing, and employment on account of race, color, religion, ancestry, national origin, age, sex, physical handicap, marital status, or place of birth.

SAN FRANCISCO

The city and county of San Francisco has created the "Human Rights Commission," declaring as a matter of policy San Francisco's opposition to discrimination on the grounds of race, religion, color, ancestry, age, sex, sexual orientation, disability, or place of birth. The Human Rights Commission may certify any complaint of discrimination to the City Attorney for appropriate legal action to eliminate such discrimination.

MINNEAPOLIS

In addition to prohibiting discrimination on the normal bases, the Minneapolis Civil Rights Commission prohibits discrimination on the basis of affectional preference.

5-5.   Conclusion

The first question that should be resolved is, therefore, whether a particular employer is covered or subject to the jurisdiction of any Equal Opportunity Law.

The second issue is which laws are applicable. Thus, employers should be aware of whether their locality has an Equal

Opportunity Law and/or agency, as well as what aspects of state and federal law apply.

Generally, those portions of the state, federal, and local Equal Opportunity Laws which are most favorable to the employee apply.

Example: In Minneapolis, Minnesota any and all of the following Equal Opportunity Laws can apply to employer and employee. Federal law prohibits discrimination on the basis of race, color, creed, sex, pregnancy, national origin, age, or handicap. In addition to these, Minnesota state law prohibits discrimination on the basis of equal pay, marital status, and status in regard to public assistance. A City of Minneapolis ordinance not only prohibits discrimination on these grounds, but also prohibits discrimination on the basis of affectional preference. Accordingly, a hotel doing business in the City of Minneapolis, Minnesota with one or more employees would be subject to the Minneapolis Civil Rights Commission, the Minnesota Department of Human Rights, and the United States Equal Opportunity Commission. The combination and amalgamation of the laws would prohibit the hotelier from discriminating on the basis of race, color, national origin, creed, religion, sex, equal pay, pregnancy, marital status, age, physical handicap/disability, mental handicap, status in regard to public assistance, and affectional preference.

While it is true that the federal agency will often defer to the state agency, which will in turn defer to the city agency, the effect is still the potential of "a triple investigation" in some situations. Equal opportunity administrative agencies are coordinating to a greater degree than in the past, but employers should be prepared for *de novo* investigations when a charging party files with more than one agency.

5-6   Chart of State Equal Opportunity Laws and Agencies

EQUAL OPPORTUNITY LAWS

Protected Groups / State Agencies

State Agencies (with required number of employees):

- 1 Comm'n. for Human Rights
- 15 Civil Rights Division
- Comm. on Human Resources
- 5 Fair Employment Practices Comm'n.
- 6 Civil Rights Comm'n.
- 3 Comm'n. on Human Rights Opportunities
- 4 Human Relations Comm'n.
- Comm'n. on Human Rights
- Comm'n. on Human Relations
- Council on Human Relations
- 1 Dept. of Labor & Industrial Relations
- 10 Comm'n. on Human Rights
- 15 Fair Employment Practices Comm'n.
- 6 Civil Rights Comm'n.
- 4 Comm'n. on Civil Rights
- 4 Comm'n. on Civil Rights
- 8 Comm'n. on Human Rights
- 25
- Human Relations Comm'n.
- 15 Comm'n. on Human Relations
- 6 Comm'n. Against Discrimination
- 8 Civil Rights Comm'n.
- 1 Depts. of Human Rights/Civil Rights
- 6 Comm'n. on Human Rights
- 1 Comm'n. for Human Rights
- 15 Equal Opportunity Comm'n.

Protected Groups (row categories):

Required Employees; Retaliation; National Guard Service; Military Service; Liability; Unfavorable Military Discharge; Political Affiliation; Matriculation; Arrest; Public Assistance Status; Family Responsibilities; Mental Handicap; Hemoglobin C Trait; Medical Condition; Faulty Eye Sight; Physical Handicap Disability; Weight; Personal Appearance; Height; Age; Sexual Orientation; Marital Status; Pregnancy; Equal Pay; Sex; Religious Creed; Religion; Creed; Place of Birth; Ancestry; National Origin; Color; Race

States:

Alabama, Alaska, Arizona, Arkansas, California, Colorado, Connecticut, Delaware, District of Columbia, Florida, Georgia, Hawaii, Idaho, Illinois, Indiana, Iowa, Kansas, Kentucky, Louisiana, Maine, Maryland, Massachusetts, Michigan, Minnesota, Mississippi, Missouri, Montana, Nebraska

Protected Groups

States / **State Agencies**

Protected Groups (column headers): Required Employees · Retaliation · National Guard Service · Military Service Liability · Unfavorable Military Discharge · Political Affiliation · Matriculation · Arrest · Public Assistance Status · Family Responsibilities · Mental Handicap · Hemoglobin C Trait · Medical Condition · Faulty Eye Sight · Physical Handicap Disability · Weight · Personal Appearance · Height · Age · Sexual Orientation · Marital Status · Pregnancy · Equal Pay · Sex · Religious Creed · Religion · Creed · Place of Birth · Ancestry · National Origin · Color · Race

States	State Agencies
Nevada	15 Comm'n. on Equal Rights of Citizens
New Hampshire	6 Comm'n. for Human Rights
New Jersey	Division on Civil Rights
New Mexico	4 Human Rights Comm'n.
New York	4 Comm'n. on Human Rights
North Carolina	Human Relations Comm'n.
North Dakota	1 Comm'n. on Labor
Ohio	4 Civil Rights Comm'n.
Oklahoma	15 Human Rights Comm'n.
Oregon	Civil Rights Division
Pennsylvania	4 Human Relations Comm'n.
Rhode Island	4 Comm'n. for Human Rights
South Carolina	Human Affairs Comm'n.
South Dakota	Divison of Human Rights
Tennessee	Comm'n. for Human Development
Texas	Equal Employment Opportunity Office
Utah	25 Industrial Comm'n.
Vermont	1 Civil Rights Divison
Virginia	Div. Human Resources
Washington	8 Human Rights Comm'n.
West Virginia	12 Human Rights Comm'n.
Wisconsin	Equal Rights Divison
Wyoming	2 Fair Employment Practices Comm'n.

COPYRIGHT © 1979
CBI Publishing Co.

Protected Groups specifically designated under state law; where federal law will also apply if Protected Group is race, color, religion, national origin, sex, pregnancy, equal pay, age, or handicap (government contractors).

☒ Protected Groups under federal law; where there is no state law on the subject.

6.

Procedures and Administration

6-1. Introduction

Equal Opportunity Laws are implemented by administrative agencies generally empowered to investigate, make administrative determinations for or against the employer, issue right-to-sue letters or the equivalent jurisdictional prerequisite to suit, file agency lawsuits, and enter into consent decrees.

Most agencies proceed in the following manner:

· Negotiated preinvestigation settlement or no-fault stage
· Investigation
· Finding of probable cause to believe that there was or was not discrimination
· Issuance of right-to-sue letter or jurisdictional evidence of charging party's right to file suit or agency determination to file suit
· Lawsuit and/or settlement

6-2. U.S. EEOC—Summary Charts

U.S. EEOC Personnel Structure

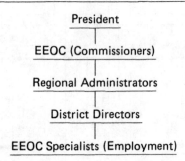

President

EEOC (Commissioners)

Regional Administrators

District Directors

EEOC Specialists (Employment)

Typical EEOC Procedure*

Filing of EEOC Charge within 180 days
of alleged unlawful employment practice

EEOC Charge served upon employer
within 10 days of filing

EEOC attempts "no fault" procedure

EEOC investigation

EEOC Determination

Expiration of 180 days and
Notice of Right to Sue

Lawsuit instituted within
90 days of receipt of
Right-to-Sue Letter

6-3. Wage & Hour Division, Employment Standards Administration, U.S. Department of Labor—Summary Charts

Dept. of Labor Personnel Structure

President

Secretary of Labor

Assistant Secretary of Labor
for
Employment Standards

Wage & Hour Administrator

Wage & Hour Division

Regional Administrator

Area Director

Compliance Specialists

*Please note that if a State Equal Opportunity Agency is involved, the EEOC may defer. Furthermore, the EEOC charge filing may occur 300 days after the alleged unlawful employment practice, or within 30 days after the state has terminated its processing, whichever is earlier.

Typical Wage & Hour Investigation

Filing of Complaint
With Wage & Hour Division

Investigation by Compliance Specialists

Conferences

Final Conference

Position Statement
of
Employer

Lawsuit filed within
2 years of alleged
unintentional violation
and within 3 years of
willful violation

6-4.   State Equal Opportunity Agency's Procedures—Chart
Pennsylvania Human Relations Commission

THE PROCEDURE OF PROCESSING COMPLAINTS

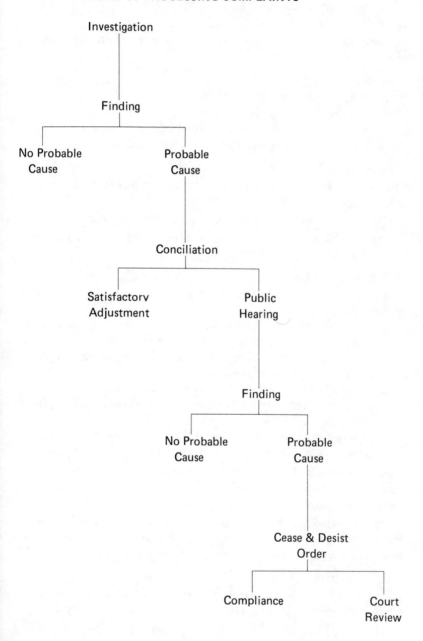

THE COMPLAINT
Complaints may be filed by:
1) the aggrieved person(s)
2) the Commission itself
3) the Attorney General of Pennsylvania
4) an employer

The complaint may include the charge of pattern and practice of discrimination.

THE INVESTIGATION
A Commission staff member must:
1) interview you and other witnesses.
2) have access to pertinent records and documents and review them.
3) make an on-site inspection of your facilities and operations.

THE FINDINGS
After the investigation of the allegations of discrimination, the Commission makes a finding of:

No probable cause . . . and moves to dismiss the complaint.

Probable cause . . . and acts to correct the discriminatory practice and its effects.

THE CONCILIATION
If the investigation substantiates the complaint, then you or your organization will be required:
1) to make available to the complainant and/or others the previously denied housing, employment, schooling or services.
2) to compensate the complainant and/or others for any losses incurred because of the discrimination.
3) to remedy any injustices caused in the violation of the PHR Act.
4) to correct practices which have had an adverse effect on persons protected by the PHR Act.
5) to take other affirmative action needed to eliminate the effects of discrimination and to effectuate the purposes of the PHR Act.

These terms of adjustment may be embodied into a formal conciliation agreement or a consent order which have the same effect as a final order issued after a public hearing.

In the vast majority of cases the actual adjustment of a complaint takes place during the conciliation without a public hearing. You will be informed by mail of the Commission's official closing of your case.

THE PUBLIC HEARING
When the complaint is not successfully resolved during the conciliation, the Commission may convene a public hearing at which testimony under

oath is heard, a decision reached, and a legally enforceable order issued. You and the complainant each has the right to appeal this order to the Commonwealth Court.

THE PENALTIES

The ignoring or willful violation of Commission orders are misdemeanors, punishable by fines of $100 to $500, and/or imprisonment not exceeding 30 days.

The same penalties apply to those who interfere with a Commission representative in the performance of duty.

6-5.   Chronology of a Discrimination Case

I have litigated extensively in this area, including over a dozen federal and state courts in different states. The following represents a summary chronology of events of an actual federal court discrimination lawsuit. It should be noted that this case involved no unusual complexities and would be considered a simple lawsuit by most attorneys experienced in labor litigation.

CHRONOLOGY OF A DISCRIMINATION CASE

Date	Event	Elapsed Time Between Events	Total Elapsed Time
April 1970	Employment practice—discharge of employee X for poor performance—employee files EEOC charge on day of discharge, alleging unlawful discharge due to race	–	–
June 1970	EEOC attempts "predetermination settlement" (now called no-fault or negotiated settlement)	2 mos.	2 mos.
April 1971	EEOC formal investigation begins and interrogatories are served on company by letter (this process may occur at an earlier stage due to increased efficiency of the EEOC today)	10 mos.	12 mos.

January 1972	EEOC issues determination finding that there is reasonable cause to believe that the hotel had discriminated against employee X on account of race in its unlawful discharge	8 mos.	20 mos.
April 1972	Employee X hires attorney and files a complaint as plaintiff against hotel in a United States District Court	3 mos	23 mos.
May 1972	Formal interrogatories, depositions, other forms of discovery, pleadings, motions, etc., begin	1 mo.	24 mos.
May 1973	Continued pleadings, discovery, motions, hearings on motions, depositions, etc.	12 mos.	36 mos.
February 1974	Trial of case before United States District Judge (3 days)	8 mos.	44 mos.
March 1974	Posttrial written proposed findings of fact and conclusions of law, written arguments, memorandum of authorities and briefs filed with United States District Judge	1 mo.	45 mos.
June 1974	Decision in favor of employer hotel	3 mos	48 mos.
July 1974	Appeal filed by plaintiff to the United States Court of Appeals	1 mo.	49 mos.
October 1974	Appellate briefs filed by plaintiff-appellant and by defendant-appellee	3 mos.	52 mos.
May 1975	Oral argument before the United States Court of Appeals (panel of three Circuit Court Judges)	7 mos.	59 mos.
June 1975	Decision of United States Court of Appeals in favor of employer hotel	1 mo.	60 mos.

5 Years

Note: This sample chronology of a simple discrimination lawsuit covers a period of five years from the date of the discharge until final resolution. The hotel was subjected to over three years of federal court litigation to justify the discharge of one employee for poor performance. The total expense and lost time, legal fees, and administrative cost was in excess of

$50,000! While the hotel employer can often recover court costs (deposition costs, transportation and travel expenses of witnesses, expert witness testimony fees, photostatic reproduction costs, etc.), it is rare for a successful defendant employer to recover attorney's fees from the unsuccessful plaintiff. On the other hand, if the plaintiff wins, he/she can recover back pay, attorney's fees, and all costs of the action.

III.
CATEGORIES OF DISCRIMINATION

7.

Sex Discrimination

7-1. Introduction and Definition

This section of the book begins with sex discrimination, since it is clearly the most pervasive form of discrimination, one that has existed for centuries and continues to exist.

Sex is often defined in dictionaries as follows:

1. Either of the two divisions of organisms distinguished as male or female; males or females (especially men or women) collectively. 2. The character of being male or female; all of the things which distinguish a male from a female. 3. Anything connected with sexual gratification or reproduction or the urge of these, especially the attraction of individuals of one sex for those of the other.

While sex discrimination is obviously the preferential or disparate treatment of individuals on account of sex, the overwhelming majority of cases involve discrimination against females. Accordingly, the phrase "sex discrimination" connotes women. Indeed, while I have litigated extensively in the area of sex discrimination, the number of such cases brought by men pales into insignificance when compared to the number instituted by or on behalf of women.

Sex discrimination cases involve more money than any other form of discrimination. It appears, moreover, that the number of sex discrimination lawsuits will increase at an even greater rate than it has in the past, and certainly at a greater rate than any other category.

In the hospitality and foodservice industries, women have

had a difficult time advancing in management until recent years. Today, women generally represent an increasing percentage of graduates of hotel administration schools.

The Bureau of the Census has reported that more than 60 percent of all employed women are working in service industries, including hotels, motels, restaurants, foodservice institutions, schools, hospitals, entertainment and recreation facilities, and other personal service industry facilities. Additionally, the percentage of women who work annually has risen from about 40 percent in 1952 to more than 60 percent in 1979. The percentage of men who work annually, on the other hand, has gone from about 87 percent in 1950 to 85 percent in 1979.

Women are fast becoming the majority in the number of total workers in America. Seventy-five percent of all employees in hotels and personal service jobs are women. Similarly, 75 percent of all employees in the medical–health industry are women.

Since this majority concentrates primarily in industries relevant to this book, it is incumbent upon hoteliers, restaurateurs, and institutional employers to appreciate fully the impact of these statistics on employee relations policies, practices, and procedures.

Other factors such as the increase in divorces, the need and desire for both men and women to bring home a paycheck, and increased emphases on the elimination of sex discrimination in public accommodations, housing, credit extension, and, of course, employment, make the influence of women geometrically more important. Hence, employers should recognize that blatant and subtle forms of sex discrimination will become increasingly costly, both in the judicial setting and in the marketplace.

The Women's Bureau of the Employment Standards Administration of the U.S. Department of Labor compiled the following "myths" and "realities" regarding women:

The Myth	**The Reality**
A woman's place is in the home.	Homemaking in itself is no longer a full-time job for most people. Goods and services formerly produced in the

The Reality (cont.)

home are now commercially available; laborsaving devices have lightened or eliminated much work in the home.

Today more than half of all women between 18 and 64 years of age are in the labor force, where they are making a substantial contribution to the nation's economy. Studies show that 9 out of 10 girls will work outside the home at some time in their lives.

Women aren't seriously attached to the labor force; they work only for extra pocket money.

Of the nearly 34 million women in the labor force in March 1973, nearly half were working because of pressing economic need. They were either single, widowed, divorced, or separated, or had husbands whose incomes were less than $3,000 a year. Another 4.7 million had husbands with incomes between $3,000 and $7,000.*

Women are out ill more than male workers; they cost the company more.

A recent Public Health Service study shows little difference in the absentee rate due to illness or injury: 5.6 days a year for women compared with 5.2 for men.

Women don't work as long or as regularly as their male co-workers; their training is costly and largely wasted.

A declining number of women leave work for marriage and children. But even among those who do leave, a majority return when their children are in school. Even with a break in employment, the average woman worker has a worklife expectancy of 25 years as compared with 43 years for the average male worker. The single woman averages 45 years in the labor force.

*The Bureau of Labor Statistics estimate for a low standard of living for an urban family of four was $7,386 in autumn 1972. This estimate is for a family consisting of an employed husband aged 38, a wife not employed outside the home, and 8-year-old girl, and a 13-year-old boy.

Studies on labor turnover indicate that net differences for men and women are generally small. In manufacturing industries the 1968 rates of accessories per 100 employees were 4.4 for men and 5.3 for women; the respective separation rates were 4.4 and 5.2.

Married women take jobs away from men; in fact, they ought to quit those jobs they now hold.

There were 19.8 million married women (husbands present) in the labor force in March 1973; the number of unemployed men was 2.5 million. If all married women stayed home and unemployed men were placed in their jobs, there would be 17.3 million unfilled jobs.

Moreover, most unemployed men do not have the education or the skill to qualify for many of the jobs held by women, such as secretaries, teachers, and nurses.

Women should stick to "women's jobs" and shouldn't compete for "men's jobs."

Job requirements, with extremely rare exceptions, are unrelated to sex. Tradition rather than job content has led to labeling certain jobs as women's and others as men's. In measuring 22 inherent aptitudes and knowledge areas, a research laboratory found that there is no sex difference in 14, women excel in 6, and men excel in 2.

Women don't want responsibility on the job; they don't want promotions or job changes which add to their load.

Relatively few women have been offered positions of responsibility. But when given these opportunities, women, like men, do cope with job responsibilities in addition to personal or family responsibilities. In 1973, 4.7 million women held professional and technical jobs, another 1.6 million worked as nonfarm managers and administrators. Many others held supervisory jobs in offices and factories.

The employment of mothers leads to juvenile delinquency.	Studies show that many factors must be considered when seeking the causes of juvenile delinquency. Whether or not a mother is employed does not appear to be a determining factor.
	These studies indicate that it is the quality of a mother's care rather than the time consumed in such care which is of major significance.
Men don't like to work for women supervisors.	Most men who complain about women supervisors have never worked for a woman.
	In one study where at least three-fourths of both the male and female respondents (all executives) had worked with women managers, their evaluation of women in management was favorable. On the other hand, the study showed a traditional/cultural bias among those who reacted unfavorably to women as managers.
	In another survey in which 41 percent of the reporting firms indicated that they hired women executives, none rated their performance as unsatisfactory; 50 percent rated them adequate; 42 percent rated them the same as their predecessors; and 8 percent rated them better than their predecessors.

Source: U.S. Department of Labor, Employment Standards Administration, Women's Bureau, May 1974 (revised).

Thus we can see this an extremely important and growing area of Equal Opportunity Law.

Q. What is sex discrimination?

A. In the hospitality and foodservice industries, sex discrimination is engaging in an employment practice which affects one sex differently from the other. Whether sex discrimination is unlawful depends upon whether the different treatment resulting from the employment practice is unfavorable to one sex. Generally, both sexes should be treated equally, unless there is a reasonable, job-related justification and/or a bona fide occupational qualification [BFOQ]. Laws prohibiting sex discrimination generally do not protect homosexuals, transsexuals, transvestites, and those with sexual preferences other than heterosexuality from discrimination on that basis alone. However, institutional employers who are *public employers* generally must prove that an employment practice adverse to homosexuals, transsexuals, and/or transvestites is relevant to the job. Title VII of the Civil Rights Act does not prohibit *private employers* from discriminating on the basis of homosexuality, transsexuality, or transvestism.

7-2.   Laws and Agencies

Federal law generally prohibits both discrimination in employee relations on the basis of sex and paying one sex less money than another for a substantially similar job. State laws often go beyond that, also prohibiting discrimination on the basis of marital status, pregnancy, and so forth.

The EEOC is the prime agency enforcing Equal Opportunity Laws prohibiting sex discrimination.

7-3.   Varieties of Sex Discrimination

REFUSAL TO HIRE

Employers have been accused and have been found liable for unlawful refusal to hire on account of sex.

Example: The use of height/weight and lifting requirements which are not job-related and the use of stereotypes that result in adverse treatment are discriminatory. Not hiring females for waitress positions at fine restaurants during evening hours is sex discrimination, if the waitress is otherwise qualified. Almost every hotelier and restaurateur which has refused to hire a female for a waitress or foodservice attendant position at a fine restaurant at night has lost or settled the case.

Example: Refusal to hire women in management or supervisory positions because they require travel is generally unlawful sex discrimination. Likewise, the refusal to hire a female for a managerial position involving the supervision of both men and women is clearly sex discrimination.

EQUAL PAY FOR EQUAL WORK

Paying one sex less money than another sex for a substantially similar job which requires the same amount of *skill, effort, responsibility,* and *is performed under similar working conditions,* is a violation of the Equal Pay Act. Thus, the rule is simply that there should be equal pay for equal work regardless of sex.

Example: Waiters and waitresses should be paid equally; house attendants and room attendants (housemen and maids) performing substantially similar functions should be paid equally, regardless of what their job classification designation is; stewards and stewardesses should generally be paid equally, likewise, pursers and flight attendants; sales representatives/ account executives, male and female, should generally be compensated equally; nurses' aids and orderlies performing substantially equal work in skill, effort, and responsibility and under similar working conditions should receive equal pay (but factual situations vary greatly in this area).

Management trainees, department heads, and other supervisors should receive equal pay regardless of sex, based upon their experience, job-related qualifications, ability, and worth to the company.

GROOMING STANDARDS

Q. May hotels and restaurants have different grooming standards for men than for women?

A. Generally yes. The courts generally uphold an employer's grooming standards which are tailored to each sex.

Example: Employers have been allowed to require male employees to wear their hair shorter than female employees. A similar result was reached in the case of flashy jewelry. Men may be prohibited from wearing beards as a general rule. A few hotel chains prohibit beards as a matter of corporate policy.

The key is simply that grooming standards must be reasonable as they apply to both sexes, and not reasonable as to one sex but unreasonable to the other sex.

THE FRINGE BENEFITS

While there are cases supporting different treatment in terms of eligibility for certain fringe benefits and the amount of the benefits, as a general rule employers in the hospitality and foodservice industries provide equal benefits regardless of sex and should continue to do so.

Accordingly, collective bargaining agreements and company health and welfare and pension plan programs should be examined to eliminate different treatment. Generally, even though women live longer than men, contributions should be on an employee basis and not because of sex. Furthermore, eligibility should be on an employee basis and should not differentiate on account of sex.

PREGNANCY

The definition of "sex" within Title VII of the Civil Rights Act of 1964, as amended, includes a prohibition against discrimination because of pregnancy, childbirth, or any medical conditions related to pregnancy. Thus, federal law prohibits pregnancy discrimination.

Example: Differentiation on account of pregnancy is being specifically prohibited by statute or regulation at the state level in increasing numbers as well as being prohibited by federal law. Therefore, maternity and pregnancy benefits should relate to other disability benefits and leaves of absence for male employees. Generally, the hospitality and foodservice industries have not differentiated in this regard.

DISCHARGES

The most common variety of unlawful sex discrimination occurs when an employer discharges an employee because of his/her sex or a sex-related characteristic.

Example: To discharge an employee due to pregnancy in and of itself is sex discrimination. Requiring the wife to resign when two people are employed in the same hotel would be sex discrimination unless the same rule applied to the husband. Thus, antinepotism rules, whether on a hotel-wide basis or a departmental basis, can be unlawful sex discrimination if these rules do not apply regardless of sex.

Example: If a hotel has a very high percentage of females in the work force, but maintains an employment policy which has the impact of discriminating against females with small children and not males with small children, this would probably be unlawful.

SEXUAL ORIENTATION

Generally speaking, federal Equal Opportunity Law does not specifically protect homosexuals, bisexuals, transsexuals, and transvestites from discrimination on those bases by employers. However, consistent with earlier discussions of the hospitality and foodservice industries, it is generally a practical mistake for employers to discriminate against individuals because of sexual orientation for that reason alone.

There are some state and local Equal Opportunity Laws which could be interpreted to protect individuals on account of sexual orientation.

Example: There are a few cases where individuals with serious physical and/or mental sexual conditions have argued that discrimination because of their condition is handicap discrimination. Once they establish their problem is a form of "gender dysphoria," an argument along these lines can be at least maintained. Individuals with Klinefelter's syndrome, a chromosomal abnormality, also could maintain discrimination on the basis of handicap should they be discharged because of that alone. At the Erickson Education Foundation in Baton Rouge, La., Johns Hopkins University, Baltimore, Md.; and

Stanford University, Stanford, Calif.; studies are being made on the question of gender dysphoria. Obviously, the more statistical evidence obtained, the greater the likelihood that a court would consider it unreasonable to discharge someone because of a particular sexual orientation.

Generally, however, sex discrimination legislation applies to heterosexuals, i.e., heterosexual males and heterosexual females.

Minneapolis, Minn., among other localities, does prohibit discrimination on the basis of *affectional preference*, which appears to protect individuals against discrimination because of various forms of sexual orientation or preference. One should check the local ordinance in this regard.

Example: Recent courts have upheld the right of employers to discharge or refuse to hire effeminate males, holding that Title VII of the Civil Rights Act does not forbid such discrimination based upon affectional or sexual preference.

EXTORTION OF SEXUAL FAVORS

An increasingly publicized example of sex discrimination occurs when a male supervisor requires sexual favors from female subordinates as a condition of employment or continued employment opportunities. This is one of the most serious varieties of sex discrimination: It is simply sexual extortion.

Not only is it violative of Equal Opportunity Laws as sex discrimination, but if it amounts to extortion, it could be both a civil wrong (tort) as well as a crime.

Example: The management official who required the female subordinate to provide sexual favors in order to gain the promotion he has promised her is clearly committing unlawful sex discrimination. The question, however, is whether his actions bind the employer hotel or restaurant. Generally, a court will hold that management is bound by the acts of its supervisors if they are acting under authority of management or "apparent authority." Courts have ruled both ways on this question. In the hospitality and foodservice industries, however, our experience is such that it would be difficult for management to argue that it did not have general knowledge of such activities, absent a clearly defined policy to the contrary.

Accordingly, management should affirmatively disavow any condonation or support of sexual extortion in order to exculpate the hotel.

Example: A prestigious hotel was sued for approximately $1 million for allegedly engaging in sham discharges, including discharging and disciplining employees for their refusal to engage in sexual activities with their superiors. Obviously, these are merely allegations, which must be proved by preponderance of the evidence in a court of law. However, one need not analyze the situation in depth before realizing the distaste and unfavorable publicity accompanying the defense of such a lawsuit.

There are examples of male management extorting sexual favors from females, as well as female managers extorting sexual favors from males. To date, I am unaware of any reported decisions involving homosexuals.

All employee relations policy manuals should reflect a carefully drafted statement, such as the following:

All employees, managerial and non-supervisory, are prohibited from demanding, indirectly or directly, sexual favors of any kind whatsoever. This policy applies in particular to supervisors. Violation of this policy may be just cause for dismissal.

7-4.   Statistics and Recordkeeping

Employers should maintain accurate statistics on the number of men and women in various job classifications. While it is not required that an employer hire on the basis of sex quotas, it is helpful periodically to analyze whether a particular sex is being statistically excluded from a desirable job classification.

Example: A luxury, convention hotel, which has no females on the executive committee or in department head positions could have a more difficult time defending a case brought by an experienced female supervisor for unlawful refusal to promote to a top managerial position.

While the EEOC has issued regulations requiring that employment applications be on file for two years (up from six months), the Wage & Hour Division of the U.S. Department of

Labor requires wage information to be maintained for three years. Further, it is important to have a uniform recordkeeping retention requirement for all employment information.

There are varying requirements for records depending upon the category of discrimination. However, it is the recommendation of this author that records be maintained as to the sex of all employees in all job classifications, management and non-supervisory, for five years.

Additionally, the personnel department should examine trends annually to determine whether there are deficiencies or obvious gaps developing concerning males and females in particular job classifications. This should not be done, again, to fulfill some cosmetic quota system. However, it should be undertaken to furnish top management with an accurate preventive law analysis of the sexual makeup of the work force in the various job classifications.

Employers should be familiar with general statistics on males and females in the Standard Metropolitan Statistical Area (SMSA), particularly as it relates to females. Both the Bureau of Labor Statistics and the Bureau of the Census provide information for employers in their SMSA, data which are generally applicable to large urban areas.

Example: As of July 1, 1975, the female population of the United States was 109 million, representing 51.3 percent of the total population. Since 1910 the female population has grown faster in each decade than the male population.

Thus, since women outnumber and outlive men, there are serious implications for employee relations programs that do not take into account both the growing number of females in the work force and the number of older women who are employed.

Since there were approximately 5.6 million more females than males in 1978, it is important to consider projections of future excesses. Most conservative estimates predict the excess of women over men will be approximately 6.5 million by 1985 and between 6.9 million and 7.9 million by 2000. Again, the implications of these statistics in the areas of sex and age discrimination are profound.

There have been dramatic statistical increases in the migration of women as well as in the number of women who are

Table 1. Size of Labor Force by Age and Sex: 1950, 1960, 1970, and 1974

(Noninstitutional population. Numbers in thousands)

Sex and age	Number in labor force				Change, 1950 to 1974	
	1974	1970	1960	1950	Number	Percent
TOTAL, 16 YEARS AND OVER						
Women	35,892	31,560	23,272	18,412	+17,480	+94.9
Men	57,349	54,343	48,870	45,446	+11,903	+26.2
Ratio: women/men	0.63	0.58	0.48	0.41	(X)	(X)

Table 2. Labor Force Participation Rates by Age and Sex: 1950, 1960, 1970, and 1974

(Noninstitutional population)

Sex and age	Labor force participation rates[1]				Percent change, 1950 to 1974
	1974	1970	1960	1950	
TOTAL, 16 YEARS AND OVER					
Women	45.7	43.4	37.8	33.9	+34.8
Men . . . .[2]	79.4	80.6	84.0	86.8	- 8.5
Ratio: women/men[2]	0.58	0.54	0.45	0.39	(X)

Table 3. Number in Labor Force and Labor Force Participation Rates by Sex and Marital Status: 1950, 1960, 1970, and 1975

(Numbers in thousands)

Sex and marital status	1975	1970	1960	1950	Percent change, 1950 to 1975
Number in Labor Force					
Single:					
Women	8,464	6,965	5,401	5,621	+50.6
Men	12,233	9,545	8,473	9,898	+37.5
Ratio: women/men	0.69	0.73	0.64	0.63	(X)
Married, spouse present:					
Women	21,111	18,377	12,253	8,550	+146.9
Men	39,516	39,138	35,757	32,912	+20.1
Ratio: women/men	0.53	0.47	0.34	0.26	(X)
Other ever married:[1]					
Women	6,932	5,891	4,861	3,624	+91.3
Men	4,091	2,938	2,845	2,616	+56.4
Ratio: women/men	1.69	2.01	1.71	1.39	(X)
PERCENT DISTRIBUTION					
Labor Force Participation Rates					
Single:					
Women	56.7	53.0	44.1	50.5	+12.3
Men	67.1	60.7	55.5	62.6	+7.2
Ratio: women/men[2]	0.85	0.87	0.79	0.81	(X)
Other ever married:[1]					
Women	40.7	39.1	40.0	37.8	+7.7
Men	65.2	54.2	59.3	63.0	+3.5
Ratio: women/men[2]	0.62	0.72	0.67	0.60	(X)

[1] Includes widowed, divorced, and married, spouse absent.

[2] Ratios of labor force participation rates.

Note: Data relate to the total population (including institutional) 14 years old and over for 1950 and 1960, to the total population 16 years old and over in 1970, and to the noninstitutional population 16 years old and over in 1975. The male Armed Forces living off post or with their families on post are included in all years.

Source: U.S. Department of Commerce, Bureau of the Census, *Current Population Reports*, Series P–50, No. 29 and U.S. Department of Labor, Bureau of Labor Statistics, *Special Labor Force Reports*, Nos. 130 and 13 and November 1975 *Monthly Labor Review*.

Table 4. Projected Size of Labor Force by Age and Sex: 1980, 1985, and 1990

Sex and Age	Number in labor force (thousands)				Change, 1974 to 1990	
	1974 (actual)	1980	1985	1990	Number	Percent
TOTAL, 16 YEARS AND OVER						
Women..........	35,892	39,219	41,699	43,669	+7,807	+21.8
Men..........	57,349	62,590	66,017	68,907	+11,558	+20.2

Table 5. Occupation of Employed Persons 14 Years and Over by Sex: 1960 and 1970
(Numbers in thousands)

Occupation	1970			1960			Change, 1960 to 1970	
	Women	Men	Women/ men ratio	Women	Men	Women/ men ratio	Women	Men
Total employed[1]	29,170	48,139	0.61	21,172	43,467	0.49	+7,998	+4,672
Service workers	4,424	3,640	1.22	2,963	2,791	1.06	+1,461	+849
Bartenders	39	159	0.26	19	153	0.12	+20	−3
Health service workers	1,045	140	7.46	587	120	4.89	+458	+20
Personal service workers	776	393	1.97	481	424	1.13	+295	−31
Protective service workers	58	895	0.06	26	674	0.04	+32	+221
Private household workers.......	1,052	37	28.43	1,657	61	27.16	−605	−24

[1] Includes employed persons with occupation not reported.

Note: Because some occupations are not included in this table, subgroups may not add to total for major occupational categories.

Source: U.S. Department of Commerce, Bureau of the Census, 1970 Census of Population, Vol. I, Part 1(D).

Table 6. Industry of Employed Persons 14 Years Old and Over by Sex: 1950, 1960, and 1970

(Numbers in thousands)

Industry	1970			1960			1950		
	Women	Men	Women/men ratio	Women	Men	Women/men ratio	Women	Men	Women/men ratio
Total employed[1]	29,170	48,139	0.61	21,172	43,467	0.49	15,773	40,662	0.39
Personal services	2,341	953	2.46	2,777	1,085	2.56	2,301	1,164	1.98
Private households	1,082	122	8.87	1,729	188	9.20	1,395	206	6.77
Hotels and motels	323	247	1.31	258	245	1.05	256	271	0.95
Laundering, cleaning, and other garment services	326	212	1.54	355	266	1.33	371	324	1.15
Beauty and barbar shops	440	209	2.11	282	214	1.32	183	201	0.91

[1] Includes persons with industry not reported.

Note: Because some industries are not included in this table, subgroups do not always add to major industrial divisions.

Source: U.S. Department of Commerce, Bureau of the Census, *1970 Census of Population*, Vol. I, Part 1(D) and Technical Paper 18, *Changes Between 1950 and 1960 Occupation and Industry Classifications.*

Source: U.S. Dept. of Commerce, Bureau of the Census, a Statistical Portrait of Women in the United States; and U.S. Dept. of Labor, Bureau of Labor Statistics.

independent, i.e., those who are divorced or who never married. Furthermore, the number of females with college degrees and advanced degrees is increasing at a much greater rate than that for men.

Most significantly, the labor force participation of women has been one of the strongest indications of changing social and economic roles in the United States. Between 1950 and 1974 the number of women workers nearly doubled, while the number of men in the labor force increased by only about one-fourth.

The preceding excerpts from the Bureau of the Census charts and tables illustrate one of the most dramatic changes the U.S. labor force has ever experienced.

Q. What job classifications and situations in the hospitality and foodservice industries create the most potentially serious sex discrimination problems?

A. Refusal to hire males in traditionally female positions, such as cocktail waiter/waitress jobs; refusal to promote women to top management positions, such as general manager or department head; extortion of sexual favors (directly or indirectly); equal pay for equal work violations, such as paying housemen more than maids; refusal to hire women at night in fine restaurants, are all examples of problem areas in the hospitality and foodservice industries from the standpoint of sex discrimination.

Example: Female sex is not a BFOQ for position of cabin or flight attendant, and airline's failure to hire men is violation of Title VII.

Example: Refusal to consider women for a so-called strenuous job is not a BFOQ defense, since the hotel must have a reasonable basis for concluding that all or substantially all women would be unable to perform the job before sex could be a BFOQ defense.

Example: So-called female protective laws, which set maximum limits on hours women may work, and the weights they may be called upon to lift, have been superseded by Title VII as such state laws result in unlawful sex discrimination.

Example: "Help wanted—Male" and "Help wanted—Female" advertising classifications are violations of Equal

Opportunity Laws forbidding sex discrimination in employment.

Example: Where an employer does not generally discriminate against a protected group, but discriminates against a sub-group within a protected group, the courts have referred to this as sex-plus discrimination. The sex-plus principle is discriminatory—for example, applying "no marriage" rules solely to stewardesses or female flight attendants and not to male employees is illegal sex discrimination. Furthermore, this airline corporate policy could not be justified as a BFOQ because of customer preference.

Example: A company cannot exclude women with preschool children from employment opportunities unless it also excludes men with preschool children.

Example: Refusal to hire or the discharge of pregnant women, unmarried or married, can result in illegal sex discrimination, violation of equal protection, an unconstitutional invasion of her right to privacy, and, where applicable, race discrimination.

Example: Requirements that a pregnant woman cease working at a definite inflexible time prior to delivery, and remain on leave for a specified period after birth, have almost always been held unlawful.

POST NOTICES PROHIBITING SEX DISCRIMINATION

MAINTAIN AN ONGOING ANALYSIS OF THE SEXUAL COMPOSITION OF EACH JOB CLASSIFICATION

CORPORATE POLICIES FAVORING THE UPWARD UTILIZATION OF WOMEN IN MANAGEMENT ARE DESIRED

SEX DISCRIMINATION IS OFTEN SUBTLE, BUT BLATANTLY EXPENSIVE

ELIMINATE THE APPEARANCE OF IMPROPRIETY WITH RESPECT TO SEXUAL EXTORITON

8.

Race Discrimination

8-1.   Introduction

Racial discrimination against blacks in the hospitality and food-service industries has resulted in a plethora of lawsuits. However, due to aggressive socioeconomic policies, these industries are eliminating the vestiges of racial discrimination against blacks in a progressive manner.

Q. What is race?

A. "An ethnical stock; a great division of mankind having in common certain distinguishing physical peculiarities constituting a comprehensive class appearing to be derived from a distinct primitive source. A tribal or national stock; a division or subdivision of one of the great racial stocks of mankind distinguished by minor peculiarities." (Black's Law Dictionary)

Q. What is race or color discrimination?

A. It is unlawful race or color discrimination to maintain an employment policy, practice, or procedure which directly or indirectly affects employees on account of their race or color.

Example: The well known *Griggs* v. *Duke Power Company* case held that requiring all prospective employees to have a high school diploma had an adverse impact on blacks, since fewer blacks graduated from high school in North Carolina (the situs of the action) than whites. Thus, any employment practice which has the consequence of an adverse impact on a minority *and which is not job-related* is violative of Title VII of the Civil Rights Act.

Obviously, to refuse to hire an individual because he/she is black (or white) is prohibited race discrimination. The blatant forms of race discrimination, e.g., refusal to hire because of race, refusal to promote because of race, are not difficult to spot. It is the more subtle forms that result in litigation.

8-2. Laws and Agencies

Q. What laws and agencies are involved with race or color discrimination?

A. The laws involved are as follows:

Fourteenth Amendment, United States Constitution
Title VII, Civil Rights Act of 1964
Civil Rights Act of 1866
Thirteenth Amendment, United States Constitution
Civil Rights Act of 1871
The various state laws

Race or color discrimination is specifically prohibited under state Equal Opportunity Laws in all but a few states. It is prohibited by federal law in all fifty states and the District of Columbia.

Q. What agencies enforce race or color discrimination prohibitions?

A. The EEOC is the most significant agency enforcing the law against race discrimination, but, as indicated above, most states and the District of Columbia have Equal Opportunity agencies which enforce the state law. Additionally, the Office of Federal Contract Compliance Programs [OFCCP] does enforce government regulations prohibiting race or color discrimination on the part of government contractors and subcontractors.

8-3.   Varieties of Race or Color Discrimination

EDUCATION

As indicated above, if an employment policy, such as an educational requirement, has an adverse impact against a minority (blacks) *and* such educational requirement *is not job-related,* it can result in unlawful race discrimination.

In the hospitality and foodservice industries educational requirements are generally unnecessary and not job-related.

Q. What educational requirements may create race or color discrimination problems?

A. Requiring all managerial applicants to have college degrees or hotel/motel administration program degrees may result in race discrimination if it is not clear that such educational requirements are job-related. This is particularly true, in the hospitality and foodservice industries, since many individuals in managerial positions do not have college degrees or hotel school degrees. Thus, one is hard-pressed to establish that a degree from a hotel school is necessarily job-related. Accordingly, promotional opportunities should generally be open to all, regardless of education.

Hospitality and foodservice industries, probably more than any other, should base promotional and hiring opportunities on clearly established job-related qualifications, such as experience, actual job performance, and the recommendation of managers who have observed the performance of the prospective manager.

ARREST OR COURT RECORDS

Generally, utilizing arrest or court records to exclude prospective applicants has an adverse impact on blacks, since the statistics reflect that more blacks are arrested and have court records than whites. Therefore, such a policy could result in race discrimination. Furthermore, several states specifically prohibit the use of arrest or court records in the selection process, e.g., Hawaii, California, Illinois, Massachusetts, New Mexico, North Dakota, and Washington State.

Q. How can an employer prohibit criminals from becoming employed?

A. A safe approach is to ask on the application form the following question: "Have you been convicted of a felony within the last five years?"

Hotels, in particular, need to screen individuals with job-related criminal felony records, e.g., a convicted rapist, burglar, etc. Hotels are held to an extremely high standard of care with respect to the liability to guests for improper selection of employees resulting in injuries or property loss to guests. Therefore, while Equal Opportunity Laws prohibiting race or color discrimination and the "adverse impact" admonition of *Griggs* v. *Duke Power Company* make it difficult for employers to prohibit the hiring of individuals with arrest or court records, one can usually avoid hiring of convicted felons without running afoul of these laws.

TESTING

Employment tests have resulted in many race discrimination cases. Accordingly, any test should be clearly job-related.

Example: Typing tests are generally approved. Skills tests regarding the performance of waiters/waitresses are generally lawful. Voice clarity and enunciation tests for PBX operators are also permissible. Additionally, tests for potential front-desk representatives operating computerized reservations systems are lawful.

Thus, tests should be based upon actual job skills and performance.

MEDICAL CONDITION

Some forms of medical status questions may result in race discrimination.

Example: Questions concerning blood type or hemoglobin C trait, indicating a propensity toward sickle cell anemia, may be prohibited handicap discrimination, medical condition discrimination, as well as race or color discrimination against blacks.

Employers should be objective in their medical, grooming, and general appearance requirements for employees.

Example: Prohibiting certain hair styles, e.g., wearing pigtails, may be unlawful race discrimination, if it only has an adverse impact upon blacks and is not job-related.

ECONOMIC AND "MORAL-RELATED" REQUIREMENTS

Where a hotel or restaurant requires that employees with children born out of wedlock be terminated, this can result in sex discrimination charges. Furthermore, if it is established that this policy affects blacks more regularly than whites, it could also result in (and has) race discrimination.

Similarly, inquiries about the credit status or welfare status of a prospective applicant could have an adverse impact on blacks, since the statistics reflect that more blacks have credit problems and have been on welfare than whites. Again, the standard is whether this employment policy has an adverse impact on a minority (blacks) and is not job-related.

DISCRIMINATION IN FAVOR OF BLACKS OR AGAINST WHITES

Obviously, under the Bakke decision of the Supreme Court, discrimination on the basis of race means exactly that, i.e., preferential treatment in favor of one race to the exclusion of another race or color can be prohibited race discrimination, regardless of whether it affects blacks or whites.

Title VII of the Civil Rights Act of 1964 specifically prohibits preferential treatment in § 703(j), which states in pertinent part as follows:

Nothing contained in this title shall be interpreted to require any employer . . . to grant preferential treatment to any individual or to any group because of the race, color, religion, sex, or national origin of such individual or group on account of an imbalance which may exist with respect to the total number or percentage of persons of any race, color, religion, sex, or national origin employed by any employer.

8-4.   Statistics and Recordkeeping

Statistics reflect that during the past thirty years blacks have comprised approximately 19 to 20 percent of all employees in the hotel industry; and blacks comprise more than 30 percent of all employees in urban hotels.

It is also a common statistical fact that blacks have comprised a very high percentage of employees in the following job classifications: maids, housemen, porters, laundry employees, door service employees, dishwashers, kitchen help, bus-service employees.

On the other hand, blacks have occupied a low percentage of those employed in the following job classifications: hosts/hostesses, maitre d's, waitresses, chefs, front-desk clerks, clerical employees, managerial employees.

Again, while race discrimination may involve blacks, whites, orientals, and others, the overwhelming majority of race discrimination cases in the hospitality and foodservice industries involve lawsuits and charges brought by black employees and prospective black employees.

An excellent study by University of Pennsylvania's Wharton School of Finance and Commerce called *The Negro In The Hotel Industry* indicated that in 1967 twelve selected cities ranked as follows in percentage of blacks in the total population compared to the percentage of blacks in hotel employment:

City	Blacks in Population in 1965		Blacks in Hotel Employment in 1967	
	RANK	%AGE	RANK	%AGE
Washington, D.C.	1	63.2%	3	52.1%
New Orleans	2	41%	1	54.4%
Atlanta	3	38.4%	4	50.7%
St. Louis	4	36.9%	2	52.3%
Philadelphia	5	29.5%	6	33.4%
Chicago	6	26.7%	5	38.6%
Miami	7	25.8%	11	13.2%

City	RANK	%AGE	RANK	%AGE
Houston	8	25%	7	31.2%
Los Angeles	9	18.2%	8	26.7%
New York	10	15.7%	10	19.7%
San Francisco	11	13.5%	9	22.1%
Minneapolis	12	3.4%	12	11.8%

Source: Adapted from E.C. and K.S. Koziara, *The Negro in the Hotel Industry*, by permission. The Racial Policies of American Industry, Report No. 4, published by the Industrial Research Unit of the Wharton School, 1968. Copyright © by the trustees of the University of Pennsylvania.

While these rankings are still illustrative of the situation—with Atlanta, Washington, D.C., New Orleans, and St. Louis in the top percentiles—Atlanta in the late seventies employs one of the highest percentages of blacks in the hotel industry, as well as a great number of blacks compared to most other cities.

Statistics such as these should be compiled and updated regularly by every major hospitality employer. One need not establish a quota system. However, if the facts reflect that your city has a very high percentage of blacks in hotel employment and your property does not, the statistical evidence of racial discrimination may be difficult to overcome in a lawsuit.

Obviously, these statistics should be maintained by major hospitals and health-care centers and public assembly facilities as well. Since these facilities are usually located in large urban areas, racial statistics should be monitored.

It is suggested that all records of racial status be maintained for five years and evaluated at least annually.

MONITOR THE NUMBER OF RACIAL MINORITIES IN VARIOUS JOB CLASSIFICATIONS TO AVOID RELEGATING PARTICULAR MINORITIES TO LIMITED JOB CLASSIFICATIONS

PROMOTE AN ATMOSPHERE FREE OF RACIAL JOKES, EPITHETS, AND SLURS

9.

National Origin Discrimination

9-1.   Introduction

Located in large metropolitan areas, the most prominent health care and public assembly facilities usually employ people of varied national origins. Indeed, hotels and restaurants employ individuals from all over the world to a greater extent than any other industry. Discrimination by hospitality and foodservice companies on the basis of national origin is an anathema to these businesses. Furthermore, there are very few cases where hotels and restaurants have been found liable for national origin discrimination.

National origin discrimination is defined to mean the following:

Discrimination based on the country from where an individual or his/her forebears comes; and

Discrimination against an individual who possesses the cultural or linguistic characteristics common to an ethnic national group.

9-2.   Laws and Agencies

Federal law generally prohibits discrimination in employment practices on the basis of national origin. The primary agency enforcing this law is the EEOC. Thus, Title VII and §§ 1981 and 1983 (nineteenth-century civil rights laws) have been used to support national origin discrimination lawsuits.

9-3.   Varieties of National Origin Discrimination

The EEOC includes the following varieties of national origin discrimination in a company's employment practices:

- Language requirement;
- Marriage or association with a member of the protected class;
- Membership in an organization promoting the rights of the protected class;
- Attendance at a school or church indicating membership in the protected class;
- Having a surname indicative of a class; and
- Various height and weight requirements.

Each case is obviously analyzed on its own merits. Some factors which may be considered national origin discrimination are actually not fixed; that is, they are capable of being changed regardless of one's national origin, e.g., clothing, religion, language, and proclivity for special foods. Other factors may be unchangeable, such as the physical characteristics of individuals of a particular national origin. However, there is no absolute rule concerning this distinction between "mutable" and "immutable" characteristics.

LANGUAGE REQUIREMENTS

The EEOC has issued opinions that employers may not prohibit employees from speaking languages other than English, unless it is clearly established that such a requirement is a justified business necessity.

In hotels and motels, it is generally reasonable to require that an employee be able to communicate with guests and patrons adequately to perform his/her job.

Similarly, hospitals and health-care centers sometimes require employees to be bilingual to perform their jobs.

Note: Hispanic-Americans are fast becoming the most numerous of all minorities in the United States. Therefore, in areas with substantial Hispanic populations, employers should consider communications in both Spanish and English in all policies, practices, and procedures.

NATIONAL ORIGIN, ANCESTRY, OR PLACE OF BIRTH

States have used the terms "national origin," "ancestry," and "place of birth" to ensure a broad prohibition against national origin discrimination. Some states use all three designations as protected groups to eliminate semantic and legalistic arguments concerning coverage.

Sometimes Chinese, Italian, French restaurants, and so forth, require individuals of specific national origins to the detriment of those, however qualified, of different national origins.

The general rule prohibits a refusal to hire an individual for any kind of job on the basis of his/her national origin. Obviously, if it is a business necessity to speak Chinese, then this may be a requirement. However, this is not to say that an individual's national origin is the requirement.

Example: Hospitals have maintained policies of patient segregation whereby minority employees are confined to contact with minority patients. While it would not be a violation of the national origin discrimination prohibition to require that certain employees be bilingual in order to facilitate the performance of their duties with patients who spoke primarily Chinese, it could be prohibited conduct to limit a Chinese-speaking employee to Chinese-speaking patients.

HEIGHT AND WEIGHT REQUIREMENTS

Hotels, restaurants, and institutions will be hard-pressed to justify any height or weight requirements. Furthermore, such requirements may have an adverse impact on individuals of a particular national origin and are therefore prohibited.

DISCRIMINATORY COMMENTS

Example: Condonation of "Polish" jokes; acquiescence in derogatory stereotypes and epithets by supervisors or management, and discriminatory insults are all examples of evidence of national origin discrimination. If an individual is subjected to an adverse employment practice in an atmosphere of discriminatory stereotypes and epithets, the company's defense will be that much more difficult.

Accordingly, all employers should eliminate an atmosphere of employee relations that tolerates discriminatory language.

CITIZENSHIP

It may be a violation of the Equal Opportunity Law if an employer requires that all be United States citizens where there is an adverse impact on a particular national origin protected group and the citizenship requirement is not job-related. However, citizenship in and of itself is not a protected group in America. Thus, the term "national origin" does not include the term "citizenship."

Example: A prominent hotel was accused of "national origin discrimination" when it fired an individual who was a citizen of Brazil. When it became apparent that the individual's national origin was actually Lebanese, then the plaintiff amended his pleadings to accuse the hotel of discrimination against a Brazilian citizen from Lebanon in favor of another employee who happened to be a Bahamian. Thus, to be found liable for national origin discrimination, the plaintiff would have had to prove that the hotel discharged the plaintiff because he was a Brazilian citizen from Lebanon and not from the Bahamas. Obviously, this absurd case was dismissed.

BONA FIDE OCCUPATIONAL QUALIFICATION

An individual's national origin may be a bona fide occupational qualification (BFOQ) in the case of a chef. Obviously, if a restaurant advertises that it is French or Chinese, it should be permitted to hire a French or Chinese chef. BFOQ can be used to justify authenticity in such a situation but will be strictly construed on a very narrow basis. For instance, one could certainly not use the chef argument to hire exclusively French waiters, when qualified candidates apply who are from countries other than France, familiar with French service, and conversive with French.

9-4.   Statistics and Recordkeeping

The statistics on the number of hotel and restaurant employees from other countries is staggering. These industries employ more individuals of foreign origin than any other.

Furthermore, prominent chefs, foodservice executives, and hoteliers from other countries are often the pride of the establishment due to the tremendous experience and heritage of hospitality service and foodservice in other parts of the world.

Records should be maintained of individuals' national origins, ancestries, and places of birth in order to monitor whether the employer is relegating a particular national origin group to a particular job or department.

Again, it is the recommendation that all records be maintained for at least five years.

10.

Religious Discrimination

10-1. Introduction and Definition

The term "religion" is defined in the law to include the following:

All aspects of religious observance and practice, as well as belief, unless an employer demonstrates that he is unable to reasonably accommodate to an employee's or prospective employee's religious observance or practice without undue hardship on the conduct of the employer's business. (Title VII, §701(j))

Whether a particular belief is protected as "religion" is not limited to traditional or parochial concepts of religion. Therefore, sincerely meaningful religious beliefs, although in no way connected with established or organized churches, would be protected.

Hospitality and foodservice companies appear to be generally nondiscriminatory with respect to religion.

Generally, an employer must make reasonable attempts to accommodate any conflicts between the requirements of an employee's religion and his/her job. However, the employer is not required to endure an undue hardship in order to accommodate reasonably religious beliefs.

10-2. Laws and Agencies

The law involved is, of course, Title VII of the Civil Rights Act prohibiting discrimination in employment practices on account

80

of religion. Various state laws also prohibit discrimination on the basis of one's creed, religion, and/or religious creed.

Enforcement of religious discrimination prohibitions is done by the EEOC and various related state agencies.

10-3. Varieties of Religious Discrimination

REASONABLE ACCOMMODATION

The primary authority for all religious discrimination prohibitions is Title VII, although the first Amendment to the U.S. Constitution also states:

Congress shall make no law respecting an establishment of religion, or prohibiting the free exercise thereof . . .

Case law interpreting § 701(j) confirms an affirmative duty reasonably to accommodate an employee's religious beliefs.

Therefore, if an employee's religious belief is sincere and the practice of that belief results in an employment action adverse to that employee, the employer has committed religious discrimination unless he/she can prove that any further reasonable accommodations would cause an undue hardship on the employer's business.

Each case is clearly handled on an *ad hoc* basis.

SABBATH DAY SCHEDULING

Most religious discrimination cases occur because of a conflict between the employee's Sabbath day and his/her work schedule.

Example: Trans World Airlines v. *Hardison,* 14 FEP Cases 1697 (1977), is the main case in this area. TWA operates a maintenance base twenty-four hours per day, 365 days per year, and whenever an employee's job in that department is not filled, an employee must be shifted from another department or a supervisor must cover the job, even if the work in other areas may suffer. Plaintiff Hardison studied the religion known as the Worldwide Church of God, one of whose tenets is that one must observe the Sabbath by refraining from work from sunset on Friday until sunset on Saturday. When Hardison informed his supervisor of his religious conviction, the supervisor agreed that the union steward should seek a job swap for Hardison or a change of days off. Hardison was trasferred to a shift which permitted him to observe his Sabbath. However, when Hardison bid on another job within TWA, he no longer had sufficient seniority to observe the Sabbath regularly. The union objected to violating the seniority provisions of the collective bargaining agreement in order to accommodate Hardison. The Supreme Court held that an employer's duty under Title VII to accommodate to religious needs of employees does not require it to take steps inconsistent with an otherwise valid collective bargaining agreement or to deny shift in job preference of other workers. The Court further stated that requiring an employer to bear more than *de minimus* cost in order to give an employee his Sabbath off is an undue hardship within the meaning of the law.

UNION MEMBERSHIP

An employee has no obligation whatsoever to join a union if such is contrary to his/her religious beliefs, even in the face of a collective bargaining agreement provision compelling union membership in a non–right-to-work state. One's religious belief may prohibit union membership, but not financial support of unions. In any event, a reasonable accommodation could be made by allowing a charitable contribution equal to union dues.

CONSTRUCTIVE DISCHARGE

Where an employer's policy or practice affronts an employee's sincere religious beliefs and the employee "resigns" as a result, the plaintiff could argue that he/she was constructively discharged because of religion.

Example: Where a bank employee was required to attend monthly staff meetings which were preceded by a "nondenominational" devotional (conducted by a Baptist minister), the employee refused to attend the meetings as an affront to her atheistic beliefs. Her beliefs in atheism were sincere and practiced by her. A United States Court of Appeals held that she had been constructively discharged and was entitled to reinstatement, back pay, and attorney's fees.

Employers should be equally as cosmopolitan and open-minded about employee's respective religious beliefs as their national origin.

There have been no major religious discrimination cases in the hospitality and foodservice industries.

10-4. Statistics and Recordkeeping

Almost every religion, established or otherwise, is represented in the complement of employees at a luxury, convention hotel in the large cities of the United States. Furthermore, statistics and records should be maintained for approximately five years concerning whether employees of particular religious persuasions are in particular job classifications or fully integrated into all jobs in the work force.

11.

Age Discrimination

11-1. Introduction

Any employment practice which results in discriminatory treatment of persons between the ages of forty (40) and seventy (70) is unlawful age discrimination. Thus, it is unlawful to fail or refuse to hire, discharge, reduce wages, or otherwise discriminate against an employee or prospective employee on account of his/her age if the individual is at least forty (40) and has not reached seventy (70) years of age.

11-2. Laws and Agencies

Administered by the EEOC, the Age Discrimination in Employment Act of 1967, as amended, prohibits all forms of discrimination in employment practices against people between forty (40) and seventy (70) years of age.

Additionally, the overwhelming majority of states specifically prohibit discrimination against individuals below forty (40) and above seventy (70) years of age. Check your local laws.

All hospitality and foodservice employers are covered if they employ twenty or more persons and affect interstate commerce.

11-3. Varieties of Age Discrimination

The most common example of age discrimination occurs in advertisements; resulting in the claim of an unlawful refusal to hire on account of age.

Example: Some examples are job advertisements using terms such as "age 20 to 30," "young," "boy," "recent graduate."

Individuals within the protected age group who apply for positions with such discriminatory or "fatal" language in the job advertisement will have a strong case if they are not hired.

The age discrimination prohibition even bars preference on the basis of age if both job applicants are in the protected age group.

Example: If one job applicant is forty-five (45) years of age and another is sixty-five (65) years of age, the employer may not give preference to the younger of the two applicants. It is unlawful to give preference to one person over another on account of age whenever the person discriminated against is within the protected age group.

FACTORS OTHER THAN AGE

The age discrimination law does authorize differentiations based upon reasonable factors other than age. While each case is determined on an *ad hoc* basis, there are certain factors which may be evidence of "reasonable factors":

- Physical fitness requirements necessary for specific jobs and uniformly applied;
- Production quantity or quality evaluation, provided job-relatedness can be established and the requirements are uniformly applied;
- Educational level which is job related and uniformly applied;
- Working hours conditions;
- Job-related, validated employee tests; and
- A prohibition against hiring relatives of employees (please note that such prohibitions may themselves be violative of various state Equal Opportunity Laws).

Each age discrimination case will be decided on its own merits, depending upon the proof of each side.

BONA FIDE SENIORITY SYSTEM

The age discrimination law authorizes different treatment on the basis of age if pursuant to the terms of a bona fide seniority system which is not a subterfuge to evade the purpose of the law. A bona fide seniority system must have the following characteristics:

- The system must be based on length of service as the primary criterion;
- The system should accord those with longer service greater rights;
- The system cannot have the effect of perpetuating past age discrimination; and
- The system must have been communicated to the employees and applied uniformly, regardless of age.

Additionally, bona fide employee benefit plans involving pension plans, retirement funds, etc., may not be used as a subterfuge to evade the age discrimination law.

EXECUTIVE EXEMPTION

Executives between the ages of sixty-five (65) and seventy (70) are exempt for the law's increased upper age limit if the following conditions are satisfied:

- The executive is a top-level employee who for at least two years prior to retirement is in a bona fide high policymaking or executive position; and
- The executive is entitled to an immediate, nonforfeitable retirement benefit equivalent to a straight-life annuity of $27,000.

Additionally, employees may be involuntarily retired so long as the retirement is pursuant to the terms of a bona fide retirement or pension program.

11-4. Statistics and Recordkeeping

Approximately 1 million establishments employing 66 million persons fall within the jurisdiction within the Age Discrimination in Employment Act. Of the 95 million persons in the labor force in September 1976, 37 million were in the protected age group at that time, forty (40) to sixty-five (65). On the other hand, by the year 2000, the number of persons in this age group will increase to more than 79 million—an increase of more than 16 million in the last decade of this century—and will comprise approximately 48 percent of the population twenty-five (25) years of age and over. Furthermore, by 2000 about 12 percent of the population will be over 65, compared with 10.4 percent in 1975.

Generally, the number of age discrimination cases will increase, as has the number of sex discrimination lawsuits. Furthermore, the number of sex and age discrimination cases brought by females within the protected age group will increase dramatically in the next ten years.

As indicated earlier, the most common discriminatory practice in the area of age discrimination is illegal advertising, followed by refusals to hire and illegal discharges.

Example: In the hospitality and foodservice industries, there are potential age discrimination problems involving front-desk clerks, waiters/waitresses, cocktail waitresses, sales and account representatives, hosts/hostesses, concierges, and any individual coming into immediate contact with guests and patrons. Employers who are inclined to select younger individuals in these job classifications on account of their youthful age may create the potential for lawsuits.

In short, there will continue to be marked increases in the number of age discrimination lawsuits. Therefore, employers should be alert to any potential problem areas. Maintain age records for employees in the protected age group for five years.

EDUCATE ALL DEPARTMENT HEADS AND KEY SUPERVISORS ABOUT AGE DISCRIMINATION

POST THE AGE DISCRIMINATION POSTER AND REQUIRE THAT IT BE STUDIED

PROMOTE AN ATMOSPHERE OF RESPECT FOR INDIVIDUALS OF ALL AGES

CONSULT YOUR ATTORNEY TO DETERMINE THE APPLICABLE PROTECTED AGE GROUPS

12.

Handicap Discrimination

12-1. Introduction

Generally, an individual is considered legally handicapped if he/she suffers substantial limitations on "major life activities."

The Rehabilitation Act of 1973, as amended, defines a "handicapped individual" to mean any individual who:

(A) has a physical or mental disability which for such individual constitutes or results in a substantial handicap to employment and (B) can reasonably be expected to benefit in terms of employability from vocational rehabilitation services provided pursuant to subchapter I and III of this chapter. For the purposes of subchapters IV and V of this chapter, such term means any person who (A) has a physical or mental impairment which substantially limits one or more of such person's major life activities, (B) has a record of such impairment, or (C) is regarded of having such an impairment. (29 U.S.C. §706(6))

Since many jobs within hospitality and foodservice businesses involve constant movement, as well as contact with guests and patrons, many individuals with mobility handicaps have gravitated toward other industries with stationary positions.

12-2. Laws and Agencies

The primary federal statute involved is the Rehabilitation Act of 1973, as amended, which requires federal contracts worth more than $2,500 to contain a provision obligating the contractor to "take affirmative action to employ and advance in employment qualified handicapped individuals."

Thus, an employer must be a government contractor to be covered by this federal law prohibiting handicap discrimination. Note, however, that the overwhelming majority of state Equal Opportunity Laws include physical handicap/disability, medical condition, faulty eyesight, blood type, or mental handicap as a protected group in employment practices.

The federal law is administered by the Office of Federal Contract Compliance Programs of the U.S. Department of Labor (OFCCP). If a hospitality of foodservice facility is a government contractor, there are affirmative action requirements, as well as sanctions for noncompliance, such as contract debarment and judicial action for injunctive relief.

However, there is no right of a private plaintiff to sue a government contractor for noncompliance. On the other hand, since an employee's handicap status is generally a protected group under state Equal Opportunity Laws, hotels, restaurants, and institutions should examine in detail what agency at the state or local level has jurisdiction over handicap discrimination.

12-3. Varieties of Handicap Discrimination

The varieties of handicap discrimination include all forms of physical and mental handicaps.

Example: Handicaps include faulty eyesight, paraplegia and neuromuscular conditions, asthma and allergy conditions, hypertension and other cardiovascular conditions, epilepsy, diabetes, spinal and abdominal defects, gastrointestinal conditions, genitourinary conditions, retardation, and speech and hearing problems. Mental handicap is also protected under federal law and government contractors must reasonably accommodate individuals with mental problems, unless the government contractor can demonstrate that such an accommodation would impose an undue hardship on the conduct of the contractor's business. Several states prohibit discrimination on the basis of psychiatric condition.

If the physical or mental handicap substantially impairs the employee from performing his/her job adequately, then even government contractors are not obligated to create an undue hardship on their business.

Since many institutional foodservice operations are government connected, as are many hospitals, health-care facilities, and public assembly facilities, these employers should generally recognize the rules against handicap discrimination. The employer should make a reasonable effort to accommodate the handicapped employee before taking any adverse employment action.

Example: A claim of discrimination on the basis of rheumatoid arthritis handicap was rejected, since the plaintiff was incapable of performing her job efficiently at the time of discharge. On the other hand, handicap discrimination was found on the basis of an asthma handicap because the plaintiff was performing the job efficiently at the time of discharge. Handicap discrimination has been found on the basis of diabetes.

Example: In a 1978 case in New Jersey an employer illegally discriminated against a heart attack victim by refusing to reemploy him, despite the lack of evidence that he was physically unable to perform his former job duties. The employer's opinion of unfitness was not reasonably arrived at, where it was based solely on a company physician's recommendations and where these recommendations were made without a physical examination and without knowledge of the job to which the employee was seeking reinstatement.

Example: In a 1978 case in Wisconsin a taxicab company improperly rejected a cab driver applicant because he was missing a hand and part of his forearm. There was no evidence that the condition of the driver's arm presented a safety hazard or otherwise impaired the applicant's ability to perform the job. His past successful employment as a cab driver indicated that his limited use of the arm did not affect his job performance.

12-4. Statistics and Recordkeeping

Depending upon the definition of handicap, the number of adults with some form of handicap is probably less than 10 million as of 1979.

Government contractors and employers in states specifically protecting handicapped employees as a group should maintain accurate records concerning recruitment of handicapped individuals, retention, separation, and efforts of reasonable accommodation. Again, it is the recommendation that all records be kept for at least five years.

Government contractors must have a written affirmative action program.

13.

Veteran and Military Status Discrimination

13-1. Introduction

The definition of a veteran generally includes all persons who served in the military during times of war, regardless of whether they participated in combat. However, generally veterans' preferences are not broad enough to cover reservists.

Federal Equal Opportunity Law generally does not require private employers to take affirmative action in employing veterans, absent government-contractor status. Furthermore, only a few states protect veterans or military status under Equal Opportunity Laws.

Example: Illinois Equal Opportunity Law protects individuals from discrimination on account of an unfavorable discharge, while New Jersey protects individuals from discrimination because of military service liability and South Carolina protects individuals from discrimination because of national guard service.

On the other hand, every state law, as well as the federal government, supports affirmative action for veterans in government employment.

Thus, if the hotel, restaurant, or institution is not a government contractor and is not located in a state which creates a preference for veterans and those with military service liability, generally there is no legal requirement to hire veterans preferentially or protect those with military service obligations.

On the other hand, if the hotel, restaurant, or institution is a government contractor, there are very specific veteran preferences required by federal law. Furthermore, many hospitals and health-care facilities are specifically owned by counties and municipalities receiving federal funds and covered by federal veterans preference statutes. Similarly, public assembly facilities are under a governmental obligation to take affirmative action with respect to veterans and those with military status.

All government contractors with annual contracts of $10,000 are covered by the Vietnam-Era Veterans' Readjustment Assistance Act of 1974. Nondisabled Vietnam-era veterans were entitled to preferential treatment in government employment and in employment with government contractors until 1979, if they came within the definition of a Vietnam veteran, generally covering service between August 5, 1964, and May 7, 1975.

On the other hand, the classification "disabled veteran" continues to be covered under this law. A disabled veteran is defined as a person entitled to disability compensation under Veterans Administration Regulations where the disability was 30 percent or more, or a person whose discharge or release from active duty was for a disability that occurred in the line of duty.

A qualified disabled veteran is a disabled veteran who is capable of performing the job with reasonable accommodation to his/her disability.

13-2. Laws and Agencies

Laws which have been passed to give preferential treatment to and protect the rights of veterans include the following:

- Servicemen's Readjustment Act of 1944
- Veterans' Readjustment Assistance Act of 1952
- Veterans' Readjustment Benefits Act of 1966
- Universal Military Training and Service Act of 1967
- Vietnam-Era Veterans' Readjustment Assistance Act of 1974

Preferential requirements for veterans and disabled veterans are generally enforced by OFCCP of the U.S. Department of Labor, as well as the Office of Veterans Reemployment Rights (OVRR).

Private employers subject to the Military Selective Service

Act are required to give certain reemployment rights concerning seniority, vacations, pensions, promotions, etc., to veterans subject to selective service obligations. Thus, should the military draft be reinstituted, employers should identify those individuals seeking to be reemployed after military service.

Example: The Supreme Court of the United States has held that the Military Selective Service Act requires that the benefits and advancements that would have inured to the benefit of an employed individual will not be denied a veteran simply because of his absence in military service.

Example: Military service time must be added to total length of service time in computing severance pay. A similar result was reached in a case involving vacation and holiday pay.

The United States Department of Labor generally handles conciliation efforts and litigation responsibility for the Military Selective Service Act. On the other hand, the U.S. Department of Justice has litigation responsibility for enforcement of the Vietnam-Era Veterans' Readjustment Assistance Act of 1974.

13-3. Varieties of Veteran and Military Status Discrimination

Generally, returning veterans are entitled to their "rightful place," if the employer is covered by the Military Selective Service Act and subject to veterans' reemployment regulations.

DISCHARGE

Individuals incurring service-connected injuries, if employed by a covered employer, are entitled to "reasonable accommodation" even if they cannot perform the exact same job they had prior to military service.

Example: An individual discharged a few weeks after enlisting in the military was entitled to reemployment and back pay as a returned veteran, since a federal court held that his employer discharged him before he was to report to active duty to avoid incurring veteran reemployment rights obligations.

Thus, an individual may be awarded his "rightful place" with respect to reemployment, pay rates, seniority rights, and so forth.

SENIORITY

Example: An employee who had been reemployed by the defendant employer at his preservice position was laid off. He would not have been laid off if he had been properly credited with the seniority due him when he was reemployed; thus he was entitled to reinstatement.

Please note that disabled veterans may also file complaints under various statutes and regulations protecting individuals from handicap discrimination.

VETERANS' PREFERENCE AND SEX DISCRIMINATION

Employers are invited to consider that extreme veterans' preference could result in sex discrimination, since very few veterans are female. Therefore, an employment policy or practice preferring veterans must be balanced against any adverse impact on the protected group of women from the standpoint of sex discrimination. Since veteran status is generally not job-related, any adverse impact on women as a result of a policy of veteran preference would likely be sex discrimination.

13-4. Statistics and Recordkeeping

There are more than 30 million veterans in the United States. Furthermore, for almost forty years men have accounted for well over 95 percent of all military personnel. Hence, serious questions of sex discrimination are raised from a statistical analysis. Each employer should analyze the veterans in his/ her work place from the standpoint of potential sex discrimination against women.

Again, it is recommended that records be kept at least five

years on veteran status of employees, job applicants, and former employees.

Government contractors must have a written affirmative action program and notify employees of various veterans' preferences and veterans' reemployment rights.

On the other hand, many hotels, motels, restaurants, and clubs are not subject to or covered by veterans' preference laws. Even if an employer is not covered, however, it is obviously good practice to maintain a nondiscriminatory employment policy with respect to veterans.

DETERMINE WHETHER YOU ARE COVERED BY VETERANS' PREFERENCE LAWS

DEVELOP A POLICY ON VETERANS AND EMPLOYEES WITH MILITARY OBLIGATIONS

14.

Union Preference Discrimination

14-1. Introduction

It is a violation of federal labor law to discharge an employee or otherwise adversely affect his/her employment relationship on account of his/her being a member of a union or active on behalf of a union. This is true regardless of whether the employer is unionized and the particular state is a right-to-work state.

If an employer is unionized, the union is the authorized collective bargaining representative to negotiate on behalf of all employees in the bargaining unit wages, hours of work, and other conditions of employment. Furthermore, union representatives and shop stewards generally have the right to act on behalf of aggrieved employees. If management discriminates against employee-shop stewards because of their advocacy on behalf of aggrieved employees, this may be subject to an unfair labor practice charge of discrimination in violation of federal labor law.

Closed shops which require all employees to join a union upon being employed are prohibited in all states and under federal labor law. Union shops which authorize a collective bargaining agreement provision requiring that employees join the union after thirty (30) days of employment are authorized in approximately thirty (30) states.

There are approximately twenty (20) states, however, which have right-to-work laws. These states are:

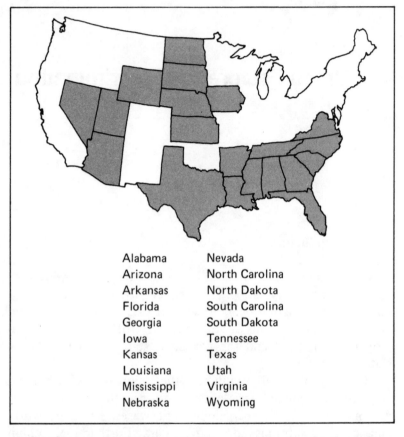

Alabama	Nevada
Arizona	North Carolina
Arkansas	North Dakota
Florida	South Carolina
Georgia	South Dakota
Iowa	Tennessee
Kansas	Texas
Louisiana	Utah
Mississippi	Virginia
Nebraska	Wyoming

Right-to-work states prohibit collective bargaining agreement provisions which make union membership a condition of employment. Hotels, restaurants, and most institutional facilities would be prohibited in right-to-work states from agreeing to any contract provision resulting in compulsory unionism, such as a union shop.

Thus, right-to-work laws prohibit employers (and unions) from discrimination against or in favor of employees because of union status or preference.

14-2. Laws and Agencies

Obviously, whether a state has a right-to-work law is very relevant to you as an employer. If your facility is in a right-to-work state, it is often a misdemeanor to require an employee to join a union as a conditon of employment.

If there is no state prohibition, federal labor law merely prohibits closed shops but not union shops.

The National Labor Relations Act of 1935, as amended, protects employees from discrimination on account of union preference or status. The National Labor Relations Board enforces federal labor law. An employee discriminated against on account of his/her union preference or status may file a charge alleging that his/her employer has committed an unfair labor practice.

This charge will be investigated by the National Labor Relations Board. The Regional Director of the National Labor Relations Board will decide whether to issue a complaint. If a complaint is issued, a hearing will be set before an Administrative Law Judge, who will determine whether the employer committed an unfair labor practice by discriminating in employment practices on account of the employee's union preference or status. The judge's decision may be reviewed by the National Labor Relations Board, which decision may in turn be reviewed by a United States Court of Appeals. The Court of Appeals decision may be appealed to the U.S. Supreme Court.

14-3. Varieties of Union Preference or Status Discrimination

Nonunion companies may be found to have discriminated on account of union preference or status by discharging an employee for union advocacy. Federal labor law authorizes employees to bargain collectively or to refrain therefrom and also to engage in concerted activity with the view towards unionization.

Of course employees may be discharged for violations of company rules, so long as the alleged "violation" is not found to be merely a subterfuge to stymie a union campaign.

Example: So-called no solicitation/distribution rules often have been found to be discriminatory in their application. Where an employer discharges an employee for distributing union authorization cards during his/her break time or free time but does not discipline employees for soliciting for employee gifts, United Way contributions, football pools, and the like, an otherwise valid rule may be unlawful as applied.

It is recommended, therefore, that the following simple rule be utilized in this regard: *Working time is for work.*

Unionized companies may be found to have discriminated against employees on account of their union advocacy.

Example: Where a shop steward pursues a grievance and the supervisor adversely changes the shop steward's shift schedule, hours of work, or the like, it has been held to be union status discrimination which would be an unfair labor practice.

On the other hand, a unionized company in a right-to-work state may be found to have discriminated against an employee if it tries to persuade a worker to join the union through indirect pressure or adversely affecting his/her working conditions.

Thus, a unionized company in a right-to-work state should neither encourage nor discourage employees concerning union membership.

On the other hand, in a non–right-to-work state a unionized employer may encourage and in fact agree to a union shop provision in the contract concerning union membership.

14-4. Statistics and Recordkeeping

The primary union involved in the hospitality and foodservice industries is the Hotel & Restaurant Employees & Bartenders International Union, AFL-CIO. This union represents almost 500,000 hotel and restaurant employees, less than 15 percent of the total number of hotel and restaurant employees.

The International Brotherhood of Teamsters is another union which has organized a substantial number of employees, particularly in the West.

The International Union of Operating Engineers (IUOE) is a union which represents many employees in the engineering department of a hotel.

Employers in all states should refrain from discrimination against employees on account of their union preference or status.

Records should be maintained at unionized companies of which employees are on union checkoff. In a non–right-to-work state where the collective bargaining agreement requires that employees join the union after thirty (30) days, records should be maintained to ensure compliance with this collective bargaining agreement provision.

IV.
EMPLOYMENT PROCESS

15.

Employment Process — Introduction

Hospitality and foodservice facilities have high turnover rates when compared to other industries. Furthermore, since personnel often determine the service shown a guest or patron, the selection and employment of individuals is fundamental to a successful hospitality or foodservice operation.

Accordingly, there should be a formal commitment to personnel function at hotels, motels, restaurants, clubs, foodservice institutions, hospitals, public assembly facilities, healthcare facilities, etc. None of these businesses is removed from the funadamental rule that good service comes from employing good people. Therefore, formalized procedures for employing qualified individuals are essential. Equal Opportunity Laws, moreover, make it even more important to establish and implement an employment process. This division of the book deals very briefly with employment process issues from a preventive law standpoint.

16.

Recruitment, Selection, and Hiring

16-1. Recruiting

Generally, recruiting for hospitality and foodservice employment should involve a broad range of sources of applicants. One should maintain records of which sources have been utilized and/or contacted.

Classified advertisements for individuals and/or jobs must be carefully drafted to avoid creating evidence of discrimination. The following examples of discriminatory terms and non-discriminatory alternatives should be considered in this regard.

Discriminatory Term	Nondiscriminatory Alternative
Attractive, Pretty, Handsome	Well-Groomed, Presentable
Barmaid	Bar Help, *Bar Waiter/Waitress
Bell Boy	Bell Hop, *Bell Man or Woman
Body Man	Body Work
Busboy, Tray Girl	Busser, Dish Bussing, Cafeteria Work, Bus Service, Feed Service Attendant
Cameraman	Camera Technician, Camera Sales
Cleaning Woman, Cleaning Lady	Cleaning
Corpsman	Paramedic, Medical Assistant

Counter Girl, Counter Boy	Counter Work
Credit Girl	Credit, *Credit Man or Woman, Credit Manager
Doorman	Doorman-Male or Female Door Attendant, Door Service
Draftsman	Drafting, *Draftsman-Male or Female
Foreman	Foreman-Male or Female
Girl Friday	General Office M/W
Handyman	Handyman or Woman, Misc. Repair
Host, Hostess	Host/Hostess
Housewife, Mother	Part-Time-School Hours
Janitor, Janitress	Janitor/Janitress, Custodian
Journeyman	Journeyman-Male or Female
Leadman	Crew Leader, Shift Leader
Masseur, Masseusse	*Masseur/Masseusse
Maid	Housekeeping, Housekeeper, Room Attendant, House-keeping Services
Maintenance Man	Maintenance Work, Engineer
Man, Woman, Girl, Boy, Male Female, Lady, Gal, Gentlemen	Person, Individual, Applicant— Man or Woman, Male or Female
Nurse	Nurse (M/W)
Partsman	Parts Work
Phone Girls	Phone Work, Phone Sales
Playboy	*Playboy/Playgirl
Pressman	Pressman/Presswoman
Repairman	Repairs, Repairwork
Salad Girl	Salad Preparation
Salesman, Saleslady, Saleswoman	Salesperson, Sales Clerk, Sales
Sheet Metal Man	Sheet Metal Worker

Stewardess	Stewardess/Steward, Cabin Attendant
Tailor, Seamstress	*Tailor/Seamstress
Usher, Usherette	*Usher/Usherette
Waiter	*Waiter/Waitress, Foodservice

*Nondiscriminatory only when used together.

Note: Where a neutral substitute is not available for a discriminatory term (such as foreman), such term may be used if the heading or the body of the ad specifies both males and females will be considered. Obviously, one should avoid extreme discriminatory terms.

The following job classifications are often considered nondiscriminatory:

Accountant	Clerk
Accounts receivable/payable clerk	Closer
Administrator	Coffee servers
Advisor	Concierge
Aide	Consultant
Analyst	Controller
Artist	Cook
Assistant	Coordinator
Attendant	Counselor
Auditor	Custodian
Bartender	Demonstrator
Bell service	Designer
Boiler attendant	Director
Bookkeeper	Dishwasher
Bus attendant	Dispatcher
Butcher	Door service
Cabinet maker	Driver
Captain	Electrician
Caretaker	Engineer
Carpenter	Estimator
Cashier	Executive
Caterer	Food server
Chauffeur	Food service
Chef	Front desk clerk
Clerical	Garde manger

General kitchen help
General maintenance
Guard
Helper
Inspector
Instructor
Interviewer
Kitchen utility
Laundry worker
Machinist
Manager
Mechanic
Operator
Orderly
Painter
Pantry help
PBX
Photographer
Powder room attendant
Presser
Printer
Programmer

Public relations representative
Receptionist
Representative
Room service
Salad prep
Sanitation attendant
Secretary
Security officer
Servers
Sommelier
Stenographer
Stylist
Superintendent
Supervisor
Technician
Trainee
Typist
Valet and cleaning
Welder
Worker
Writer

These are a few job classification titles which are generally considered nondiscriminatory.

16-2. Selecting and Hiring

PREEMPLOYMENT INQUIRIES

The following chart of discriminatory and nondiscriminatory preemployment inquiries is a good guideline for most employers:

PREEMPLOYMENT INQUIRIES

Subject	Fair Preemployment Inquiries	Unfair Preemployment Inquiries
Age	Inquiries as to birth date and proof of true age are permitted.	Any inquiry not in compliance with the law which implies a preference for persons under 40 years of age.

Arrests	None	All inquiries relating to arrests.
Citizenship	Whether applicant is prevented from lawfully becoming employed in this country because of visa or immigration status. Whether applicant can provide proof of citizenship, visa, alien registration number after being hired.	Whether applicant is citizen. Requirement before hiring that applicant present birth certificate, naturalization or baptismal record. Any inquiry into citizenship which would tend to divulge applicant's lineage, ancestry, national origin, descent, or birthplace.
Convictions	(1) Inquiries concerning specified convictions which relate reasonably to fitness to perform the particular job(s) being applied for; PROVIDED that such inquiries be limited to convictions for which the date of conviction or prison release, whichever is more recent, is within 5 years of the date of the job application. (2) Where the employer believes, after careful consideration, that it is not practicable to inquire about specific convictions, the employer may inquire generally about all convictions for which the date of the conviction or prison release, whichever is more recent, is within 5 years of the date of the job application; PROVIDED that such general inquiries be accompanied by a disclaimer informing the applicant that a conviction record will not necessarily bar him or her from employment.	Any inquiry which does not meet the requirements for fair preemployment inquiries.

Family	Whether applicant can meet specified work schedules or has activities, commitments, or responsibilities that may prevent him or her from meeting work attendance requirements.	Specific inquiries concerning spouse, spouse's employment or salary, children, child-care arrangements, or dependents.
Handicap	Whether applicant has certain specified sensory, mental, or physical handicaps which relate reasonably to fitness to perform the particular job. Whether applicant has any handicaps or health problems which may affect work performance or which the employer should take into account in determining job placement.	Overgeneral inquiries, e.g., "Do you have any handicaps?" which would tend to divulge handicaps or health conditions which do not relate reasonably to fitness to perform the job.
Height and Weight	Inquiries as to ability to perform actual job requirements. Being of a certain height or weight will not be considered to be a job requirement unless the employer can show that no employee with the ineligible height or weight could do the work.	Any inquiry which is not based on actual job rements.
Marital status	None	( ) Mr. ( ) Mrs. ( ) Miss ( ) Ms. Whether the applicant is married, single, divorced, separated, engaged, widowed, etc.
Military	Inquiries concerning education, training, or work experience in the armed forces of the United States.	Type or condition of military discharge. Applicant's experience in other than U.S. armed forces. Request for discharge papers.
Name	Whether applicant has worked for this company or a competitor under a	Inquiry into original name where it has been changed by court order or marriage.

	different name and, if so, what name. Name under which applicant is known to references if different from present name.	Inquiries about a name which would divulge marital status, lineage, ancestry, national origin, or descent.
National origin	Inquiries into applicant's ability to read, write, and speak foreign languages, when such inquiries are based on job requirements.	Inquiries into applicant's lineage, ancestry, national origin, descent, birthplace, or mother tongue. National origin of applicant's parents or spouse.
Organizations	Inquiry into organization memberships, excluding any organization the name or character of which indicates the race, color, creed, sex, marital status, religion, or national origin or ancestry of its members.	Requirement that applicant list all organizations, clubs, societies, and lodges to which he or she belongs.
Photographs	May be requested after hiring for identification purposes.	Request that applicant submit a photograph, mandatorily or optionally, at any time before hiring.
Pregnancy	Inquiries as to a duration of stay on job or anticipated absences which are made to males and females alike.	All questions as to pregnancy, and medical history concerning pregnancy and related matters.
Race or color	None	Any inquiry concerning race or color of skin, hair, eyes, etc.
Relatives	Names of applicant's relatives already employed by this company or by any competitor.	Names and address of any relative other than those listed as proper.
Religion or creed	None	Inquiries concerning applicant's religious denomination, religious affiliations, church, parish, pastor, or religious holidays observed.

Residence	Inquries about address to the extent needed to facilitate contacting the applicant.	Names or relationship of persons with whom applicant resides. Whether applicant owns or rents home.
Sex	None	Any inquiry.

Note: While the law does not directly prohibit company policies governing the employment of relatives, any policy which has the effect of disadvantaging minorities, women, married couples, or other protected classes, would be a violation of the law, unless it is shown to serve a necessary business purpose.

REFERENCE CHECKS

It is important to check state and local law concerning what questions may be asked and what information may be used when making reference checks.

Example: Arrest and conviction records, military discharge records, welfare status records, bad credit reports, and the like may be prohibited information in some states and localities. Federal law prohibits the use of such materials if they form the basis for a refusal to hire an individual in a protected group and are not job-related.

Similarly, recent, relevant conviction records may be used consistent with the hotelier's and restaurateur's duty to select employees who will not in all likelihood harm guests and patrons. Since hoteliers and restaurateurs have a duty to avoid negligently selecting individuals who may cause harm to guests and patrons, conviction records of felonies committed within the last five years are generally relevant and nondiscriminatory.

Q. May polygraph examination be required as a condition of employment?

A. The trend in the hospitality and foodservice industries, as well as throughout American industry, is against the use of polygraph examinations as a condition of employment. While each state law must be examined on this subject, the number of states prohibiting the use of polygraph examinations as a condition of employment is increasing annually.

It is suggested that a similar result would be reached concerning voice stress analysis tests as a condition of employment. New York, for example, prohibits employers from using truth or falsity of statements as a means of selecting prospective employees or as a means of screening current employees.

It is recommended that in states where polygraph examinations and voice stress analysis tests are lawful, they should be utilized on an *ad hoc* basis only and not as a condition of employment.

APPLICATION FORMS

Application forms should seek only job-related information. Questions on application form which are discriminatory, regardless of their relevancy, will be taken as evidence of a policy of discrimination.

Example: Asking the age of the applicant, regardless of whether there is any intent to discriminate against individuals between the ages of forty (40) and seventy (70), will be evidence of age discrimination against all those applicants between the ages of forty and seventy who are not hired. On the other hand, asking whether an individual is at least the minimum age for the purpose of handling alcoholic beverages is clearly job related and lawful. (*See* Appendix F.)

16-3. Recordkeeping, Reports, and Posters

Employers should keep accurate records of all job applicants, including the full name of the applicant, date of interview, and job applied for.

Additionally, all Equal Opportunity Law posters should be posted in a prominent place for employees and applicants to see and read.

It is recommended that the following notice be reproduced in poster form and displayed prominently:

THE _____ HOTEL IS AN EQUAL OPPORTUNITY EM-
PLOYER AND ALWAYS ENDEAVORS TO SELECT THE BEST QUAL-
IFIED INDIVIDUAL FOR THE JOB BASED UPON JOB-RELATED
QUALIFICATIONS, AND REGARDLESS OF RACE, COLOR, CREED,
SEX, NATIONAL ORIGIN, AGE, HANDICAP, OR OTHER PRO-
TECTED GROUP UNDER FEDERAL, STATE, OR LOCAL LAW.

17.

Transfer, Promotion, and Demotion

Great care must be taken to avoid discrimination in transfers, promotions, and demotions. Frequently, employers may be charged with allegedly unlawful refusal to promote an individual on account of some protected group's status.

Example: Where a female secretary with years of experience is not even considered for the position of administrative assistant to a manager, and a young male college graduate is selected, the result may be an expensive sex discrimination lawsuit.

Therefore, in transferring, promoting, and demoting individuals ensure that the department head has adequately considered all relevant job applicants prior to the final decision.

Job-posting policies are generally very helpful in this regard. While they may require more administrative processing and more review before selecting the individual to transfer or promote, such policies provide guidelines so that a qualified individual who may want the job is not overlooked. Employees seeking transfers and promotions, moreover, are often intimately aware of any prejudices harbored by supervisors with decision-making authority. Therefore, a plaintiff in an unlawful-refusal-to-promote case often has a wealth of knowledge to use against the employer if he/she so desires.

For key positions, management should keep a record of all those individuals considered and the relevant qualifications of all candidates for the promotion.

18.

Release, Separation, Termination, and Discharge

The discharge of an employee causes more ill feeling and lawsuits statistically than all other actions in the employment process. Thus, it is crucial for employers to establish a set procedure for handling separations and discharges. It is equally essential to have an objective disciplinary procedure which encourages documentation of an employee's activities which may result in discharge.

A discharged employee in a protected group may not only file with the state and/or federal Equal Opportunity agencies but will also often file a claim for unemployment insurance. Hence, there may be numerous hearings where testimony will be taken considering the reasons for discharge. These reasons should be well documented prior to the decision to discharge.

DISCIPLINARY PROCEDURE

The most salient point of any disciplinary procedure is that it be simple enough to be objectively applied in all departments of the facility. Secondly, the disciplinary procedure should be progressive.

Example: Requiring three warning notices prior to discharge is generally considered an objective, progressive disciplinary procedure. Obviously, the warning notices should state with specificity the offense committed, the time of the offense, key witnesses involved, and the disciplinary procedure awarded at that time. Whether the employee signs the notice is normally not determinative, as long as some management representative can testify that he/she informed the employee being disciplined of the reasons and the discipline awarded.

It is recommended that there be a formal record kept of all major infractions of the rules.

Prior to discharging an employee, there should be an exit interview by the personnel director explaining the reasons for the discharge and affording the employee the opportunity to refute any allegations.

When an employee voluntarily separates himself/herself from company's employment, a responsible management representative and/or the personnel director should document the reasons for such voluntary separation.

If the employee is in a protected group, he/she may later sue the employer, alleging that working conditions were so adverse to him/her that the resignation was forced, resulting in a "constructive discharge" argument. Ample legal authority exists for a plaintiff to sue for an unlawful constructive discharge. This may be avoided by a thorough exit interview as to the reasons for resignation.

ESTABLISH A DISCIPLINARY PROCEDURE WHICH IS OBJECTIVELY ADMINISTERED BY ALL DEPARTMENTS. DISCIPLINE SHOULD BE PROGRESSIVE.

ALL EMPLOYEES SEPARATING FROM THE COMPANY, BOTH INVOLUNTARILY AND VOLUNTARILY, SHOULD BE SUBJECT TO AN EXIT INTERVIEW.

DOCUMENTATION, DOCUMENTATION, DOCUMENTATION

V.
AFFIRMATIVE EQUAL OPPORTUNITY PROGRAMS

19.

Government Contractors

Employers with federal government contracts of $50,000 or more and fifty (50) or more employees are obligated to prepare and maintain a written affirmative action program (AAP) particularly with respect to handicapped and Vietnam-era individuals and racial minorities and women. Affirmative action requirements are also applicable to those with government contracts in excess of $2,500. As indicated earlier, Section 503 of The Rehabilitation Act of 1973 requires affirmative action with respect to handicapped individuals and is administered by the OFCCP of the U.S. Department of Labor.

Governmental affirmative action requirements concerning racial minorities and women are embodied in Presidential Executive Order No. 11246, which is also administered by the OFCCP.

The most stringent affirmative action requirements affect individuals with contracts of $50,000 or more and fifty or more employees.

Thus, such an employer must have a written AAP and that program must be left on file at the employer's place of business available for inspection by employees or interested prospective employees. The $50,000 and fifty (50) employee criteria are, therefore, applicable to the Vietnam-Era Veterans' Readjustment Assistance Act of 1974, the Rehabilitation Act of 1973, and Executive Order No. 11246. Again, all are administered by the OFCCP.

Since enforcement of these affirmative action requirements has been almost exclusively through the individual complaint process to the OFCCP, the OFCCP implemented "Directed Compliance Reviews," which it "believed to be a more effective way to prevent systemic discrimination." The OFCCP states in pertinent parts:

The goal of the enforcement process is to assure that contractors take affirmative action in the employment and advancement in employment of handicapped workers, disabled veterans, and Viet Nam era veterans.

The language required by federal law and government regulations for use in the affirmative action plan is very specific. Furthermore, affirmative action plans must be updated annually consistent with work-force developments and regulations.

The OFCCP has promulgated a booklet called "Directed Compliance Review Procedures for Veterans and Handicapped Workers Affirmative Action Programs (OFCCP-24, January 26, 1978)," which describes in detail the "Directed Compliance Review."

DEBARMENT

An employer not complying with the affirmative action requirement of the federal Equal Opportunity Law and government regulations may be barred from government contract. The term "debarment" includes such actions taken by federal government to prohibit employers from receiving further federal contracts.

Sometimes the government has taken the position that it may "pass over" a contractor for alleged violations of Executive Order No. 11246.

Courts, however, have ruled that a "pass over" without a prior hearing would be unlawful, and the government could be enjoined for engaging in such action. It appears that the government may attempt to "pass over" a company without a hearing in the following situation:

If the next two contracts for which an employer is the lowest bidder are small, the Department of Labor may award those to the contractor and wait to "pass over" the company for much larger contracts. This has been so-called enforcement by economic coercion. Selective "economic coercion" obviously could have the same result as debarment.

Therefore, if a "pass over" occurs to a contractor without a hearing, it can be argued that this action is violative of the Due Process Clause of the United States Constitution.

In short, once an employer is a government contractor, affirmative action requirements are effectively enforced and should be complied with. On the other hand, serious questions have been raised by the Bakke case concerning so-called reverse discrimination. (*See* Appendix C for a sample affirmative equal opportunity program which attempts to track the Bakke case.)

The rules and regulations covering government contractors are extremely complex and enforced in the most effective way possible—debarment from federal contracts and/or "economic coercion." Therefore, it behooves all employers to determine their government contractor status.

Example: If a hotel is part of a chain and a hotel within that chain has a government contract for $100,000 a year with the Army, the OFCCP generally takes the position that all other hotels owned and/or managed by that chain are government contractors or subcontractors.

Example: If a hotel managed by a hotel management company books business in excess of $50,000 a year with a prime government contractor, such as IBM, the hotel would generally be considered to be a government subcontractor by the OFCCP.

DETERMINE GOVERNMENT CONTRACTOR STATUS AND TAKE AFFIRMATIVE ACTION STEPS AS INDICATED

POST ALL GOVERNMENT CONTRACTOR NOTICES

MAKE AFFIRMATIVE ACTION PLAN AVAILABLE FOR INSPECTION

DETERMINE GOVERNMENT CONTRACTOR STATUS WITH RESPECT TO STATE AND LOCAL GOVERNMENTS

20.

Nongovernment Contractors

Q. Is a hotel, motel, restaurant, foodservice facility, club, public assembly facility, hospital, health-care center, the like required to have a written affirmative action plan even if it does not have a federal, state, or local government contract or subcontract relationship?

A. No. There is no specific statutory or regulatory requirement that a private employer have a written affirmative action plan, unless that employer is a government contractor or subcontractor.

Q. Should private hospitality and foodservice employers have written affirmative action plans?

A. Despite the lack of a legal requirement for a written affirmative action plan, it is recommended that each employer have a written AFFIRMATIVE EQUAL OPPORTUNITY PROGRAM similar to one in Appendix C. Compliance with Equal Opportunity Law is much easier and more preventive if an employer has a written commitment embodied in a document to be updated annually.

Furthermore, a written program assists in the defense of individual and class action lawsuits.

REVERSE DISCRIMINATION

Reverse discrimination refers to preference given to minorities and women in a protected group at the expense of majority members of the protected group.

Example: Hiring a black woman at the expense of a white male who is more qualified is an example of reverse discrimination.

It is clear that the Bakke case supports the proposition that individuals should not be selected on account of race, color, creed, sex, national origin, age, or handicap. On the contrary, race, color, creed, sex, national origin, age, or handicap should not be factors in the final decision to select, promote, discharge, or otherwise engage in an employment practice.

However, many employers who have been found to have discriminated against a minority member of a protected group have been required to take affirmative action with respect to "righting the wrong" they committed against that minority member of a protected group. A similar result has been reached with respect to women. Therefore, preferential treatment in the form of affirmative action hiring "goals" may be taken to "right the wrong" that employer committed against the particular protected group or individual involved. This is generally permissible only after a judicial or regulatory determination that the employer has discriminated.

Accordingly, the employer who has not been found to have discriminated by a judicial body or the EEOC, should not take preferential action which may result in "reverse discrimination" against a majority member of the protected group involved.

Obviously, hiring quotas are generally unlawful.

Employers who maintain they are not government contractors or subcontractors should analyze the issue in detail, both practically and legally. Many luxury hotels, for instance, have established relationships with prime government contractors, resulting in hundreds of thousands of dollars of business annually. To litigate this issue both administratively and judicially is costly. A more pragmatic solution is to maintain an affirmative equal opportunity program which complies with all Equal Opportunity Law requirements and regulations but which does not result in "reverse discrimination."

**IT IS PREFERABLE TO DRAFT YOUR OWN
AFFIRMATIVE EQUAL OPPORTUNITY PROGRAM
BEFORE YOU ARE REQUIRED TO DO SO BY
A GOVERNMENT AGENCY OR A COURT**

VI.

DEFENSE

21.

Penalties and Violations

The chart opposite dramatically illustrates the cost of discrimination in selected cases from 1974 through 1976.

21-1. Back Pay

Plaintiffs who succesfully prove that they have been discriminated against by some adverse employment practice because of their protected group status are entitled to back pay, reflecting the difference between what they made and what they should have made but for the discrimination.

Example: Where a black employee was unlawfully refused a promotion on account of his race, a court later awarded him the difference between what he should have made had he received the promotion and what he actually made.

Q. What does the term "back pay" include?

A. It includes total earnings, i.e., straight time pay, overtime, shift differentials, premium pay, holiday pay, reasonable estimations of tips, fringe benefits, sick pay, health insurance premiums, vacation pay, pension and retirement benefits, uniform cleaning allowances, travel allowances, temporary housing allowances, savings plan contributions, life insurance, profit-sharing participation contributions, and nondiscretionary bonuses. In short, back pay includes all those earnings an individual would have been entitled to in whatever form, but for the discrimination.

SELECTED EQUAL OPPORTUNITY LAWSUITS—1974–1976

1974 Dollar Amount	Number Affected	Employer	Issue(s)	Action
24,100,000	1800	Northwest Airlines	Sex–Stewardess pay	Private suit
10,000,000 year	*	Bank of America	Sex–Hiring, promotion	Private suit
375,000	210	Rutgers Univ.	Sex	EEOC
210,000	172	Iowa State Univ.	Sex	Dept. of Labor
1,185	1	Boeing Co.	Sex–Lifting	Wash. State Human Rights Comm.
2,000	2	Snelling & Snelling	Sex–Referral	Wash. State Human Rights Comm.
9,000	1	Avco Financial	Sex–"Girl" reference	N.Y. State Human Rights Comm.
600,000	*	Corning Glass	Sex–Day/night shifts	Dept. of Labor/Women's Group
30,000,000	*	AT&T	Equal pay–Management	*
30,900,000	4048	9 Steel Companies	Race–Assignments	EEOC Dept. of Labor
48,000	79	Carborundum Co.	Equal pay	Dept. of Labor
10,000	1	City of Chicago	Pregnancy	Private suit
22,500	1	Ford Motor Co.	Race–Assignment	Private suit
2,550	1	Western Elec. Company	Sex–Pregnancy	Missouri Comm. of Human Rights
2,750,000	160	Std. Oil of Ca.	Age	*
21,000	1	Newsweek Magazine	Race	*
350,000	137	Eastex, Inc.	Sex–Race	Justice Dept.
87,000	2	Malden (Mass.) School Comm.	Sex–Pregnancy	Mass. Comm. Against Disc.

*Information not immediately available

1974 Dollar Amount	Number Affected	Employer	Issue(s)	Action
55,000	13	Boston Redevelopment Agency	Sex	Mass. Comm. Against Disc.
8,400	1	Rugers Univ.	Sex	N.J. Div. of Civil Rights
319,000	*	Jersey Central Power & Light	*	EEOC
26,264	1	U.S. Steel	*	Private suit
37,000	1	Cont. Trailways	Race	Private suit
60,000	1	Ford Motor Co.	Race	Private suit
62,500	*	Union Electric	Sex–Maternity leave	EEOC
2,100,000	360	Georgia Power	Race–Back pay	Justice Dept.
167,000	96	Loveman's Department Store	Sex–Equal pay	Dept. of Labor
28,000	*	Univ. of Montana	Sex–Equal pay	H.E.W.
23,000	2	Univ. of Arkansas	Sex–Equal pay	H.E.W.
100,000	750	Weyerhaeuser Lumber Co.	Sex	EEOC, Union
350,000	276	General Electric (Philadelphia)	Race	EEOC
175,000	100	East Texas Motor Freight	Race–Seniority	Justice Dept.
250,000	29	Pan Am.	Age	Dept. of Labor
275,000	93	Uniroyal	Race	EEOC
4,000,000 year	476	Quaker Oats	Race	P.U.S.H.
45,000,000	*	AT&T	*	EEOC, Justice Dept.
450,000	140	El Paso Natural Gas	Sex	EEOC
31,852	18	J.M. Fields Stores	Sex	Dept. of Labor
45,000	1	Cambridge Housing Authority	Sex	Mass. Comm. Against Disc.
102,000	70	N.Y. Telephone	Sex	Private suit

40,000	Friendly Ice Cream	Age	Dept. of Labor
100,000	Texaco	Sex	*
48,000	Container Corp. of Am.	Sex.	EEOC
30,650	Cleveland Bd. of Ed.	Sex–Maternity leave	Private suit
5,000	Temple Univ.	Reverse discrimination	
100,000	Corning Glass	Sex–Day/night Shifts	EEOC/Women's groups
70,000	Lutheran Hospital	Race, Sex	EEOC
1,000	General Motors	Race–Promotion	Private suit
40,000	Washington, D.C.	Race	Private suit
177,000	N.Y. City Newspapers and Un.	Race	Justice Dept./NAACP
800,000	Western Electric Co.	Sex	EEOC
265,000	3M	Sex	Atomic Energy Commission
920	Safeway	Sex–Male hair length	
1,535	White Mt. Reg. School Dist.	Sex	N.H. Comm. on Civil Rights
1,000,000	Safeco Insurance	Sex	Private suit
1,917,477	Companies St. Louis area	Race, Sex, et al.	EEOC
2,300	Flint Michigan School System	Sex–Maternity	Michigan Education Association
20,623,800	Numerous Emp. during FY 1974	Equal pay	Dept. of Labor
6,315,484	Numerous Emp. during FY 1974	Age discrimination	Dept. of Labor
1975			
2,000	China Dragon Restaurant	Age	N.H. Comm. on Human Rights
119,000	Starkville & Columbus (Miss.) School Districts	Race	Private suit

*Information not immediately available

Dollar Amount	Number Affected	Employer	Issue(s)	Action
17,162	1	CWA Union	Sex	Washington, D.C. Human Rights
750,000	1	Exxon	Age	Private suit
8,000	1	Duluth, Minn. bar	Sex–Dress codes	Minn. State Dept. of Human Rights
10,000	1	Dept. of Labor	Race	Civil Service Commission
13,691	1	Los Angeles Herald	Race	Calif. FEPC
2,500,000	*	AT&T	Race, Sex	EEOC
70,000	1	Univ. of Penn.	Sex–Tenure	Private suit
12,000	1	Transit Casualty Ins. Co.	Sex–Truck driving	Penn. Human Relations Comm.
50,000	9	Rainier National Bank	Sex	Private suit
12,000	1	U.S. Postal Service	Sex–Paternity	Civil Service Comm.
10,000	1	Standard Oil Co.	Age	Dept. of Labor
9,000	1	Penn. State Dept. of Welfare	Race	
95,000	*	ET&WNC Transportation Co.	Race, National Origin	EEOC
21,000	21	Ethyl Corp.	Sex	EEOC
258,000	250	Kerr Glass Mfg. Co.	Sex	EEOC
240,000	60	Container Corp. of Am.	Race, Sex	EEOC
1,800	8	Multi Line Cans, Inc.	Sex	EEOC
2,847	6	National Welders Supply	Race	EEOC
5,020	2	Treadwell Ford	Race	EEOC
10,000	2	Abbot Laboratories	Race	EEOC
1,500	2	Day Detectives, Inc.	Race, Color	EEOC
4,000	3	Dellinger, Inc.	Race	EEOC

Amount		Company	Violation	Agency
4,200	1	Stan's Sandwich Shops, Inc.	Sex	EEOC
42,705	56	South Western Pub. Co.	Race, Sex, National Origin	EEOC
16,668	1	American Koyo Corp.	Religion, National Origin	EEOC
70,000	*	Lutheran Hospital	Sex, Race	EEOC
2,502	1	D&L Transportation, Inc.	Race, National Origin	EEOC
5,000	1	Sheltering Arms Hospital	Retaliation	EEOC
20,000	12	Red Arrow Corp.	Race	EEOC
63,680	*	Metal Carbide Corp.	Sex	EEOC
12,500	2	Southland Corp.	National Origin	EEOC
9,000	1	William & Wilkins Waverly Prs.	Race, Sex	EEOC
9,500	1	Yorkwood Savings & Loan Assn.	Sex, National Origin	EEOC
3,500	1	Lorillard Corp.	Race	EEOC
4,044	1	F&M Schaefer Brewing Co.	Race, Sex, National Origin	EEOC
80,000	*	Eaton Corp.	Race, Sex	EEOC
1,000	1	Southeast Sayre	Race	EEOC
7,000	1	Otis Elevator	Race	EEOC
2,250	1	Vancouver Fed. Savings & Loan	Sex	EEOC
29,642	64	Grandview Care Homes, Inc.	Sex	EEOC
72,000	1	State Univ. College Brockport, N.Y.	Sex	Private suit
11,800	1	Compton & Sons, Inc.	Sex–Maternity	Private suit
6,750	2	Airborne Freight Corp.	Sex	N.Y. Comm. on Human Rights
159,000	*	W.T. Grant	Sex	Dept. of Labor
20,000	1	Honeywell, Inc.	Race	Private suit

*Information not immediately available

Dollar Amount	Number Affected	Employer	Issue(s)	Action
11,000	9	Unnamed Missouri Employer	Sex	Missouri Comm. on Human Rights
29,495	*	Brown Univ.	Sex	Private suit
70,000	1	Univ. of Penn.	Sex–Tenure	*
140,000	*	Mobil Oil Corp. and Union	Sex	EEOC
1,067	1	Taulman Co.	Sex	EEOC
1,150	1	NL Industries	Sex	EEOC
3,506	4	George T. Broadnax, Inc.	Race	EEOC
30,000	26	Brunswick Elec. Mem. Corp.	Race	EEOC
12,000	*	St. Joe Paper Co.	Race	EEOC
3,000	1	Coulter Electronics Inc.	Sex	EEOC
6,835	1	New England Nuclear Corp.	Race, Sex	EEOC
75,000	30	Sunshine Biscuits, Inc.	Sex	EEOC
15,000	*	Illinois Cent. & Gulf RR.	Race	Ill. Fair Em. Prac. Commission
17,500	1	Northrop	Sex–Emotional distress	Private suit
50,000	1	American Medical Internatl.	Sex–Emotional distress	Private suit
6,000	1	Wexner Brothers, Inc.	Sex, Race	N.Y. Division of Human Rights
5,249	1	Wayne Co. Bd. of Ed.	Sex–Pregnancy	*
314,000	22	Unity Frankford Rack Serv. Inc.	Sex	Private suit
20,000	1	Worcester Fnd. for Ex. Bio.	Sex	Mass. Comm. Against Disc.
14,500	1	Budd Co.	Sex	Philadelphia Human Re. Comm.
3,290	1	Calif. Growers Assn	Sex–Dress codes	

Amount	Number	Employer/Entity	Violation	Enforcing Agency
100,000	300	State of Minn.	Sex–Equal pay	Dept. of Labor
111,000,000	52,000	7,000 Conciliation Agreements in FY 1975		EEOC, State FEPCs
26,484,800	31,843	Num. Employers FY 1975	Equal pay	Dept. of Labor
6,674,403	*	Num. Employers FY 1975	Age Discrimination	Dept. of Labor

1976 to September

Amount	Number	Employer/Entity	Violation	Enforcing Agency
33,278	2	Randall State Bank (Wisc.)	Sex–Equal pay	EEOC
120,000	43	Birmingham Southern RR	Race	Private suit
11,609	6	Bayless (Mo.) School District	Sex–Maternity leave	Private suit
19,000	7	Portland Policemen's Assn.	Sex	Oregon Bureau of Labor
31,900,000	46,000	9 Steel Companies & Union	Race, Sex	EEOC
76,000	1	South Ill. Univ.	Sex–Pay	HEW
2,500	1	Endicott Johnson Corp.	Sex, Race, etc.	EEOC
5,000	*	Atlanta Airport Trans.	Sex, Race, etc.	EEOC
3,800	1	Wells Lamont Corp.	Race, Sex	EEOC
4,300	2	Delta Industries	Race	EEOC
1,485	1	Impact Plastics	Sex	EEOC
1,753	1	Roses Stores	Race	EEOC
9,000	1	St. Joe Paper Co. & Union	Race	EEOC
17,000	*	Ralston Purina Co.	Race, Color	EEOC
1,000	1	Key Chevrolet	Race, Sex	EEOC
4,000	1	Arrow Automotive	Sex	EEOC
1,822	2	Security National Bank	Race	EEOC

*Information not immediately available

Dollar Amount	Number Affected	Employer	Issue(s)	Action
5,500	*	East Bay Rest. Assn. & Union	Race	EEOC
88,814	*	Payless Drug Stores	Sex	EEOC
20,000	1	American Airlines	Religion	EEOC
500,000	*	Miami	Race, Sex, National Origin	Justice Dept.
208,126	57	Oklahoma City School Bd.	Sex, Maternity leave	Private suit
50,000	1	Western Electric	Age, National Origin	N.J. Div. of Civil Rights
63,980	15	Pay'N Save	Sex	Private suit
22,000	*	Seven Cases in 1976	Handicapped	Dept. of Labor
3,450	1	Moore Business Forms	Race	Conn. Comm. of Human Rights & Opp.
5,200	5	Meyer Brothers Drug	Race	EEOC
1,000,000	*	United Airlines	Race, Sex, National Origin	EEOC/Justic Dept.
(−) 20,000	*	Datapoint	Frivolous EEOC suit	EEOC
879,520	1,400	Wachovia Bank	Race	Private suit
14,074	1	Kansas City Ch. of Com.	Sex	Private suit
1,000	1	Consolidated Int, Inc.	Race	Ohio Civil Rights Comm.
500	1	Otis Elevator	Race–Layoff	EEOC
3,000,000	*	Merrill, Lynch	Race, Sex	EEOC
15,000	15	Amalgamated Transit Union	Race–Seniority	Private suit
10,661	1	Essex County, N.J. Voc. Bd.	Sex	N.J. Div. of Civil Rights
19,147	*	U.S. Justice Dept.	Sex	Private suit
75,000	1	Pace Univ.	Sex	N.Y. Human Rights Comm
302,000	250	Texas Agricultural Extension	Sex, Race	Justice Dept.
935,000	640	Gulf Oil	Race, Sex	EEOC/OFCC/Interior Dept.

16,309	3	Burlington Madison Yarn Co.	Sex	EEOC
6,000	*	Jockey International & Union	Race, Sex	EEOC
2,000	1	Woolf Bros., Inc.	Race	EEOC
502	*	Cato Corp.	Race	EEOC
20,000	8	Parker-Hannifin & Union	Race	EEOC
10,900	1	Aeronca	Sex	EEOC
11,123	2	McGraw Edison Co.	Religion	EEOC
6,299	4	Meyer Brothers Drug Co.	Race	EEOC
1,000	1	Havens Steel Co.	Race	EEOC
7,000	1	Kinsel Ford, Inc.	Race, Sex, Nat'l Origin	EEOC
809,492	*	Allied Maintenance Corp.	Sex	EEOC
23,633	*	Trailways of New England	Race, Sex	EEOC
4,000	*	WWM&L Union	Race	EEOC
4,779	1	Purolator Products, Inc.	Race	EEOC
6,100	1	Ashbourne School	Sex	EEOC
10,000	*	Cleveland Mills	Sex	EEOC
100,000	*	East Tenn. & West. Car. Trans	Race	EEOC
125,000	*	Santa Ana, Ca.	Race	Center for Law in the Public
17,500	1	Northrop Corp.	Sex	Private action
50,000	1	American Medical Internal.	Sex	Private action
3,000	1	Coulter Electronics, Inc.	Sex	Private action
140,000	1	Mobil Oil	Sex	EEOC
64,823	17	United Trans. Union	Race, Sex	West Va. Human Rights Comm.
2,500,000	*	AT&T	Race, Sex	EEOC
50,910	1	Kansas City Bd. of Pub. Util.	Race	Kansas Comm. on Civil Rights
8,000	1	Vandalia Butler Bd. of Ed.	Sex	Private action

*Information not immediately available

21-2. Reinstatement

Victims of discriminatory employment practices are also entitled to reinstatement if they have been unlawfully discharged. Additionally, some courts have ruled that identifiable victims of hiring discrimination are not only entitled to receive jobs but also "constructive seniority" from the date they would have been hired, but for the discrimination. Thus, seniority adjustments are authorized once a plaintiff proves discrimination.

Generally, victims of employment discrimination are entitled to be in "their rightful place" which they would have been in, but for the discrimination. To prevail on the merits of an employment discrimination case, a plaintiff must prove by a preponderance of the evidence that the adverse employment action taken against the plaintiff was on account of the plaintiff's protected group status, namely, his/her race, color, creed, sex, national origin, age, or handicap.

21-3. Injunctive Relief

Equal Opportunity Law authorizes courts to issue injunctions to prohibit a defendant employer from engaging in current and future unlawful employment practices on account of the plaintiff's protected group status.

Example: Employers have been enjoined from using discriminatory testing practices, non–job-related educational requirements, discriminatory and subjective hiring and promotion practices, etc.

While judicial remedies ordering quotas in hiring practices receive much publicity, most such decisions requiring quotas involve public employers and unions, and not private hospitality and foodservice employers.

The Bakke case, moreover, supports the proposition that employers should not hire or promote according to quotas. As a matter of fact, Title VII prohibits hiring individuals in a protected group merely because there is a statistical imbalance. On the other hand, some courts have awarded quota hiring remedies where there are severe statistical imbalances specifically attributed to past employment discrimination. Hence, where current policies appear to be nondiscriminatory but in actuality perpetuate the present effects of past discrimination, remedies bordering on "quota hiring" may be authorized.

Again, courts are prone to fashion a remedy to fit the wrong proved by the plaintiff.

Injunctive relief is an equitable remedy, just as is reinstatement. Therefore, each case will be analyzed on its own merits to determine what remedy, if any, would justify "righting the wrong."

Sometimes employees who have been discharged and who are alleging unlawful discrimination in court may seek preliminary injunction to gain back their job pending a trial of the case on the merits.

Generally, a plaintiff must establish the following to get a preliminary injunction ordering the employer to put him/her back to work pending the trial of the case on the merits:

1. That plaintiff will incur irreparable injury if he/she is not put back to work;
2. Plaintiff has a likelihood of prevailing on the merits of his/her lawsuit;
3. A balancing of the harm to the defendant employer if the preliminary injunction is issued against the degree of harm to the plaintiff if it is denied; and
4. Whether the issuance of such a preliminary injunction would further the public interest, including effectively ending the lawsuit, etc.

Defendant employers should maintain very accurate records of adverse employment decisions, since all lawsuits hinge upon who can carry their respective burdens of proof.

21-4. Class Actions

Q. What is a "class action"?

A. A class action is a lawsuit filed by one or more members of a similarly situated group of individuals to right a wrong committed against the individual which reflects a wrong committed against the group. To maintain a "class action" a representative plaintiff must establish the following:

1. The class is so numerous that joinder of all members is impractical;
2. There are questions of law or fact common to the class;
3. The claims or defenses of the representative parties are typical of the claims or defenses of the class;
4. The representative parties will fairly and adequately protect the interest of the class; and
5. The party opposing the class has acted or refused to act on grounds generally applicable to the class, thereby making appropriate final injunctive relief or corresponding declaratory relief with respect to the class as a whole; or the court finds that the questions of law or fact common to the members of the class predominate over any questions affecting only individual members, and that a class action is superior to other available methods for the fair and efficient ajudication of the controversy.

Example: A qualified waitress (female) is unlawfully refused employment as a waitress working at night in the fine restaurant of a prominent hotel. She learns that the hotel has never hired a waitress to work at night in the restaurant, but only in the daytime and in the coffee shop. She further learns that numerous other qualified waitresses have been refused employment at night in the restaurant on account of their sex. These facts could establish the basis for certification of a class action against the hotel. The class would be defined as all qualified female waitresses who were refused employment in the restaurant at night on account of their sex. Assuming the number of individuals refused is numerous, all other elements necessary for a class action would probably be satisfied.

The requirements for certification of a class are strict, since the time and expense on the court, as well as the defendant employer, are enormous. Defendant employers should avoid, if at all possible, ever becoming embroiled in class action litigation. It is the most expensive form of litigation in the Equal Opportunity Law.

Fortunately, there have been no major class action employment discrimination cases against major hotel and restaurant companies. There has been, however, a plethora of class action employment discrimination cases against airlines, hospitals, and food companies.

Example: Additional monetary damages have been awarded for emotional distress and humiliation in discrimination cases, including situations where the plaintiff was subjected to humiliation, embarrassment, and discomfort after being unlawfully arrested.

While Title VII does not authorize a plaintiff to recover punitive damages, Section 1981 and Section 1983 (nineteenth-century civil rights laws) have been held to support punitive damages, as well as damages for pain and suffering, humiliation, and embarrassment.

21-5. Punitive Damages

Although a few courts have awarded compensatory and punitive damages, as well as damages for so-called psychic distress in employment discrimination cases, the overwhelming majority of decisions supports the established general rule that neither compensatory nor punitive damages is recoverable under Title VII.

On the other hand, compensatory and punitive damages for embarrassment, humiliation, and mental anguish are authorized under Section 1981 cases. Compensatory and punitive damages are those damages awarded a plaintiff over and above the damages he/she actually incurred and necessary to make him/her "whole." They are awarded in cases where the facts establish that the plaintiff should receive more and the defendant employer should be required to pay more because of the aggravating facts established at the trial. Penalties for employment discrimination also include attorney's fees for the successful plaintiff's attorney.

Therefore, employers losing such cases will appreciate the extreme economic impact of discrimination.

PENALTIES INCLUDE BACK PAY, REINSTATEMENT, INJUNCTION, MORE LAWSUITS, ATTORNEYS' FEES, ETC.

22.

Legal Defenses and Actions

The most important defense element in an employment discrimination case is to begin preparing the employer's facts and position at the time of the adverse employment action and more thoroughly during the administrative investigation stage of the case. Obviously, it is ideal to prevent the case from arising altogether. However, adverse employment decisions are made daily in the hospitality and foodservice industries in particular. Turnover is very high; the pace is very fast. Thorough documentation is the key to proving a successful defense in an employment discrimination case several years later. This is particularly important to hotel and restaurant employers, since key management and nonsupervisory individuals knowledgeable about the adverse employment decision may be difficult to find and their memories may be foggy after the passage of time.

DEFENSE BEGINS AT THE TIME OF THE ADVERSE EMPLOYMENT ACTION

DOCUMENTATION OF FACTS AND WITNESSES IS THE KEY TO SUSTAINING THE EMPLOYMENT DECISION

22-1. BFOQ

Q. What is a "BFOQ"?

A. A bona fide occupational qualification (BFOQ) is a job-related requirement which in good faith justifies the apparent discrimination.

Example: Generally, theaters where plays are performed may require that males be hired for male roles and females be hired for female roles. The director and the audience demand authenticity of players. Therefore, the director may knowingly refuse to hire a female applying for a male role, even if she demonstrates that the audience might not "know the difference." A similar result has been reached in the case of motion picture actors and actresses.

Example: A high school diploma or other educational requirement would not be a bona fide occupational qualification for most jobs in the hospitality and foodservice industries. On the other hand, the ability to type, file, take dictation, spell, and organize work would be prime considerations for a clerical position such as secretary to the food and beverage director of a hotel.

Generally, bona fide occupational qualifications for jobs in hotels, motels, restaurants, foodservice facilities, hospitals, health-care centers, and public assembly facilities would not normally result in discrimination against some protected group.

However, the BFOQ defense has had limited success, since it is very difficult to prove. The best defense is simply proving that there was no discrimination.

22-2. Business Necessity

The so-called business necessity defense has had little success. Its theory is simply that the nature of the business necessitates the resulting discrimination against the plaintiff.

Example: Since most individuals who fly on airplanes are male, customer preference and business necessity justify airline's hiring primarily female flight attendants. The courts have uniformly ruled such a policy to be unlawful sex discrimination against men. Customer preference is generally not a justification for sex discrimination.

If an employer can establish that the essence of the business necessitates the adverse employment action resulting in discrimination to the plaintiff, possibly the court will rule for the employer. Again, it is often difficult to discern whether a judge is ruling that the defendant employer should win because the plaintiff did not prove discrimination or that the defendant employer should win because he/she proved the business necessity defense. The overwhelming majority of successful defenses to employment discrimination lawsuits are in the former category.

22-3. State Protective Laws

Q. Is it a valid defense to show the defendant employer discriminated because of a state protective law?

A. No.

Example: Where a state protective law prohibits the employment of women and children beyond certain working hours, this law would probably be struck down (as many have been) as a violation of the Equal Protection Clause of the Constitution and as sex discrimination violative of Title VII.

Therefore, state protective laws are rarely, if ever, legal defenses to employment discrimination.

22-4. EEOC Opinion

Q. Where the EEOC has issued an opinion upon which the defendant employer has relied, can this be an adequate defense?

A. While it is possible for the court to rule that the violation of Equal Opportunity Law was unintentional due to reliance upon an EEOC opinion, this situation is rare. Most EEOC opinions, as well as state Equal Opportunity Agency opinions, are very broad. Thus, these opinions would normally not be more supportive of the employer's position than the court would be.

If, on the other hand, the EEOC opinion is more supportive, it should definitely be used to persuade the court not to issue an injunction and not to find an intentional violation of law.

22-5. Mitigation of Damages

Q. What is "mitigation of damages"?

A. The phrase "mitigation of damages" is an old common-law concept which has been applied for many years in contract law and court law. Briefly, it requires the plaintiff to take reasonable steps to reduce (or mitigate) his/her damages, so that he/she will not necessarily profit from the unlawful discrimination committed against him/her by the employer. While the plaintiff should be put in his/her rightful place, the law does not permit an individual to profit from the wrong committed.

Title VII specifically provides in pertinent part as follows:

Interim earnings or *amounts earnable with reasonable diligence* by the person or persons discriminated against shall operate to reduce the back pay otherwise allowable. (Emphasis supplied.)

This is one of the most important elements to the successful defense of an employment discrimination lawsuit. If the case is not "worth" anything of significance to the plaintiff after the concept of mitigation of damages has been applied, it can usually be resolved for a small or nominal amount.

One should investigate whether the plaintiff (a discharged former employee) has a job and what he/she earns. One may further reduce back pay liability by determining "amounts earnable with reasonable diligence."

Example: An employee was discharged on account of his sex by a hotel employer. Since evidence of male sex discrimination against the plaintiff was so blatant, the plaintiff felt he would win the lawsuit. Therefore, after filing a charge with the EEOC, he retained an attorney and sued in Federal Court alleging sex discrimination on account of his male sex. However, from the date of discharge until the date of trial, plaintiff made no effort whatsoever to seek other employment. Since plaintiff was receiving a substantial monthly disability check from his military service, he did not need any interim earnings. Thus, the plaintiff did nothing to seek employment for a period of two and one-half years. The Court found the defendant hotel employer liable for sex discrimination but awarded no back pay damages to the plaintiff, because he had not mitigated his damages according to the requirements of Title VII and common law contract principles.

THE MOST SUCCESSFUL DEFENSE OF AN EMPLOYMENT DISCRIMINATION CASE IS TO PROVE THAT THERE WAS NO DISCRIMINATION

DEFENDANT EMPLOYERS SHOULD EXAMINE PLAINTIFF'S ATTEMPTS TO MITIGATE DAMAGES

23.
Preventive Law — Personnel Policies, Practices, and Procedures

23-1. Company Organizational Structure

Certainly the size of an operation will dictate whether a property can support a full-time director of personnel or industrial relations. However, it is recommended that an individual be responsible for the personnel function at all properties. The employee responsible for personnel administration should report directly to the manager of the property.

Example: The director of personnel of a luxury, convention hotel should have direct reporting responsibility to the general manager of the hotel and should be on the executive committee. These two elements are essential to a preventive commitment to equal opportunity principles. Similarly, the personnel director of a hospital should report to the administrator.

The director of personnel should be responsible for overseeing the proper execution of adverse employment actions. He/she should be contacted prior to the discharge, separation, or release of any employee and similarly should be contacted prior to the hiring of any employee.

It is fundamental that the general manager should communicate to all department heads and supervisors the importance of the personnel function at his/her property. Top management must support personnel in order to promote a preventive law attitude.

Obviously, the same principles apply at the corporate level. All major hospitality and foodservice corporations, hospitals, and public assembly facilities should have an executive, usually a vice-president, in charge of the personnel and industrial relations function. A corporate commitment to a staff professional in the industrial relations area is necessary to attract those personnel professionals capable of implementing preventive law programs and avoiding costly lawsuits.

23-2. Handbook

Employee handbooks should reflect a firm commitment to equal opportunity for all employees. Misunderstandings concerning the company can often be avoided by a well-written and presented employee handbook.

Employers spend thousands of dollars annually on numerous tangible and intangible, quantifiable benefits to employees. Frequently, however, the employees are not told of these benefits. It is part of an overall preventive law philosophy to inform employees fully about the benefits provided by the employer. The handbook is the primary vehicle for this information. (*See* Appendix D for an example of an excellent handbook.)

23-3. Disciplinary Procedure

As indicated earlier, the disciplinary procedure should be clearly defined, progressive, objectively implemented, and uniformly applied. The person responsible for the personnel function is crucial to fulfilling these requirements.

The director of personnel can become familiar with how discipline is being awarded in the food and beverage department as opposed to the housekeeping department. If there is a problem, he/she can correct the situation to ensure uniformity of discipline.

Hospitality and foodservice companies have notorious employee grapevines. Once an individual receives a disproportionate disciplinary award in comparison to a similar offense in a different department, charges of discrimination will necessarily ensue.

Additionally, employers should consider not only documenting instances of disciplinary awards, warning notices, and the like, but documenting praises of employees when they do a good job.

As always, the key to sustaining a disciplinary award is evidence. The best evidence, aside from sworn testimony, is often a well-documented file. On the other hand, a personnel file that is "too well documented" will be evidence of a vendetta against that employee and possibly the basis for a charge of discrimination.

23-4. Complaint Procedures

Every employer should have an established complaint procedure whether unionized or not. Employees should have the opportunity to complain formally with a view toward correcting the situation internally before outside third parties, such as administrative agencies and courts, are involved.

23-5. Exit Interview

Each employee who is released, terminated, dismissed, discharged, or in any manner separates himself/herself, voluntarily or involuntarily, from the employer should be interviewed.

The exit interview should be documented and placed in the employee's personnel file.

The exit interview should be implemented by the personnel professional or management representative responsible for the personnel function.

Since employees discharged for violation of rules sometimes will claim discrimination, it is helpful to determine the specifics of their claims at the earliest point possible.

Therefore, the exit interviewer should give the employee a "hearing" to again understand his/her side of the story.

Certainly an individual should receive a hearing and an opportunity to present his/her side prior to the final decision to terminate the employee. More importantly, however, it should be documented again at the exit interview stage.

If the employee reveals some facts which raise questions of discrimination or unfair treatment at the exit interview stage, then the decision to terminate the employee should be re-evaluated in light of this new evidence. While not specifically required by any statute or court decision, there are two fundamental elements of proof necessary to defend successfully an employment discrimination case involving a discharged employee:

1. The employer should be able to prove that the employee had adequate notice of whatever rules he/she was found to have violated; and
2. The employer should be able to prove that the employee had an adequate opportunity to be heard regarding his/her side of the story, including the opportunity to present witnesses contradictory to the "accusers."

23-6. Checkups and Audits

A preventive law personnel program necessarily includes regular checkups and audits. These checkups and audits can be conducted by the following individuals:

1. Corporate personnel representatives,
2. Regional personnel representatives,
3. The personnel professional responsible for the property involved,
4. The general manager or top management official of the property, and
5. An outside consultant or expert in the field.

Each of these individuals has value in terms of preventing costly lawsuits.

**AFFORD ALL EMPLOYEES AN OPPORTUNITY
TO BE HEARD PRIOR TO DISCHARGE**

**INSURE ALL EMPLOYEES ARE NOTIFIED OF
EMPLOYER'S RULES AND REGULATIONS**

**SUSPEND PENDING INVESTIGATION AND CONDUCT
THOROUGH INVESTIGATIONS PRIOR TO DISCHARGE**

24.

Union Status and Equal Opportunity Law

Whether an employer is unionized is relevant to the proper implementation of a preventive Equal Opportunity Law Program.

24-1. Nonunion Employers

Employers which are not unionized must obviously formulate and implement all personnel policies, practices, and procedures through the personnel professional responsible. Personnel directors at nonunion companies must appreciate that employees adversely affected by an employment decision have no shop steward, common union representative, or outside advocate to process their complaints and grievances. Therefore, the employee discharged for a violation of a house rule might be more inclined to file a discrimination charge than the employee at the unionized company, who may complain to the union first.

24-2. Unionized Properties

Once a property is unionized, it is helpful for the personnel director to maintain a rapport with the union officials and shop stewards.

Unions can assist in avoiding frivolous charges of discrimination in the following ways:

1. By providing a forum for candid discussions with an aggrieved employee, prior to the filing of a charge; and
2. By pointing out problems of discrimination which management may not be aware of before charges are filed.

On the other hand, unions may foment more charges of discrimination than would exist at nonunion companies in the following ways:

1. By encouraging employees to file charges of discrimination with the appropriate agency, rather than a grievance under the collective bargaining agreement; and
2. By encouraging those similarly situated to a charging party to join with him/her in filing their own charges of discrimination.

It is suggested that the collective bargaining agreement include a broad provision prohibiting discrimination such as the following:

§ 12. Equal Opportunity. The UNION AND HYATT agree there shall be no discrimination by either party which violates any local, Georgia or Federal Equal Opportunity Law.

Additionally, a contract provision requiring that the parties first complain of equal opportunity problems through the grievance and arbitration procedure will prevent, at best, and merely delay, at worst, charges of discrimination.

Since courts and agencies generally do not defer to arbitration procedures in the area of Equal Opportunity Law, the arbitration procedure, the equal opportunity prohibition, and the relevant grievance procedure must be carefully drafted to encourage courts and agencies to allow the arbitration process to come to an end before litigation ensues.

Thus, the parties could agree that the grievance and arbitration procedure would be the exclusive process for grievances in the area of Equal Opportunity Law but should also provide that the time period for filing with agencies would be tolled or postponed during the grievance and arbitration procedure.

Very few collective bargaining agreements in any industry adequately cover this subject.

Lastly, a collective bargaining agreement should recognize the joint responsibility of labor and management for violations of Equal Opportunity Laws.

Example:

Article 5
HYATT & UNION RIGHTS & RESPONSIBILITIES

§11. Recognition of Applicable Laws. Nothing contained in this Agreement shall be deemed or construed to require, directly or indirectly, HYATT to do anything inconsistent with the laws, orders, regulations, rules, or decisions of any competent governmental agency (local, Georgia or Federal) having jurisdiction over HYATT. The UNION and HYATT agree that neither will compel, force, or cause, directly or indirectly, the other respective party to do anything inconsistent with any applicable laws. Provided, furthermore, each party agrees to hold the other respective party harmless should that party cause a violation of this Section.

See THE COLLECTIVE BARGAINING HANDBOOK FOR HOTELS, RESTAURANTS, AND INSTITUTIONS (CBI Publishing Company, Inc., 1980).

ANY EQUAL OPPORTUNITY PROGRAM SHOULD INCLUDE COORDINATION WITH ANY UNIONS REPRESENTING YOUR EMPLOYEES

25.

Conclusion

Equal Opportunity Law is constantly changing. However, the basic principles set forth in this book with accompanying summaries, charts, posters, forms, etc., should afford managers with a fundamental understanding of Equal Opportunity Law principles.

However, the drafting of your forms, documents, posters, and all personnel policies, practices, and procedures should definitely be under the guidance of your attorney.

New laws and case decisions may substantially affect your equal opportunity policies.

Therefore, all employers are encouraged to implement a regular, continuing education program specifically designed for the Equal Opportunity Laws in your locale and at your property.

The following rules should be adhered to in implementing such an educational program in the areas of Equal Opportunity Law:

BECOME ACQUAINTED WITH THE BASICS OF ALL LOCAL AND FEDERAL EQUAL OPPORTUNITY LAWS

CONDUCT REGULAR EDUCATIONAL PROGRAMS FOR ALL SUPERVISORS

MAINTAIN PRECISE RECORDS OF ALL EMPLOYMENT PRACTICES AND ACTIONS

**CONDUCT REGULAR LEGAL CHECKUPS TO
REVIEW EXISTING POLICY AND TO
CONSIDER RECENT DEVELOPMENTS IN
THE LAW**

**ELIMINATE THE APPEARANCE OF IMPROPRIETY
WITH RESPECT TO ALL FORMS OF DISCRIMINATION
BY THE OPEN EXAMPLE OF TOP
MANAGEMENT**

Appendices

CAVEAT: The following materials, summaries, documents, and posters in the appendices are for illustrative purposes and are effective as of January 1, 1979. Therefore, you are encouraged to contact the relevant state or federal agency prior to making any business decision in the area of Equal Opportunity Law. Contact your attorney to assure compliance with all recent developments.

APPENDIX A

Federal Equal Opportunity Posters and Documents

Equal Employment Opportunity is the Law

DISCRIMINATION is PROHIBITED

BY THE CIVIL RIGHTS ACT OF 1964
AND BY EXECUTIVE ORDER NUMBER 11246

Title VII of the Civil Rights Act of 1964
Administered by

THE EQUAL EMPLOYMENT OPPORTUNITY COMMISSION

Prohibits discrimination because of RACE, COLOR, RELIGION, SEX or NATIONAL ORIGIN

By EMPLOYERS with 25 or more employees, by LABOR ORGANIZATIONS with a hiring hall of 25 or more members, by EMPLOYMENT AGENCIES, and by JOINT LABOR-MANAGEMENT COMMITTEES FOR APPRENTICESHIP OR TRAINING.

ANY PERSON
who believes he or she has been discriminated against
SHOULD CONTACT

THE EQUAL EMPLOYMENT OPPORTUNITY COMMISSION
1800 G Street, N.W.
Washington, D.C. 20506

OR ANY OF ITS
REGIONAL OFFICES

7101—108

Executive Order Number 11246*
Administered by

THE OFFICE OF FEDERAL CONTRACT COMPLIANCE

Prohibits discrimination because of RACE, COLOR, RELIGION, SEX, or NATIONAL ORIGIN, and requires affirmative action to ensure equality of opportunity in all aspects of employment

By all FEDERAL GOVERNMENT CONTRACTORS AND SUBCONTRACTORS, and by CONTRACTORS AND SUBCONTRACTORS PERFORMING WORK UNDER A FEDERALLY ASSISTED CONSTRUCTION CONTRACT, regardless of the number of employees in either case

ANY PERSON
who believes he or she has been discriminated against
SHOULD CONTACT

THE OFFICE OF FEDERAL CONTRACT COMPLIANCE
U.S. Department of Labor
Washington, D.C. 20210

* As amended by Executive Order Number 11375

U.S. GOVERNMENT PRINTING OFFICE : 1971—O-425-964

EQUAL EMPLOYMENT OPPORTUNITY IS THE LAW

LA LEY EXIGE IGUALDAD DE OPORTUNIDAD PARA TODOS EN EL EMPLEO

Discrimination Is Prohibited

by Title VII of the Civil Rights Act of 1964 and by Executive Orders 11246 and 11375

El Titulo VII de La Ley de Derechos Civiles de 1964 prohibe la discriminación en el empleo.

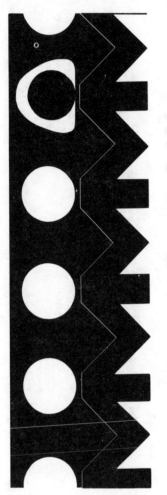

FEDERAL LAW PROHIBITS job discrimination because of RACE, COLOR, RELIGION, SEX or NATIONAL ORIGIN.

This protects employees of private employers, labor unions, employment agencies, state and local governments, and educational institutions. ANY PERSON who believes he or she has been discriminated against should contact immediately

THE U S EQUAL EMPLOYMENT OPPORTUNITY COMMISSION
2401 "E" Street, N.W.
Washington, D.C. 20506

or

any EEOC District Office listed in your local telephone directory under U S Government.

Executive Order Number 11246, issued by the President, prohibits job discrimination because of RACE, COLOR, RELIGION, SEX or NATIONAL ORIGIN, and requires affirmative action to ensure equality of opportunity in all aspects of employment.

This protects employees of any company with a contract or a subcontract with the Federal Government. ANY PERSON who believes he or she has been discriminated against should contact

THE OFFICE OF FEDERAL CONTRACT COMPLIANCE
U S Department of Labor
Washington, D C 20210

LA LEY FEDERAL PROHIBE discriminación en el empleo por motivo de su RAZA, COLOR, RELIGION, SEXO, u ORIGEN NACIONAL.

La ley proteje empleados de compañias privadas, sindicatos de trabajadores (uniones), agencias de empleo, escuelas o instituciones de educación, o para gobiernos de los estados o municipales y sus agencias. CUALQUIER PERSONA que cree que sus derechos han sido violados debe de escribir al:

THE U S EQUAL EMPLOYMENT OPPORTUNITY COMMISSION
1800 G Street, NW
Washington, D C 20506

o

cualquier oficina de distrito del EEOC. Consulte la guia local de teléfono debajo de "United States Government."

La orden ejecutiva Número 11246, del Presidente, prohibe la discriminación en el empleo por motivo de su RAZA, COLOR, RELIGION, SEXO, u ORIGEN NACIONAL y exige que ciertos patrones tomen acción positiva para garantizar igualdad de oportunidad en todos los aspectos del empleo.

Esta orden proteje a los empleados de cualquier compañia o a aquellos que trabajan para un patron que tenga un contrato o subcontrato con el gobierno Federal. CUALQUIER PERSONA que cree que un contratista a discriminado debe escribir a

"THE OFFICE OF FEDERAL CONTRACT COMPLIANCE"
U S Department of Labor
Washington, D C 20210

* GPO : 1977 O - 676- 440

equal employment opportunity is the law

Private Industry, State, and Local Government

Title VII of the Civil Rights Act of 1964, as amended, prohibits job discrimination because of race, color, religion, sex or national origin.

Applicants to and employees of private employers, state/local governments, and public/private educational institutions are protected. Also covered are employment agencies, labor unions and apprenticeship programs. Any person who believes he or she has been discriminated against should contact immediately

**The U.S. Equal Employment Opportunity Commission (EEOC)
2401 E St., N.W.
Washington, D. C. 20506**

or an EEOC District Office, listed in most telephone directories under U. S. Government.

igualdad de oportunidad en el empleo es la ley

Industrias Privadas, Gobiernos Locales y Estatales

El Título VII de la Ley de Derechos Civiles de 1964, enmendado, prohíbe la discriminación en el empleo por razón de raza, color, religión, sexo o nacionalidad de origen.

La ley protege a los empleados y solicitantes de empleo en empresas privadas, gobiernos estatales y locales e instituciones educacionales públicas y privadas. También abarca las agencias de empleo, sindicatos de trabajadores y programas de aprendizaje. Cualquier persona, tanto hombre como mujer, que crea que ha sido objeto de discriminación debe escribir inmediatamente a

**The U. S. Equal Employment Opportunity Commission (EEOC)
2401 E St., N.W.
Washington, D. C. 20506**

o a cualquier oficina regional de EEOC, las que se encuentran en las guías telefónicas locales bajo el nombre de: U. S. Government.

Federal Contract Employment

Executive Order 11246, as amended, prohibits job discrimination because of race, color, religion, sex or national origin and requires affirmative action to ensure equality of opportunity in all aspects of employment.

Section 503 of the Rehabilitation Act of 1973 prohibits job discrimination because of handicap and requires affirmative action to employ and advance in employment qualified handicapped workers.

Section 402 of the Vietnam Era Veterans' Readjustment Assistance Act of 1974 prohibits job discrimination and requires affirmative action to employ and advance in employment (1) qualified Vietnam era veterans during the first four years after their discharge and (2) qualified disabled veterans throughout their working life if they have a 30 percent or more disability.

Applicants to and employees of any company with a federal government contract or subcontract are protected. Any person who believes a contractor has violated its affirmative action obligations, including nondiscrimination, under Executive Order 11246, as amended, or under Section 503 of the Rehabilitation Act should contact immediately

**The Employment Standards Administration
Office of Federal Contract Compliance
Programs (OFCCP)
Third and Constitution Ave., N.W.
Washington, D. C. 20210**

or an OFCCP regional office, listed in most telephone directories under U. S. Government, Department of Labor. Complaints specifically under the veterans' law should be filed with the Veterans' Employment Service through local offices of the state employment service.

All complaints must be filed within 180 days from date of alleged violation.

U.S. Department of Labor
Employment Standards Administration
Office of Federal Contract Compliance Programs

OFCCP-1420
(October 1976)

Empleos En Compañías Con Contratos Federales

La Orden Ejecutiva Número 11246, enmendada, prohíbe la discriminación en el empleo por razón de raza, color, religión, sexo o nacionalidad de origen y exige acción positiva para garantizar la igualdad de oportunidad en todos los aspectos del empleo.

La Sección 503 de la Ley de Rehabilitación de 1973, prohíbe la discriminación en el empleo contra personas que sufran de impedimentos físicos o mentales y exige acción positiva en el empleo y promoción de personas que sufran de impedimentos físicos o mentales, siempre que reúnan las condiciones indispensables para el desempeño del empleo.

La Sección 402 de la Ley de 1974 de Asistencia para el Reajuste de los Veteranos de la Era de Vietnam, prohíbe la discriminación en el empleo y exige acción positiva en el empleo y promoción de (1) veteranos de la era de Vietnam, durante los primeros cuatro años después de haber sido separados del servicio activo, siempre que reúnan las condiciones indispensables para el desempeño del empleo (2) ciertos veteranos que tengan un 30 por ciento o más de impedimentos físicos o mentales mientras puedan trabajar, siempre que reúnan las condiciones indispensables para el desempeño del empleo.

La ley protege a los solicitantes de empleo y empleados de cualquier compañía que tenga un contrato o subcontrato con el gobierno federal. Cualquier persona que crea que uno de estos contratistas no ha cumplido con sus obligaciones de tomar acción positiva, incluyendo la de no discriminar, bajo la Orden Ejecutiva 11246, enmendada, o bajo la Sección 503 de la Ley de Rehabilitación, debe escribir inmediatamente a

**The Employment Standards Administration
Office of Federal Contract Compliance
Programs (OFCCP)
Third and Constitution Ave., N.W.
Washington, D. C. 20210**

o a cualquier oficina regional de OFCCP, las que se encuentran en la mayoría de las guías telefónicas bajo: U. S. Government, Department of Labor. Las reclamaciones específicamente comprendidas bajo la ley de veteranos, deben de dirigirse a Veterans' Employment Service por medio de las oficinas locales del servicio de empleo del estado.

Todas las reclamaciones deben de ser registradas dentro de los 180 días subsequentes a la fecha del supuesto acto de discriminación.

¡LA OPORTUNIDAD DEBE SER IGUAL PARA TODOS!

NO IMPORTA EL COLOR, RAZA, RELIGION ORIGEN, SEXO, O EDAD AVANZADA

La Constitución del Estado Libre Asociado de Puerto Rico, así como algunas de nuestras leyes, prohiben que se discrimine en el empleo de cualquier persona por razones de edad avanzada, color, raza, credo, sexo, origen, condición social o ideales políticos. Esta discriminación también la prohiben órdenes ejecutivas del Presidente de los Estados Unidos y Leyes Federales.

Si usted ha sido rechazado de una oportunidad de empleo, despedido de su último empleo, se le ha negado el aumento de sueldo u oportunidad de progreso en su trabajo por algunas de las razones aquí expuestas, comuníquese con nosotros.

UNIDAD ANTI-DISCRIMEN
DEPARTAMENTO DEL TRABAJO

AVENIDA BARBOSA NUM. 414, HATO REY, P.R.   00917
TELEFONOS 763-4022 / 763-4136 / 763-5151

También puede escribir a:

THE EQUAL EMPLOYMENT
OPPORTUNITY COMMISSION
NEW YORK DISTRICT OFFICE
90 CHURCH STREET
NEW YORK, NEW YORK 10007

Noticia A Los Trabajadores

Si tiene usted una queja sobre el servicio de empleos, o un asunto que trate con empleo,

- Discriminacion

- Viviendas, precauciones en el trabajo sobre peligro, contratistas de trabajo

- Sueldos, horas o condiciones de trabajo

- Violacion de Leyes Federales o Estatales de trabajo,

Hable con el encargado local del Servicio de Empleos o escriba a:

Assistant Regional Director for
Manpower (Monitor Advocate)
John F. Kennedy Bldg.
Boston, Mass. 02203

U.S. Department of Labor
Manpower Administration (USES)
601 D Street N.W.
Washington, D.C. 20213

APPENDIX B

State Equal Opportunity Laws—A Summary
Selected State Equal Opportunity Posters and Documents

The following summaries of each state's Equal Opportunity Law are obviously for illustrative purposes and are effective as of January 1, 1979. Therefore, contact the relevant state agency (addresses are included in the summaries) to keep abreast of the changes in state law, regulations, and court de-decisions. The selected posters in this Appendix are examples of several states' posters, and all state posters have not been reproduced. Contact your attorney to ensure compliance with all recent developments.

NOTE: Federal Equal Opportunity Law generally prohibits discrimination on account of race, color, creed, sex, pregnancy, national origin, age, or handicap. Thus, *the following state laws are in addition to or supplemental to these protected groups.*

ALABAMA EQUAL OPPORTUNITY LAW

LAW. No relevant Equal Opportunity Law.

ALASKA EQUAL OPPORTUNITY LAW

LAW. Alaska state laws against discrimination prohibit employment discrimination. Alaska law also prohibits the use of lie detector tests by employers.

PROTECTED GROUPS. Race, color, religion, national origin, age, physical handicap, sex, marital status, changes in marital status, pregnancy, equal pay, or parenthood.

AGENCY. Alaska State Commission for Human Rights, Equal Employment Opportunity Office, Department of Administration, Pouce Ce, Juneau, Alaska 99881

ARIZONA EQUAL OPPORTUNITY LAW

LAW. Arizona Civil Rights Act of 1965.

PROTECTED GROUPS. Race, color, religion, sex, equal pay, and national origin.

AGENCY. Arizona Civil Rights Division, Industrial Commission of Arizona, 1645 West Jefferson, Phoenix, Arizona 85007

ARKANSAS EQUAL OPPORTUNITY LAW

LAW. Arkansas has no fair employment practice law prohibiting discrimination in employment, but it does have a statute prohibiting discrimination in the payment of wages on the basis of sex.

CALIFORNIA EQUAL OPPORTUNITY LAW

LAW. California Fair Employment Practices Act generally prohibits discrimination in all employment practices.

PROTECTED GROUPS. Race, religion, color, sex, pregnancy, physical handicap, medical condition, marital status, age (40 and up), national origin, or ancestry. Employers in California are also prohibited from requiring on an initial employment application form that a record of arrest be listed. California law further prohibits the use of lie detector tests by employers. The California Fair Employment Practice Commission has issued specific guidelines on sex discrimination with which all employers should become familiar. The California FEPC has also issued a "Guide to Pre-Employment Inquiries."

AGENCY. California Fair Employment Practice Commission, Division of Fair Employment Practices, Department of Industrial Relations, Agricultural and Services Agency, State of California, 455 Golden Gate Avenue, San Francisco, California 94101

COLORADO EQUAL OPPORTUNITY LAW

LAW. Colorado Antidiscrimination Act of 1957.

PROTECTED GROUPS. Race, creed, color, sex, national origin, ancestry, age, and equal pay. The Colorado Civil Rights Commission prohibits discrimination because of pregnancy.

AGENCY. Colorado Civil Rights Commission, 312 State Services Building, 1525 Sherman Street, Denver, Colorado 80203

CONNECTICUT EQUAL OPPORTUNITY LAW

LAW. Connecticut Fair Employment Practices Act.

PROTECTED GROUPS. Race, color, religion, sex, pregnancy, age, marital status, national origin, ancestry, physical disability, equal pay. Connecticut law also prohibits the use of lie detector tests by employers.

AGENCY. Connecticut Commission on Human Rights and Opportunities, 90 Washington Street, Hartford, Connecticut 06115

DELAWARE EQUAL OPPORTUNITY LAW

LAW. Delaware Fair Employment Practices Act.

PROTECTED GROUPS. Race, creed, color, sex, national origin, and age. Delaware law also prohibits the use of lie detector tests by employers.

AGENCY. Delaware Department of Labor, Division of Industrial Relations, Anti-Discrimination Section, 2413 Lancaster Avenue, Wilmington, Delaware 19805

DISTRICT OF COLUMBIA EQUAL OPPORTUNITY LAW

LAW. District of Columbia Human Rights Law.

PROTECTED GROUPS. Race, color, religion, national origin, sex, age, marital status, personal appearance, sexual orientation, family responsibility, physical handicap, equal pay, matriculation, and political affiliation. Pregnancy discrimination is prohibited by regulation.

AGENCY. The District of Columbia Commission on Human Rights, Office of Human Rights District Building, 14th and E Streets, N.W., Room 22, Washington, D.C. 20004

FLORIDA EQUAL OPPORTUNITY LAW

LAW. Florida Human Rights Act of 1977 (replacing the Florida Human Relations Act of 1969).

PROTECTED GROUPS. Race, color, religion, sex, national origin, age, handicap, marital status, and equal pay.

AGENCY. Florida Commission on Human Relations, Department of Community Affairs, Howard Building, 2571 Executive Center Circle East, Tallahassee, Florida 32301

GEORGIA EQUAL OPPORTUNITY LAW

LAW. Georgia does not have a general statutory provision concerning equal employment opportunities. However, Georgia does have an Age Discrimination Act and an Equal Pay Act. It also has a Fair Employment Practices Act of 1978 for *state employees* prohibiting discrimination on account of race, color, religion, national origin, sex, physical handicap, age, and equal pay, and discrimination against wives whose husbands are on active duty in the military. Again, this law only applies to state employment policies.

HAWAII EQUAL OPPORTUNITY LAW

LAW. Hawaii Fair Employment Practices Act.

PROTECTED GROUPS. Race, sex, age, religion, color, ancestry, physical handicap, equal pay, and arrest or court record. Hawaii law also prohibits the use of lie detector tests by employers. Hawaii also has an elaborate "Pre-Employment Inquiry Guide" with which employers should become familiar.

AGENCY. The Hawaii Department of Labor and Industrial Relations, Hawaii District Office, State Office Building, 75 Aupuni Street, Hilo, Hawaii   96720

IDAHO EQUAL OPPORTUNITY LAW

LAW. Idaho Fair Employment Practices Act of 1969.

PROTECTED GROUP. Race, color, religion, sex, equal pay, age, and national origin. Idaho law also prohibits employers from requiring lie detector tests in certain circumstances.

AGENCY. Idaho Commission on Human Rights, State House, Boise, Idaho   83720

ILLINOIS EQUAL OPPORTUNITY LAW

LAW. Illinois Fair Employment Practices Act of 1961.

PROTECTED GROUPS. Race, color, religion, sex, national origin, physical or mental handicap unrelated to ability, ancestry, unfavorable discharge from military service, equal pay, and age. Furthermore, the Illinois constitution grants freedom from discrimination on the basis of race, color, creed, national origin, ancestry, sex in hiring and promotion practices of employers, physical or mental handicap unrelated to ability, and also provides that equal protection of the law shall not be denied or abridged on account of sex by the state or any of its local units of government. The Illinois Fair Employment Practices Commission also has issued regulations prohibiting the use of arrest/conviction records if the use of such information operates to exclude members of minority groups at a higher rate than others. Illinois law also prohibits discrimination in employment because of an individual's unfavorable discharge from military service. By regulation, Illinois FEPC guidelines prohibit discrimination on account of pregnancy.

AGENCY. Illinois Fair Employment Practices Commission, 3 West Old State Capital Plaza, Springfield, Illinois 62701

INDIANA EQUAL OPPORTUNITY LAW

LAW. Indiana Civil Rights Law, enacted in 1961 as the Indiana Fair Employment Practices Act.

PROTECTED GROUPS. Race, religion, color, sex, national origin, ancestry, handicap, age, and equal pay.

AGENCY. The Indiana Civil Rights Commission, 311 West Washington Street, Indianapolis, Indiana 46202

IOWA EQUAL OPPORTUNITY LAW

LAW. Iowa Civil Rights Act of 1965.

PROTECTED GROUPS. Age, race, creed, color, sex, national origin, religion, non–job-related physical or mental disability, and equal pay. Administrative regulations prohibit pregnancy discrimination.

AGENCY. Iowa Civil Rights Commission, 418 6th Avenue, Liberty Building, Des Moines, Iowa   50309

KANSAS EQUAL OPPORTUNITY LAW

LAW. Kansas Act Against Discrimination.

PROTECTED GROUPS. Race, religion, color, sex, national origin, ancestry, physical handicap, and equal pay. By regulation, pregnancy discrimination is prohibited.

AGENCY. Kansas Commission on Civil Rights, 535 Kansas Avenue, 5th Floor, Topeka, Kansas   66603

KENTUCKY EQUAL OPPORTUNITY LAW

LAW. Kentucky Fair Employment Practices Act of 1966.

PROTECTED GROUPS. Race, color, religion, national origin, sex, age, equal pay, and physical handicap. Administrative guidelines prohibit pregnancy discrimination.

AGENCY. Kentucky Commission on Human Rights, 600 West Walnut Street, Louisville, Kentucky   40203

LOUISIANA EQUAL OPPORTUNITY LAW

LAW. Louisiana has no general statute concerning equal employment opportunities. Louisiana state law does prohibit discrimination in employment on the basis of age.

MAINE EQUAL OPPORTUNITY LAW

LAW. Maine Human Rights Act of 1972.

PROTECTED GROUPS. Race, color, sex, physical or mental handicap, religion, ancestry, national origin, and age. Court interpretation prohibits pregnancy discrimination.

AGENCY. Maine Human Rights Commission, State House, Augusta, Maine   04330

MARYLAND EQUAL OPPORTUNITY LAW

LAW. Maryland Fair Employment Practices Act.

PROTECTED GROUPS. Race, color, religion, sex, age, national origin, marital status, physical or mental handicap, psychiatric or psychological condition, and equal pay. Maryland law also prohibits employers from using lie detector tests. Pregnancy discrimination is prohibited by regulation.

AGENCY. Maryland Commission on Human Relations, Metro Plaza at Mondawmin, Suite 300, Baltimore, Maryland 21215

MASSACHUSETTS EQUAL OPPORTUNITY LAW

LAW. Massachusetts Fair Employment Practices Law of 1946.

PROTECTED GROUPS. Race, color, religion, national origin, ancestry, age, sex, pregnancy, equal pay, physical handicap, and *foreign trade relationships*. Note that Massachusetts law uniquely prohibits discrimination by businesses engaged in foreign trade. Massachusetts law also prohibits the use of lie detector tests by employers. Massachusetts law on pregnancy discrimination is the most broad of any state law prohibition on the subject.

AGENCY. Massachusetts Commission Against Discrimination (formerly Massachusetts Fair Employment Practice Commission), 120 Tremont Street, Boston, Massachusetts 02108

MICHIGAN EQUAL OPPORTUNITY LAW

LAW. Michigan Civil Rights Act.

PROTECTED GROUPS. Religion, race, color, national origin, age, sex, pregnancy, height, weight, marital status, handicap, and equal pay. Michigan law also limits the use of lie detector tests by employers, prohibiting the discharge of an employee solely because of the refusal to take a polygraph examination. The law also prohibits discharges because of an alleged or actual opinion that the employee did not tell the truth during a polygraph examination.

AGENCY. The Michigan Civil Rights Commission, Michigan Department of Civil Rights, Stoddard Building, 10th Floor, 125 West Allegan Street, Lansing, Michigan 48933

MINNESOTA EQUAL OPPORTUNITY LAW

LAW. Minnesota Human Rights Act.

PROTECTED GROUPS. Race, color, creed, religion, sex, pregnancy, marital status, status with regard to public assistance, disability, age, national origin, and equal pay. Minnesota law also regulates the use of lie detector tests, prohibiting the use of polygraph tests, voice stress analysis, or any tests purporting to test the honesty of any employee or prospective employee.

AGENCY. Minnesota Department of Human Rights, 200 Capitol Square Building, St. Paul, Minnesota 55101

MISSISSIPPI EQUAL OPPORTUNITY LAW

LAW. Mississippi has no statutes whatsoever concerning equal opportunity or equal employment opportunities. Mississippi does prohibit discrimination because of physical handicap in *state employment.*

MISSOURI EQUAL OPPORTUNITY LAW

LAW. Missouri Fair Employment Practices Act.

PROTECTED GROUPS. Race, creed, color, religion, sex, national origin, ancestry, and equal pay. Missouri FEPC sex discrimination guidelines prohibit pregnancy discrimination.

AGENCY. Missouri Commission on Human Rights, P.O. Box 1129, Jefferson City, Missouri 65101

MONTANA EQUAL OPPORTUNITY LAW

LAW. Montana Fair Employment Practices Act of 1965.

PROTECTED GROUPS. Race, religion, creed, marital status, color, national origin, age, physical or mental handicap, sex, pregnancy, and equal pay. Montana law regulates the use of lie detector tests by employers by prohibiting such usage as a condition of employment or continuation of employment.

AGENCY. The Montana Human Rights Commission, Room 404, Power Block, Last Chance Gulch, Helena, Montana 59601

NEBRASKA EQUAL OPPORTUNITY LAW

LAW. Nebraska Fair Employment Practices Act of 1965.

PROTECTED GROUPS. Race, color, religion, sex, disability, marital status, national origin, age, and equal pay.

AGENCY. Nebraska Equal Opportunity Commission, Fifth Floor, 301 Centennial Mall South, Lincoln, Nebraska 68509

NEVADA EQUAL OPPORTUNITY LAW

LAW. Nevada Fair Employment Practices Act.

PROTECTED GROUPS. Race, color, religion, sex, age, national origin, physical or visual handicap, and equal pay.

AGENCY. Nevada Commission on Equal Rights, Executive Center, 1515 East Tropicana Avenue, Suite 590, Las Vegas, Nevada 89158

NEW HAMPSHIRE EQUAL OPPORTUNITY LAW

LAW. New Hampshire Law Against Discrimination of 1965.

PROTECTED GROUPS. Age, sex, race, creed, color, marital status, physical or mental handicap, national origin, ancestry, religious creed, and equal pay. N.H. Human Rights Commission guidelines prohibit pregnancy discrimination.

AGENCY. The New Hampshire Commission for Human Rights, 66 South Street, Concord, New Hampshire 03310

NEW JERSEY EQUAL OPPORTUNITY LAW

LAW. New Jersey Law Against Discrimination of 1945.

PROTECTED GROUPS. Race, color, creed, national origin, ancestry, age, marital status, sex, nationality, liability for service in the U.S. Armed Forces, physical handicap, and equal pay. New Jersey law also prohibits the use of lie detector tests by employers. The New Jersey Division on Civil Rights has promulgated a booklet entitled "Questions and Answers on Pre-Employment Inquiries" which is the finest the author has observed by any state agency.

AGENCY. New Jersey Division on Civil Rights, Department of Laws and Public Safety, 436 East State Street, Trenton, New Jersey 08608

NEW MEXICO EQUAL OPPORTUNITY LAW

LAW. New Mexico Human Rights Act of 1969.

PROTECTED GROUPS. Race, color, religion, sex, age, national origin, ancestry, and physical or mental handicap.

AGENCY. The New Mexico Human Rights Commission, 120 Villagra Building, Sante Fe, Mexico 87503

NEW YORK EQUAL OPPORTUNITY LAW

LAW. New York Human Rights Law (originally titled The New York Against Discrimination of 1951).

PROTECTED GROUPS. Race, creed, sex, disability, marital status, color, national origin, age, blindness, certain criminal offenses, pregnancy, and equal pay. The use of psychological stress evaluator examinations to determine the truth or falsity of statements as a means of selecting prospective employees or of screening current employees is prohibited.

AGENCY. New York Division of Human Rights, Administrative Office, Two World Trade Center, New York, New York   10047

NORTH CAROLINA EQUAL OPPORTUNITY LAW

LAW. North Carolina Equal Employment Practices Act of 1977.

PROTECTED GROUPS. The North Carolina Equal Employment Practices Act of 1977 declares that it is the public policy of North Carolina to protect the right of all persons to seek and hold employment without discrimination based on race, religion, color, national origin, age, sex, or handicap. North Carolina law also prohibits discrimination on account of the sickle cell trait or hemoglobin C trait.

AGENCY. North Carolina Human Relations Council, Department of Administration, 116 West Jones Street, Raleigh, North Carolina   27603

NORTH DAKOTA EQUAL OPPORTUNITY LAW

LAW. North Dakota has no general statute concerning equal employment opportunities. North Dakota law does prohibit discrimination in pay based on sex, a law barring sex discrimination against women jockeys, and a law prohibiting discrimination on the basis of age.

AGENCY. North Dakota Commissioner of Labor, State Capitol, Bismark, North Dakota   58501.

OHIO EQUAL OPPORTUNITY LAW

LAW. Ohio Fair Employment Practices Law of 1959.

PROTECTED GROUPS. Race, color, religion, sex, national origin, handicap, ancestry, age, and equal pay.

AGENCY. Ohio Civil Rights Commission, 220 Parsons Avenue, Columbus, Ohio   43215

OKLAHOMA EQUAL OPPORTUNITY LAW

LAW. Oklahoma Civil Rights Act of 1968.

PROTECTED GROUPS. Race, color, religion, national origin, sex, and equal pay. Interpretative guidelines prohibit pregnancy discrimination.

AGENCY. Oklahoma Human Rights Commission, P.O. Box 52945, Jim Thorpe Office Building, Oklahoma City, Oklahoma   73152

OREGON EQUAL OPPORTUNITY LAW

LAW. Oregon Fair Employment Practices Act.

PROTECTED GROUPS. Race, religion, color, national origin, sex, pregnancy, childbirth, related medical conditions, marital status, certain juvenile records, age, equal pay, and mental or physical handicap. The Oregon law also prohibits employers from utilizing lie detector tests. Oregon law also prohibits an employer from refusing to hire or from terminating the employment of an individual solely because another member of that individual's family presently works for that employer.

AGENCY. Oregon Bureau of Labor, Civil Rights Division, Room 479, State Office Building, 1400 S.W. 5th Avenue, Portland, Oregon   97201

PENNSYLVANIA EQUAL OPPORTUNITY LAW

LAW. Pennsylvania Human Relations Act of 1961 (amended as The Pennsylvania Fair Employment Practice Act of 1955).

PROTECTED GROUPS. Race, color, religious creed, ancestry, handicap, disability, age, sex, national origin, and equal pay. Pennsylvania law also prohibits the use of lie detector tests. Pennsylvania Human Relations Commission regulations prohibit pregnancy discrimination.

AGENCY. Pennsylvania Human Relations Commission, 100 North Cameron Street, Second Floor, Harrisburg, Pennsylvania 17101

PUERTO RICO EQUAL OPPORTUNITY LAW

LAW. Puerto Rico Fair Employment Practices Act.

PROTECTED GROUP. Age, race, color, creed, sex, birth, or social position.

AGENCY. The Equal Employment Opportunity Commission, New York District Office, 90 Church Street, New York, New York 10007

RHODE ISLAND EQUAL OPPORTUNITY LAW

LAW. Rhode Island Fair Employment Practices Act.

PROTECTED GROUPS. Race, color, religion, sex, physical handicap, country of ancestral origin, age, and equal pay. Rhode Island law also prohibits the use of lie detector tests. Pregnancy discrimination is prohibited by regulation.

AGENCY. Rhode Island Commission for Human Rights, 244 Broad Street, Providence, Rhode Island 02903

SOUTH CAROLINA EQUAL OPPORTUNITY LAW

LAW. South Carolina Human Affairs Law.

PROTECTED GROUPS. South Carolina Law prohibits *state agencies or departments or local subdivisions thereof* from discriminating against individuals concerning employment rights because of race, creed, color, sex, age, or national origin. However, the South Carolina law does not prohibit discrimination against any of these protected groups by private employers, even though the South Carolina law does establish procedures to resolve discriminatory practices in both private and public employment through conference, conciliation, and persuasion.

AGENCY. South Carolina Human Affairs Commission, 1111 Belleview Street, P.O. Drawer 11528, Columbia, South Carolina 29211

SOUTH DAKOTA EQUAL OPPORTUNITY LAW

LAW. South Dakota Human Relations Act of 1972.

PROTECTED GROUPS. Race, color, creed, religion, sex, ancestry, national origin, and equal pay. Pregnancy discrimination is prohibited by regulation.

AGENCY. South Dakota Department of Commerce and Consumer Affairs, Division of Human Rights, State Capitol, Pierre, South Dakota 57501

TENNESSEE EQUAL OPPORTUNITY LAW

LAW. Tennessee Fair Employment Practices Law of 1978.

PROTECTED GROUPS. Race, creed, color, religion, sex, national origin, physical handicap, faulty eyesight, mental handicap, and equal pay.

AGENCY. Tennessee Commission for Human Development, C3-305 Cordell Hull Building, Nashville, Tennessee 37219

TEXAS EQUAL OPPORTUNITY LAW

LAW. Texas has no general statute protecting employees from employment discrimination. However, Texas law does protect physically handicapped persons from employment discrimination, as well as mentally handicapped and visually handicapped individuals. Furthermore, Texas does have an equal pay for equal work law.

UTAH EQUAL OPPORTUNITY LAW

LAW. Utah Anti-Discriminatory Act of 1965.

PROTECTED GROUPS. Race, color, sex, age, religion, ancestry, national origin, and equal pay.

AGENCY. Anti-Discrimination Division, Utah Industrial Commission, 350 East 500 South, Salt Lake City, Utah 84111

VERMONT EQUAL OPPORTUNITY LAW

LAW. Vermont Fair Employment Practices Act.

PROTECTED GROUPS. Race, color, religion, ancestry, national origin, sex, place of birth, physically handicapped persons, and equal pay.

AGENCY. Vermont Civil Rights Division, 109 State Street, Pavilion Office Building, Montpelier, Vermont 05602

VIRGINIA EQUAL OPPORTUNITY LAW

LAW. Virginia does not have a general statute concerning equal employment opportunities.

PROTECTED GROUPS. Virginia law does require the payment of equal compensation for equal work, regardless of sex, and prohibit employment discrimination based on an individual's physical handicaps. Furthermore, Virginia law does regulate the use of lie detector tests by employers, prohibiting the questioning of prospective employees concerning their sexual activities and requiring employers to furnish the results of any lie detector tests taken by employees and prospective employees and any conclusions drawn from the tests from the employee or applicant, if requested. Virginia law does prohibit employers from requiring prospective employees to provide information concerning any arrest or criminal charges that have been expunged from the prospective employee's record.

WASHINGTON EQUAL OPPORTUNITY LAW

LAW. Washington Law Against Discrimination.

PROTECTED GROUPS. Age, sex, marital status, race, creed, color, national origin, the presence of any sensory, mental, or physical handicap and equal pay. Washington law also prohibits the use of lie detector tests by employers. Pregnancy discrimination is prohibited by regulation.

AGENCY. Washington State Human Rights Commission, Evergreen Plaza Building, Capitol Way at 7th Avenue, Olympia, Washington 98504

WEST VIRGINIA EQUAL OPPORTUNITY LAW

LAW. West Virginia Human Rights Act of 1967.

PROTECTED GROUPS. Race, religion, color, national origin, ancestry, sex, blindness, age, and equal pay.

AGENCY. West Virginia Human Rights Commission, State Capitol, Charleston, West Virginia 25305

WISCONSIN EQUAL OPPORTUNITY LAW

LAW. Wisconsin Fair Employment Act.

PROTECTED GROUPS. Age, race, color, handicap, sex, creed, national origin, arrest record or conviction record, ancestry, and equal pay. Pregnancy discrimination is prohibited by regulation.

AGENCY. Wisconsin Department of Industry, Labor and Human Relations, Equal Rights Division, 201 East Washington Avenue, Madison, Wisconsin 53702

WYOMING EQUAL OPPORTUNITY LAW

LAW. Wyoming Fair Employment Practices Act of 1965.

PROTECTED GROUPS. Race, sex, creed, color, national origin, ancestry, and equal pay.

AGENCY. Wyoming Fair Employment Practices Commission, Barrett Building, 4th Floor, Cheyenne, Wyoming 82002

A GUIDE FOR APPLICATION FORMS AND INTERVIEWS UNDER THE

EMPLOYMENT PRACTICES LAW
CHAPTER 378, HAWAII REVISED STATUTES

PRE-EMPLOYMENT INQUIRY GUIDE

SUBJECT	LAWFUL INQUIRIES	UNLAWFUL INQUIRIES
1. NAME		Inquire about the name which would indicate applicant's lineage, ancestry, marital status, national origin or descent. Inquire into previous name of applicant where it has been changed by court order or otherwise. Mr., Mrs., Miss, or Ms.
2. ADDRESS OR DURATION OF RESIDENCE	Applicant's address. Inquire into place and length of current and previous addresses. "How long a resident of this State or city?"	Specific inquiry into foreign addresses which would indicate national origin.
3. BIRTHPLACE	"Can you after employment submit a birth certificate or other proof of U.S. citizenship?"	Birthplace of applicant. Birthplace of applicant's parents, spouse or other relatives. Requirement that applicant submit proof of birth document prior to hiring.
4. AGE	If a minor, require proof of age in form of a work permit or a certificate of age. Require proof of age by birth certificate after being hired. Inquire whether or not the applicant meets the minimum age requirement set by law.	Requirement that applicant state age or date of birth. Requirement that applicant produce proof of age in the form of a birth certificate or baptismal record.
5. RELIGION	An applicant may be advised concerning normal hours and days of work.	Applicant's religious denomination or affiliation, church, parish, pastor or religious holidays observed. "Do you attend religious services or a house of worship?" Applicant may not be told, "This is a Catholic/Protestant/Jewish/atheist/etc. organization." Applicant may not be told that employees are required to work on religious holidays which are observed as days of complete prayer by members of their specific faith. Any inquiry to indicate or identify religious denomination or customs.
6. RACE OR COLOR		Applicant's race. Color of applicant's skin, eyes, hair, etc., or other questions directly or indirectly indicating race or color. Applicant's height.
7. PHOTOGRAPH	May be required after hiring for identification.	Require photograph before hiring.
8. CITIZENSHIP	"Are you a citizen of the United States?" "If you are not a U.S. citizen, have you the legal right to remain permanently in the U.S.? Do you intend to remain permanently in the U.S.?"	"Of what country are you a citizen?" Whether applicant or his parents or spouse are naturalized U.S. citizens. Date when applicant or parents or spouse acquired U.S. citizenship. Requirement that applicant produce his naturalization papers or first papers.
9. ANCESTRY OR NATIONAL ORIGIN	Language applicant reads, speaks or writes fluently.	Applicant's nationality, lineage, ancestry, national origin, descent or parentage. Nationality of applicant's parents or spouse; maiden name of applicant's wife or mother. Language commonly used by applicant. "What is your mother tongue?" How applicant acquired ability to read, write or speak a foreign language.
10. EDUCATION	Applicant's academic, vocational, or professional education; school attended.	Any inquiry asking specifically the nationality, racial or religious affiliation of a school. Dates of attendance and/or graduation from school.
11. EXPERIENCE	Applicant's work experience. Other countries visited.	
12. CONVICTION, ARREST, AND COURT RECORD		Ask or check into person's arrest, court or conviction record if not substantially related to functions and responsibilities of the prospective employment.
13. RELATIVES	Name of applicant's relatives already employed by this company. "Do you live with your parents?"	Name and addresses of guardian of minor applicant.
14. NOTICE IN CASE OF EMERGENCY	Name and address of person to be notified in case of accident or emergency.	Relationship of person to be notified in case of emergencies.
15. ORGANIZATION	Inquiry into membership in organizations providing the name or character of the organization does not reveal the race, religion, color, physical handicap, marital status or ancestry of the applicant. What offices are held, if any.	The names of organizations to which the applicant belongs if such information would indicate through character or name the race, religion, color, or ancestry of the membership.
16. REFERENCES	"By whom were you referred for a position here?" Names of persons willing to provide professional and/or character references for applicant.	Require the submission of a religious reference.
17. SEX	Only if required by business necessity.	Sex of the applicant. "Are you expecting?" or "Are you pregnant?" Applicant's weight.
18. PHYSICAL HANDICAP	Any illnesses that may interfere with your job duties.	Whether applicant has a physical handicap or defect. "Have you collected workers' compensation for a previous illness or injury?"
19. MARITAL STATUS		Whether single, married, divorced, widowed, separated, etc. Names and ages of spouse and children. Spouse's place of employment.
20. MISCELLANEOUS	Notice to applicants that any misstatements or omissions of material facts in the application may be cause for dismissal.	Require resume containing unlawful information.

ANY INQUIRY IS FORBIDDEN WHICH, ALTHOUGH NOT SPECIFICALLY LISTED AMONG THE ABOVE, IS DESIGNED TO ELICIT INFORMATION AS TO RACE, COLOR, ANCESTRY, AGE, SEX, RELIGION, PHYSICAL HANDICAP, MARITAL STATUS, OR ARREST AND COURT RECORD UNLESS BASED ON A BONA FIDE OCCUPATIONAL QUALIFICATION.

State of New Hampshire

COMMISSION FOR HUMAN RIGHTS

THE LAW AGAINST DISCRIMINATION IN EMPLOYMENT

The Law Against Discrimination declares that no person shall be denied the right to work because of race, color, religious creed, national origin, ancestry, sex, age, marital status or physical or mental handicap. This law, however, does not restrict an employer, a labor organization, or an employment agency from establishing occupational qualifications. The law does require that the same standards of qualification be applied equally to all persons.

THE FOLLOWING ARE NOT AFFECTED BY THE LAW:

1. An employer with fewer than six persons in his employ.

2. A club exclusively social, or a fraternal, charitable, educational or religious association or corporation which is not organized for a private profit.

3. An individual employed by his parents, spouse or child or in the domestic service of any person.

The term "Employer" includes the State and all political sub-divisions, boards, departments, and commissions thereof.

IT IS AN UNLAWFUL EMPLOYMENT PRACTICE
(Unless based upon a bona fide occupational qualification)

FOR AN EMPLOYER:

1. To ask any question before employment, answers to which directly or indirectly disclose the race, color, religious creed, national origin, ancestry, sex, age, marital status or physical or mental handicap, of the applicant.

2. To print or circulate any advertisement which directly or indirectly specifies any limitation because of race, color, religious creed, national origin, ancestry, sex, age, marital status or physical or mental handicap, of any prospective applicant for employment.

3. To discharge or refuse to hire any individual because of race, color, religious creed, national origin, ancestry, sex, age marital status or physical or mental handicap.

4. To act unfairly against any individual in matters relating to compensation, terms, conditions, or privileges of employment because of race, color, religious creed, national origin, ancestry, sex, age, marital status or physical or mental handicap.

FOR A LABOR ORGANIZATION:

1. To exclude from full membership rights or to expel from membership any individual because of race, color, religious creed, national origin, ancestry, sex, age, marital status or physical or mental handicap.

2. To discriminate in any way against any of its members or against any employer or any individual employed by an employer.

FOR AN EMPLOYMENT AGENCY:

1. To ask questions before employment, answers to which directly or indirectly disclose the race, color, religious creed, national origin, ancestry, sex, age, marital status or physical or mental handicap, or any applicant for employment.

2. To print, circulate, advertise, or publish any material which directly or indirectly expresses any limitation upon employment because of the race, color, religious creed, national origin, ancestry, sex, age, marital status or physical or mental handicap of the prospective applicant

3. To accept or process job orders from employers which limit or specify the race, color, religious creed, national origin, ancestry, sex, age, marital status or physical or mental handicap of any applicant for employment.

FOR EMPLOYEES:

To offer resistance to the employment of any individual because of race color, religious creed, national origin, ancestry, sex, age, marital status or physical or mental handicap.

FOR ANYONE:

1. Whether a person, employer, labor organization, or employment agency: To discharge, refuse to employ, or to expel any individual because he has opposed any practices forbidden by the Law Against Discrimination, or has testified or assisted in any proceeding under that Law.

2. Whether an employer or an employee or other person: to aid, abet, incite compel, or coerce the doing of any of the acts forbidden under The Law Against Discrimination.

COMPLAINTS

Complaints may be filed in person at, or mailed to, the offices of the New Hampshire Commission for Human Rights, 66 South Street, Concord, N. H. 03301

SECTION II OF THE LAW AGAINST DISCRIMINATION REQUIRES EVERY EMPLOYER, EMPLOYMENT AGENCY, AND LABOR UNION SUBJECT TO ITS PROVISIONS TO POST THIS NOTICE OR A NOTICE OTHERWISE APPROVED BY THE NEW HAMPSHIRE COMMISSION FOR HUMAN RIGHTS IN A CONSPICUOUS PLACE OR PLACES ON THEIR PREMISES.

QUESTIONING APPLICANTS
FOR EMPLOYMENT

A Guide for Application Forms
and Interviews under the

OHIO FAIR EMPLOYMENT PRACTICES ACT

JOHN J. GILLIGAN
Governor

Distributed by

OHIO CIVIL RIGHTS COMMISSION

220 Parsons Avenue

Columbus. Ohio 43215

INQUIRIES BEFORE HIRING	LAWFUL	UNLAWFUL
1. NAME	Name.	Inquiry into any title which indicates race, color, religion, sex, National origin or ancestry.
2. ADDRESS	Inquiry into place and length of current and previous addresses.	Specific inquiry into foreign addresses which would indicate national origin.
3. AGE	A. Request proof of age in form of work permit issued by school authorities. B. Require proof of age by birth certificate after hiring.	Require birth certificate or baptismal record before hiring.
4. BIRTHPLACE OR NATIONAL ORIGIN		A. Any inquiry into place of birth. B. Any inquiry into place of birth of parents, grandparents or spouse. C. Any other inquiry into national origin.
5. RACE OR COLOR		Any inquiry which would indicate race or color.

INQUIRIES BEFORE HIRING	LAWFUL	UNLAWFUL
6. SEX		Any inquiry which would indicate sex.
7. RELIGION — CREED		A. Any inquiry to indicate or identify denomination or customs. B. May not be told this is a Protestant (Catholic or Jewish) organization. C. Request pastor's recommendation or reference.
8. CITIZENSHIP	A. Whether a U.S. Citizen B. If not, whether intends to become one. C. If U.S. residence is legal. D. If spouse is citizen. E. Require proof of citizenship after being hired.	A. If native-born or naturalized. B. Proof of citizenship before hiring. C. Whether parents or spouse are native-born, or naturalized.
9. PHOTOGRAPHS	May be required after hiring for identification purposes.	Request photograph before hiring.
10. EDUCATION	A. Inquiry into what academic, professional or vocational schools attended. B. Inquiry into language skills, such as reading and writing of foreign languages.	A. Any inquiry asking specifically the nationality, racial or religious affiliation of a school. B. Inquiry as to what is mother tongue or how foreign language ability was acquired, unless necessary for job.
11. RELATIVES	Inquiry into name, relationship and address of person to be notified in case of emergency.	Any inquiry about a relative which is unlawful.
12. ORGANIZATION	A. Inquiry into organization memberships, excluding any organization, the name or character of which indicates the race, color, religion, sex, national origin or ancestry of its members. B. What offices are held, if any.	Inquiry into all clubs and organizations where membership is held.
13. MILITARY SERVICE	A. Inquiry into service in U.S. Armed forces. B. Rank attained. C. Which branch of service. D. Require military discharge certificate after being hired.	A. Inquiry into military service in armed service of any country but U.S. B. Request military service records.
14. WORK SCHEDULE	Inquiry into willingness to work required work-schedule.	Any inquiry into willingness to work any particular religious holiday.
15. OTHER QUALIFICATIONS	Any question that has direct reflection on the job to be applied for.	Any non-job related inquiry that may present information permitting unlawful discrimination.
16. REFERENCES	General personal and work references not relating to race, color, religion, sex, national origin or ancestry.	Request references specifically from clergymen or any other persons who might reflect race, color, religion, sex, national origin or ancestry of applicant.

I. Employers acting under approved Affirmative Action Programs or acting under orders of Equal Employment law enforcement agencies of federal, state, or local governments may be exempt from some of the prohibited inquiries listed above only to the extent that these inquiries are required by such programs, agreements or orders.

II. Federal Defense Contracts: Employers having Federal defense contracts are exempt to the extent that otherwise prohibited inquiries are required by Federal Law for security purposes.

III. Any inquiry is forbidden which, although not specifically listed among the above, is designed to elicit information as to race, color, religion, sex, national origin or ancestry in violation of the law.

Rev. 5-74—20M

TO BE POSTED IN A CONSPICUOUS PLACE

STATE OF NEW JERSEY   DEPARTMENT OF LAW & PUBLIC SAFETY

DIVISION ON CIVIL RIGHTS

NEW JERSEY LAW GUARANTEES
EQUAL EMPLOYMENT OPPORTUNITY

"All persons shall have the opportunity to obtain employment without discrimination because of race, creed, color, national origin, ancestry, age, sex, marital status, or physical handicap, subject only to the conditions and limitations applicable alike to all persons."

THIS OPPORTUNITY IS RECOGNIZED AND DECLARED TO BE A CIVIL RIGHT

N.J.S.A. 10:5-1 et seq., and 10:2-1 et seq.

- **A QUALIFIED PERSON** can <u>not</u> be denied employment because of race, color, religion, place of birth, age, ancestry, sex, marital status, physical handicap, or liability for military service.

- **EMPLOYERS** can <u>not</u> discriminate in recruiting, employment interviews, hiring, upgrading, setting working conditions or discharging.

- **LABOR ORGANIZATIONS** can <u>not</u> deny membership to qualified persons or discriminate in apprentice training programs.

• EMPLOYMENT AGENCIES

can **not** discriminate in job referrals, ask pre-employment questions or circulate information which limits employment because of race, color, religion, ancestry, place of birth, age, sex, marital status, physical handicap, or liability for military service.

• NEWSPAPERS

can **not** publish discriminatory employment advertisements.

If you have experienced discrimination report it immediately to any of the offices listed below.

Reprisals can **not** be taken against you for making a complaint.

Violation of the law may result in a fine, imprisonment, or both.

FOR ADDITIONAL INFORMATION CONTACT

THE NEW JERSEY DIVISION ON CIVIL RIGHTS

DEPARTMENT OF LAW AND PUBLIC SAFETY

TRENTON OFFICE
436 East State Street
Trenton, New Jersey 08608
Tel. 609-292-4605

CAMDEN OFFICE
530 Cooper Street
Camden, N. J. 08102
Tel. 609-964-0011

PATERSON OFFICE
370 Broadway
Paterson, N. J.
Tel. 201-345-1465

NEWARK OFFICE
1100 Raymond Boulevard
Newark, New Jersey 07102
Tel. 201-648-2700

The Commonwealth of Massachusetts
COMMISSION AGAINST DISCRIMINATION
EXECUTIVE DEPARTMENT
THE FAIR PRACTICE LAW

The Fair Practice Law declares that no person shall be denied the right to work because of race, color, religious creed, national origin, sex, age or ancestry. This law, however, does not restrict an employer, a labor organization, or an employment agency from establishing qualifications. The law does require that the same standards of qualification be applied equally to all persons.

THE FOLLOWING ARE NOT COVERED BY THE LAW:

1. An employer with fewer than six persons in his employ.
2. A club exclusively social, or a fraternal, or religious association or corporation which is not organized for private profit, a charitable or educational association or corporation that is operated by or connected with a religious organization.
3. An individual employed by his parents, spouse or child or in the domestic service of any person.

The term "Employer" includes the Commonwealth and all political sub-divisions, boards, departments and commissions thereof.

The amendment concerning age prohibits discrimination against employees and persons seeking employment between forty and sixty-five years of age.

It Is An Unlawful Practice
(Unless based upon a bona fide occupational qualification determined by the Commission)

For An Employer:

1. To ask any questions before employment, answers to which directly or indirectly disclose the race, color, religious creed, national origin, sex, age or ancestry of the applicant.
2. To print or circulate any advertisement which directly or indirectly specifies any limitation because of race, color, religious creed, national origin, sex, age or ancestry of any prospective applicant for employment.
3. To discharge or refuse to hire any individual because of race, color, religious creed, national origin, sex, age or ancestry.
4. To act unfairly against any individual in matters relating to compensation, terms, conditions or privileges of employment because of race, color, religious creed, national origin, sex, age or ancestry.
5. To fail to undertake in good faith affirmative action programs in the areas of recruitment and hiring to promote equal employment opportunity and to remedy the effects of past discrimination in employment.

For A Labor Organization:

1. To exclude from full membership rights or to expel from membership any individual because of race, color, religious creed, national origin, sex, age or ancestry.

For An Employment Agency:

1. To ask questions before employment, answers to which directly or indirectly disclose the race, color, religious creed, national origin, sex, age or ancestry of any applicant for employment.
2. To make any statements to a prospective employer which disclose the race, color, religious creed, national origin, sex, age or ancestry of the prospective applicant for employment.
3. To print, circulate, advertise or publish any material which directly or indirectly expresses any limitation upon employment because of the race, color, religious creed, national origin, sex, age or ancestry of the prospective applicant.
4. To accept or process job orders from employers which limit or specify the race, color, religious creed, national origin, sex, age or ancestry of any applicant for employment. (Any employer, employment agency or labor organization may request an opinion from the Commission concerning whether any existing or proposed requirement for employment or for membership in such organization is a bona fide occupational qualification).

For Insurance or Bonding Companies:

1. For any person engaged in the insurance or bonding business, or his agent, to make any inquiry or record of any person seeking a bond or surety bond conditioned upon the faithful performance of his duties or to use any form of application, in connection with the furnishing of such bond, which seeks information relative to the race, color, religious creed, national origin or ancestry of the person to be bonded.

For Employees:

1. To offer resistance to the employment of any individual because of race, color, religious creed, national origin, sex, age or ancestry.

For Anyone:

1. Whether a person, employer, labor organization or employment agency; to discharge, refuse to employ or to expel any individual because he has opposed any practices forbidden by the Fair Practice Law or has testified or assisted in any proceeding under that Law.
2. Whether an employer or an employee or other person: to aid, abet, incite, compel or coerce the doing of any of the acts forbidden under the Fair Practice Law.

Pre-Employment or Post-Employment inquiries may be made under certain conditions as outlined in the Commission's Guidelines and Regulations, Publication No. 605.

Complaints

Complaints may be filed in person at, or mailed to the office of the Massachusetts Commission Against Discrimination at 120 Tremont Street, Boston, 139 Chandler Street, Worcester, 145 State Street, Springfield or 222 Union Street, New Bedford.

SECTION 7 OF THE FAIR PRACTICE LAW REQUIRES EVERY EMPLOYER, EMPLOYMENT AGENCY, AND LABOR UNION SUBJECT TO ITS PROVISIONS TO POST THIS NOTICE OR A NOTICE OTHERWISE APPROVED BY THE MASSACHUSETTS COMMISSION AGAINST DISCRIMINATION IN A CONSPICUOUS PLACE OR PLACES ON THEIR PREMISES.

Form CAD-1 (Rev. 1-70) 25M-6-70-047128

Kansas Law Provides
EQUAL
OPPORTUNITY

without regard to

RACE, RELIGION, COLOR, SEX, PHYSICAL HANDICAP,

NATIONAL ORIGIN or ANCESTRY

report discrimination to:

**KANSAS COMMISSION
ON CIVIL RIGHTS**

535 Kansas Ave. — 5th Floor
Topeka, Kansas 66603
Phone: (913) 296-3206

or

212 South Market
Wichita, Kansas 67202
Phone: (316) 265-9624

in

**Recruitment •
Hiring • Placement •
Promotion • Transfer •
Training and Apprenticeship •
Compensation •
Layoff • Termination •
Physical Facilities •**

Nondiscrimination Of Wage Payments Based On Sex
(KRS 337.420 to 337.433 and KRS 337.992)

DEFINITIONS:

EMPLOYEE --

Any individual employed by any employer, including but not limited to individuals employed by the State or any of its political subdivisions, instrumentalities, or instrumentalities of political subdivisions.

EMPLOYER --

A person who has eight or more employees within the State in each of twenty or more calendar weeks in the current or preceding calendar year and an agent of such a person.

WAGE RATE--

All compensation for employment, including payment, in kind and amounts paid by employers for employee benefits, as defined by the Commissioner in regulations issued under this Act.

PROHIBITION OF THE PAYMENT OF WAGES BASED ON SEX:

The employer is prohibited from discriminating between employees of opposite sexes in the same establishment by paying different wage rates for comparable work on jobs which have comparable requirements. This prohibition covers any employee in any occupation in Kentucky. Any employer violating this Act shall not reduce the wages of any employee in order to comply with the Act.

No employer can discharge or discriminate against any employee for the reason that the employee sought to invoke or assist in the enforcement of this Act.

EXEMPTIONS FROM COVERAGE:

A differential paid through an established seniority system or merit-increase system is permitted by the Act if it does not discriminate on the basis of sex.

Employers subject to the Fair Labor Standards Act of 1938, as amended, are excluded "when that act imposes comparable or greater requirements than contained" in this Act. However, to be excluded, the employer must file with the Commissioner of the Kentucky Department of Labor a statement that he is covered by the Fair Labor Standards Act of 1938, as amended.

ENFORCEMENT OF LAW AND POWER TO INSPECT:

The Commissioner of Labor or his authorized agent has the power to enter the employer's premises to inspect records, compare character of work and operations of employees, question employees, and to obtain any information necessary to administer and enforce this Act.

The Commissioner or his authorized representative has the power to hold hearings, subpoena witnesses or documentary evidence, and examine witnesses under oath. If a person fails to obey a subpoena, the circuit court of the judicial district wherein the hearing is being held may issue an order requiring the subpoena to be obeyed. Failure to obey the court order may be punished as a contempt of that court.

COLLECTION OF UNPAID WAGES:

Any employer who violates this Act is liable to the employee or employees affected in the amount of the unpaid wages. If the employer violates this Act willfully by reducing wages in order to comply with it, he is liable for an additional equal amount as liquidated damages. The court may order other appropriate action, including reinstatement of employees discharged in violation of this Act.

The employee or employees affected may maintain an action to collect the amount due. At the written request of any employee, the Commissioner of Labor may bring any legal action necessary to collect the claim for unpaid wages in behalf of the employee.

An agreement between an employer and employee to work for less than the wage to which such employee is entitled will not bar any legal action or a voluntary wage restitution.

STATUTE OF LIMITATIONS:

Court action under this Act may be commenced no later than six months after the cause of action occurs.

POSTING OF LAW:

All employers subject to this Act shall post this abstract in a conspicuous place in or about the premises wherein any employee is employed.

PENALTIES:

"Any person who discharges or in any other manner discriminates against an employee because such employee has:

"(a) made any complaint to his employer, the Commissioner, or any other person, or

"(b) instituted or caused to be instituted any proceeding under or related to this Act, or

"(c) testified or is about to testify in any such proceedings, shall, upon conviction thereof, be subject to a fine of not less than five-hundred dollars, or by imprisonment for not more than six months, or by both such fine and imprisonment."

Commissioner
Kentucky Department of Labor

Division of Labor Standards
Informational Copy

FAILURE TO POST THIS ORDER WHERE ALL EMPLOYEES
MAY READ IT IS A CRIMINAL VIOLATION

THE MAINE HUMAN RIGHTS ACT GUARANTEES...

Equal Employment Rights

EQUAL EMPLOYMENT RIGHTS

1. The RIGHT to freedom from discrimination in employment.

2. The opportunity for an individual to secure employment without discrimination . . is declared to be a CIVIL RIGHT.

The Maine Human Rights Act prohibits discrimination because of race, color, religion, age, national origin, sex, ancestry, or physical or mental handicap.

UNLAWFUL EMPLOYMENT DISCRIMINATION

1. For any employer to fail or refuse to hire an applicant

2. For any employer to discharge an employee

3. For any employer to discriminate against an employee with respect to recruitment, tenure, promotion, transfer, or compensation

4. For any employment agency to fail or refuse to classify properly or refer for employment an applicant

5. For any labor organization to exclude from apprenticeship or membership an applicant

6. For any employer, employment agency, or labor organization prior to employment or admission to membership of an individual to ask questions, keep a record, use application form, issue any notice, employ a quota system

7. For any employer, employment agency, or labor organization to retaliate against a person who has opposed a violation of the Maine Human Rights Act.

Because of race, color, religion, age, national origin, sex, ancestry, or physical or mental handicap.

HUMAN RIGHTS

STATE HOUSE, AUGUSTA, MAINE
207 289 2326   04330

IF YOU FEEL YOU HAVE BEEN DISCRIMINATED AGAINST, CONTACT THE COMMISSION OFFICE.

STATE OF INDIANA
EQUAL JOB OPPORTUNITY

WHAT
IS
PROHIBITED?

The Indiana Civil Rights Law prohibits discrimination
against persons in any aspect of their employment or
in their attempts to obtain employment when the discrimination is due to race, religion, color, sex,
national origin or ancestry, or handicap.

Practices of unequal treatment and those requirements
unrelated to the job which produce an unequal effect
are forbidden. The Commission may order that any
income loss suffered by a person protected by this law
be paid.

WHO
IS
COVERED?

1. Employers of six or more persons (except not-for-
    profit corporations or associations organized ex-
    clusively for fraternal or religious purposes).
2. The State of Indiana and any of its political or
    civil subdivisions.
3. Unions and other labor organizations.
4. Employment agencies.

WHAT IS
THE TIME LIMIT
FOR FILING?

Persons who feel they have suffered discrimination as
defined above should file a signed, notarized complaint
with the Indiana Civil Rights Commission not longer
than 90 days from the date of the alleged act or acts
of discrimination, or 90 days from the date of the termination of a published and meaningful grievance procedure provided by a respondent employer or labor union,or
90 days from notification of a local commission's
final decision on the same complaint. All available
details about the matter should be supplied, including
any known documents or where they may be found and names
and addresses of any witnesses.

INDIANA CIVIL RIGHTS COMMISSION
311 West Washington Street
Indianapolis, Indiana 46202

Telephone: 1-317-633-4855,5741, 5573, 5763, 5312

MARYLAND COMMISSION ON HUMAN RELATIONS

The Complaint

A Commission representative will hear your complaint and determine whether or not is is within the Commission's jurisdiction to investigate.

The representative will help you draft the wording of the complaint and prepare it in legal form for your review, approval and notarized signature.

Your complaint will be logged and then investigated by an assigned investigator, who will keep you advised of the progress of your case.

The Investigation

The investigator will interview the respondent (the person ultimately responsible for the alleged discrimination) and other witnesses, in addition to reviewing pertinent records and documents.

The investigator may ask you to clarify certain aspects of the complaints in the light of any new information. Remember, if you should learn or remember any additional information, contact the investigator immediately.

The investigation may either find:

1. no probable cause, and dismiss the complaint

or

2. probable cause, and proceed to correct the discriminatory act(s) and its effects.

The Conciliation

If the investigation reveals that the charges are valid, the Commission will attempt to remedy the problem through conciliation and negotiation with the Respondent. Respondent must:

1. cease and desist from the specific discriminatory act,

2. implement whatever actions or programs the Commissions deems necessary to end the discriminatory act(s),

and

3. restore to the charging party losses that occurred during the discriminatory act or policies.

The Public Hearing

Whenever there is a failure to reach a voluntary settlement, the Commission may convene a public hearing. Testimony under oath is heard, witnesses are called, evidence submitted, a decision rendered, and a legally enforceable order issued.

The complainant and the respondent have the right to appeal this order to the Courts.

Basic Complaint Process

Complaint Reception
1. Filed Directly
2. Deferrals Accepted from Federal Agencies
3. Commission Initiated Complaints

Investigation and Determination

Finding of No Probable Cause (Case Closed)

Administrative Closure
1. Complaint Withdrawn
2. Lack Jurisdiction
3. Cannot Locate (Case Closed)

Finding of Probable Cause

Conciliation – To Remedy Alleged Discrimination

Successful Conciliation Agreement Signed (Case Closed)

Unsuccessful Conciliation - Finding of No Agreement

Public Hearing

No Discrimination Found Order Dismissing the Complaint (Case Closed)

Discrimination Found Order to Cease and Desist and Take Affirmative Action

Orders Complied With (Case Closed)

Refusal to Comply With Order Institute Litigation In The Appropriate Equity Court

Court Confirmation (Case Closed)

Possible Appeal to Higher Court

La Ley En Michigan

PROHIBE

LA DISCRIMINACION

EN TRABAJO, EDUCACION, VIVIENDAS, ACOMODACION PUBLICA, SERVICIO PUBLICO O EN EL CUMPLIMIENTO DE LA LEY

POR MOTIVOS DE RELIGION, RAZA, COLOR DE LA PIEL, NACIONALIDAD, EDAD, SEXO O INHABILIDAD FISICA

LAS PERSONAS A QUIENES SE LES NIEGUE OPORTUNIDADES IGUALES BASANDAS EN DICHAS CONDICIONES PUEDEN PRESENTAR SUS QUEJAS A

LA COMISIÓN DE DERECHOS CIVILES DE MICHIGAN
En las oficinas locales del distrito, situadas en Battle Creek, Benton Harbor, Detroit, Flint, Grand Rapids, Jackson, Lansing, Muskegon, Pontiac y Saginaw.

Póngase en un lugar bien visible

Michigan Law

PROHIBITS

DISCRIMINATION

IN EMPLOYMENT, EDUCATION, HOUSING, PUBLIC ACCOMMODATION, PUBLIC SERVICE OR LAW ENFORCEMENT

BASED ON RELIGION, RACE, COLOR, NATIONAL ORIGIN, AGE, SEX OR HANDICAP

PERSONS DENIED EQUAL OPPORTUNITY BASED ON THESE CONDITIONS MAY FILE A COMPLAINT WITH THE

MICHIGAN CIVIL RIGHTS COMMISSION
District offices located in Battle Creek, Benton Harbor, Detroit, Flint, Grand Rapids, Jackson, Lansing, Muskegon, Pontiac and Saginaw.

Must be posted in a conspicuous place

DISCRIMINATION

because of RACE, CREED, COLOR, RELIGION, NATIONAL ORIGIN, SEX OR ANCESTRY

IS PROHIBITED
by Law in Missouri

Missouri's Fair Employment Practices Act applies to
- **private employers with 6 or more employees**
- **all apprenticeship or training programs**
- **all labor organizations**
- **all employment agencies, public or private**
- **all state and local government agencies**

IF YOU
BELIEVE YOU HAVE BEEN
UNLAWFULLY DISCRIMINATED AGAINST
CONTACT

Missouri Commission on Human Rights

P. O. Box 1129
Jefferson City, Missouri 65101
Phone (314) 751-3325

615 E. 13th Street
Kansas City, Missouri 64106
Phone (816) 274-6491

Suite 727
508 North Grand Boulevard
St. Louis, Missouri 63103
Phone (314) 534-7090

103 E. Center Street
P. O. Box 784
Sikeston, Missouri 63801
Phone (314) 471-8566

A STATE AGENCY

" . . . all persons are created equal and are entitled to equal rights and opportunities under the law . . . to give security to these things is the principal office of government and . . . when government does not confer this security, it fails in its chief design."

CONSTITUTION OF MISSOURI
Art. 1. Sec. 2

MONTANA LAW PROHIBITS

DISCRIMINATION

IN
Creed or Religion
Age
Sex
Race, national origin, or color
Handicap, physical or mental
Political belief (Government Involved)
Marital Status

AREA
Employment
Training or education
Housing
Public accommodations
Financing
Government services
Retaliation (for Human Rights Complaint)

FOR INFORMATION CALL

(406)-449-2884

MONTANA
HUMAN
RIGHTS
COMMISSION

ROOM **404**, POWER BLOCK, LAST CHANCE GULCH, HELENA, MONTANA 59601 • TELEPHONE 406/449-2884

STATE OF NEW MEXICO
HUMAN RIGHTS COMMISSION

New Mexico Prohibits
DISCRIMINATION

in EMPLOYMENT, HOUSING,
PUBLIC ACCOMMODATIONS,
and CONSUMER CREDIT

for reasons of: race, religion,
ancestry, national origin, sex, age,
and mental or physical handicap.

Nuevo México Prohibe
DISCRIMINACIÓN

en EMPLEO, RENTAS, COMPRAS
de CASA o DOMICILIOS PUBLICOS y
CREDITO dado al CONSUMIDOR

por causa de raza, color, religion,
origen nacional, sexo, edad
o disabilidad fisica y mental.

HUMAN RIGHTS COMMISSION
120 Villagra Building
Santa Fe, New Mexico 87503
Phone: 827-2713

The New Mexico Human Rights Commission Requests Your Cooperation by Posting This Abstract of the New Mexico
Human Rights Act in a Conspicuous Place.

In the State of Oregon it is <u>UNLAWFUL</u> to discriminate against or treat unequally certain classes of persons in the following areas:

EMPLOYMENT

Employers may not discriminate on the basis of race, sex, age (18 - 65), religion, national origin, color, or because of a mental or physical handicap unrelated to job performance.

All employers, public and private; labor unions; and employment agencies are covered by the law.

Discrimination is forbidden in hiring, promotion, demotion, re-employment lay-offs, firing; in salary and wages, benefits, and all other terms and conditions of employment; in inequality in on-the-job treatment; in advertising for employes.

HOUSING

No one who sells, rents or leases a house, apartment, or any other real property may discriminate on the basis of: race, sex, marital status, color, religion, national origin, or because of a mental or physical handicap. Not even a private home owner.

Acts forbidden by the law are: refusal to sell, lease or rent; expelling or evicting a current or potential tenant, lessee, or buyer from any housing; discrimination in the price of the property or in any other terms, privileges or services relating to the sale or use of the housing; attempting to discourage sale or rental; or advertising in a way which indicates the landlord

IN CASE
OF
DISCRIMINATION

CONTACT

OREGON
BUREAU OF LABOR
CIVIL RIGHTS DIVISION

| PORTLAND | SALEM | EUGENE |
| 229-5741 | 378-3297 | 686-7623 |

or seller prefers persons of a particular race, sex, marital status, etc.

PUBLIC ACCOMMODATIONS

It is unlawful for any place of public accommodation to refuse or deny admission to, make any distinctions or restrictions, or extend its services and privileges in an unequal manner on the basis of race, sex, marital Status, religion, national origin, color, or because of a person's having a mental or physical handicap.

A place of public accommodation means any place or person offering goods and services to the public. This not only includes places of recreation, such as restaurants, bars and motels, but includes retail stores, banks, insurance companies and other businesses and also includes credit extended to the public-at-large in the form of charge accounts, mortgages, loans, and installment purchase's.

VOCATIONAL, PROFESSIONAL & TRADE SCHOOLS

Vocational, professional, and trade schools are private businesses licensed by the State of Oregon.

Such schools may not refuse admission or discriminate in giving instruction on the basis of race, color, sex, marital status, religion, or national origin.

OTHERS COVERED BY CIVIL RIGHTS LAWS

1. Injured workers who are refused reinstatement or re-employment, upon recovery, to available positions suitable to their abilities; or

injured workers who have been discriminated against because they have applied for or used workmens' compensation benefits.

2. Employes who report, complain of, or oppose unsafe or unhealthy working conditions prohibited by law or regulation, who are discriminated or retaliated against for making such a complaint.

IF YOU BELIEVE YOU HAVE BEEN UNLAWFULLY DISCRIMINATED AGAINST, you or your lawyer may file a formal complaint with the Civil Rights Division of the Oregon Bureau of Labor.

Simply visit any of our field offices, which are listed on the back of this brochure, and file a complaint -- listing the reason for and circumstances under which you believe the discrimination occurred.

If, after investigating your complaint, our staff finds substantial evidence of unlawful discrimination, the Division will represent you in obtaining the remedies you are entitled to under the law. This might be obtaining a job or housing you were denied, including compensation for any financial hardship you suffered because of the discrimination.

The Division will first try to settle your complaint through a process of conference and conciliation. If this fails, and the discriminating party refuses to settle, your case will go to a public hearing, in which both sides present evidence, under oath, and a decision is rendered.

Form PHRC-20—25M—5-75   3

Commonwealth of Pennsylvania

EMPLOYMENT PROVISIONS
PENNSYLVANIA HUMAN RELATIONS ACT

(Act of October 27, 1955, P.L. 744, as amended)

PURPOSE OF PROVISIONS

The purpose of the employment provisions of the Pennsylvania Human Relations Act is to prevent and eliminate unlawful discriminatory practices in employment because of race, color, religion, ancestry, age (40-62), sex, national origin, non-job related handicap or disability, or willingness or refusal to participate in abortion or sterilization.

UNLAWFUL DISCRIMINATORY PRACTICES

It is unlawful — on the basis of the factors listed above — for an employer, labor union or employment agency to:

1. Deny any person an equal opportunity to obtain employment, to be promoted and to be accorded all other rights to compensation, tenure and other conditions and privileges of employment.

2. Deny membership rights and privileges in any labor organization.

3. Deny any person equal opportunity to be referred for employment.

PARTIES SUBJECT TO THE ACT

The employment provisions of the Pennsylvania Human Relations Act apply to: (1) Employers of 4 or more persons, including units of state and local government; (2) Labor organizations, and (3) Employment agencies.

WHO MAY FILE A COMPLAINT

Complaints may be filed by any of the following: (1) An individual who believes he or she has been discriminated against; (2) The Pennsylvania Human Relations Commission; (3) The Attorney General of Pennsylvania, or (4) An employer whose employes hinder compliance with the provisions of the Act.

PARTIES EXEMPT FROM THE ACT

The employment provisions of the Pennsylvania Human Relations Act do not apply to: (1) any person employed in agriculture or domestic service; (2) any individual who, as part of his or her employment, resides in the personal residence of the employer; (3) any individual employed by his or her parents, spouse or child.

WHO MUST POST THIS NOTICE

Every employer, labor organization and employment agency subject to the employment provisions of this Act is required by law to post this notice. The notice must be placed in an easily-accessible and well-lighted location customarily frequented by applicants, employes or members.

WARNING: Removing, defacing, covering up or destroying this notice is a violation of the Pennsylvania Penal Code and may subject you to fine or imprisonment.

WHERE COMPLAINTS MAY BE FILED AND INFORMATION OBTAINED

——————————— PENNSYLVANIA HUMAN RELATIONS COMMISSION ———————————

HEADQUARTERS OFFICE: 100 N. Cameron Street — 2nd Floor
Harrisburg, Pennsylvania 17101
(717) 787-4410

PITTSBURGH
Room 810
4 Smithfield Street
(412) 565-5395

HARRISBURG
First Floor
301 Muench Street
(717) 787-9780

PHILADELPHIA
101 State Office Building
Broad and Spring Garden Streets
(215) 238-6940

No es el color, la religión, el sexo, la raza o la edad...

lo que cuenta es la destreza!

La Constitución del Estado Libre Asociado de Puerto Rico, así como algunas de nuestras leyes, prohiben que se discrimine en el empleo de cualquier persona por razones de edad avanzada, color, raza, credo, sexo, origen, condición social o ideales políticos. Esta discriminación también la prohiben órdenes ejecutivas del Presidente de los Estados Unidos y Leyes Federales.

Si usted ha sido rechazado de una oportunidad de empleo, despedido de su último empleo, se le ha negado aumento de sueldo u oportunidad de progreso en su trabajo por algunas de las razones aquí expuestas, comuníquese con nosotros.

UNIDAD ANTI-DISCRIMEN
DEPARTAMENTO DEL TRABAJO

AVENIDA BARBOSA NUM. 414, HATO REY, P.R. 00917
TELEFONOS 763-4022 / 763-4136 / 763-5151

También puede escribir a:

THE EQUAL EMPLOYMENT
OPPORTUNITY COMMISSION
NEW YORK DISTRICT OFFICE
90 CHURCH STREET
NEW YORK, NEW YORK 10007

STATE OF WEST VIRGINIA

NOTICE

THE WEST VIRGINIA HUMAN RIGHTS ACT

Prohibits

Discrimination in Employment

and

Places of Public Accommodations

Based on

RACE, RELIGION, COLOR, NATIONAL ORIGIN, ANCESTRY, SEX, AGE (40 to 65) OR BLINDNESS

AND

Discrimination in Housing

Based on

RACE, RELIGION, COLOR, NATIONAL ORIGIN, ANCESTRY, SEX OR BLINDNESS

For Further Information or to File a Complaint, Call, Write or Visit:

WEST VIRGINIA HUMAN RIGHTS COMMISSION

MAIL ADDRESS
STATE CAPITOL
CHARLESTON, WEST VIRGINIA 25305

TELEPHONE
304 — 348-2616

OFFICE LOCATION
1036 QUARRIER STREET
215 PROFESSIONAL BUILDING
CHARLESTON, WEST VIRGINIA 25301

POST

State of California
Edmund G. Brown Jr., Governor

Department of Industrial Relations

DIVISION OF FAIR EMPLOYMENT PRACTICES

DISCRIMINATION IN EMPLOYMENT

Because of

- Race
- Color
- Ancestry
- Religious Creed
- National Origin
- Sex
- Physical Handicap
- Medical Condition
- Age*
- Marital Status

IS PROHIBITED BY LAW

The California Fair Employment Practice Act—
(Sections 1410-1432, Labor Code)

- permits job applicants to file complaints with the Fair Employment Practice Commission (FEPC) against an employer, employment agency, or labor union which fails to grant equal opportunity as required by law.

- requires employers not to discriminate against any job applicant or worker in hiring, promotion, assignment, or discharge. On-the-job segregation is also prohibited, and employers may file complaints against workers who refuse to cooperate in compliance.

- requires employment agencies to serve all applicants equally; to refuse discriminatory job orders; to refrain from prohibited pre-hiring inquiries or help-wanted advertising.

- requires unions not to discriminate in member admissions or dispatching to jobs.

- forbids any person to interfere with efforts to comply with the Act.

- authorizes the FEPC to work affirmatively with cooperating employers to review hiring and recruiting practices in order to expand equal opportunity.

(* Discrimination because of age is prohibited for ages 40 ████.)

REMEDIES to individuals, or penalties for violation may include: hiring, back pay, promotion, reinstatement, cease-and-desist order, or a fine.

JOB APPLICANTS AND WORKERS: If you believe you have experienced discrimination, FEPC will investigate without cost to you and without publicity.

For information contact any of the following offices of the Division of Fair Employment Practices:

San Francisco	Los Angeles	San Diego	Fresno	Sacramento	San Bernardino
30 Van Ness	322 W. 1st St.	1350 Front	467 N. Van Ness	926 J Street	303 W. 3rd St.
557-2005	620-2610	236-7405	488-5373	445-9918	383-4698

This notice must be conspicuously posted in hiring offices, on employee bulletin boards, in employment agency waiting rooms, union halls, etc. For extra copies write FEPC, Box 603, San Francisco 94101.

CALIFORNIA FAIR EMPLOYMENT PRACTICE COMMISSION
John A. Martin, Jr., Chairperson

APPENDIX C

Sample Affirmative Equal Opportunity Program

CAVEAT: Affirmative action and affirmative equal opportunity programs are subject to intense scrutiny by the courts and relevant agencies. Thus, because of the dynamic nature of this aspect of Equal Opportunity Law, it is essential that your lawyer draft these programs as well as guidelines for implementation.

AFFIRMATIVE EQUAL OPPORTUNITY PROGRAM
JANUARY 1, 19 ___ TO DECEMBER 31, 19 ___

Adopted by _____
            Board Chairman and President
        This _____ day of December, 19 ___

TABLE OF CONTENTS

Affirmative Equal Opportunity Program

I.   Purpose and Policy

A.   PURPOSE OF AFFIRMATIVE EQUAL
OPPORTUNITY PROGRAM
_____ (hereinafter referred to as _____)
adopts this affirmative equal opportunity program as a set of specific equal opportunity policies, practices, and procedures to
which _____ is committed. This document is
_____ Affirmative Equal Opportunity Program.

B.   EQUAL OPPORTUNITY POLICY
_____ is an equal opportunity employer and al-
ways selects the best-qualified individual for the job based upon
job-related qualifications, regardless of race, color, creed, sex, national origin, age, handicap, status in regard to economic assistance, marital status, pregnancy, veteran status, or other protected
group under federal, state (_____) or local, city,
county or parish Equal Opportunity Law. It is _____
express purpose to comply fully with all prohibitions against discrimination, both statutory and judicial.

C.   OBJECTIVE
The _____ Affirmative Equal Opportunity Pro-
gram objective is to eliminate the appearance of impropriety with
respect to discrimination either for or against any protected group.

This objective calls for achieving full utilization of individuals within protected groups at all levels of management and non-management according to the normal progression for all employees of _____ . Thus, this objective calls for a work environment free of discrimination.

_____ objective and the practical implementation of this affirmative equal opportunity program shall not include the imposition of quotas, discrimination in favor of or against any particular protected group, as required by statutory and case law.

However, _____ Affirmative Equal Opportunity Program is a positive program of inclusion rather than exclusion.

D.   EQUAL EMPLOYMENT PROGRESS

_____ has had an extensive commitment to equal employment and equal treatment of employees since its founding in _____ .

In addition to internal and external employment-related programs, _____ has been active and influential in organizing and assisting business, community, and public agencies in solving community programs. _____ has earned recognition for its accomplishments in this field from many organizations.

Examples:

_____

_____

_____

_____

_____

_____

1.   *Background*

2.   *Protected Group Progress*

3.   *Summary*

II.   **Program Implementation and Communications**

A.   **INTERNAL PROGRAM COMMUNICATIONS**
    1. *Handbooks.*
_____ Affirmative Equal Opportunity Policy
Statement has been incorporated in all management handbooks,
supervisory guides and instructions, and employee handbooks.
    2. *Bulletins.*
_____ Affirmative Equal Opportunity Policy
Statement and Program are featured periodically in employee
newspapers, magazines, bulletins, and other reports. Additionally, _____ urban affairs activities are periodically presented to employees through existing company news
media, special bulletins, and brochures.
    3. *Meetings.*
Special meetings and seminars are held with all _____
management employees for the express purpose of informing
them about _____ Affirmative Equal Oppor-
tunity Program. The agendas of these meetings and seminars include a statement from _____ , Board Chair-
man, and President, _____ , supporting the
program. Management responsibility for the program's effec-
tiveness is specifically stated. All management employees attend
meetings and receive information several times annually on
_____ Affirmative Equal Opportunity Program.
    4. *Managerial Orientation.*
New management employees are oriented to _____
Affirmative Equal Opportunity Program within One Hundred
Twenty (120) days of their employment.
    5. *Nonsupervisory Orientation.*
_____ Affirmative Equal Opportunity Pro-
gram is communicated to all nonmanagement and nonsupervisory
employees at orientation programs, staff meetings, and other

sessions. These orientation presentations explain how employees can take advantage of _____ wage, benefit, and personnel policies and its affirmative equal opportunity program. Employee responsibility is detailed and includes an opportunity for employees to discuss the program and the maintaining of employee attendance. There is a document in each employee's file confirming his/her receipt of employee orientation material, including _____ Affirmative Equal Opportunity Policy Statement.

     6. *Nondiscriminatory Communications.*
All communications within _____ are nondiscriminatory.

     7. *Annual Personnel Conference.*
Management and other employees engaged in personnel, employment, placement, training, promotions, separations, and transfers, receive additional training on applicable federal, state, and local Equality Opportunity Laws and case decisions. Furthermore, _____ conducts an annual personnel conference for all personnel professionals within _____ , at which time an extensive review of all Equal Opportunity Laws is conducted.

     8. *Annual General Manager's Conference.*
_____ conducts an annual General Manager's Conference which includes a personnel presentation, including recent developments in Equal Opportunity Law, as well as update on _____ Affirmative Equal Opportunity Program.

B.   EXTERNAL POLICY COMMUNICATIONS
     1. All major recruiting sources, including those organizations primarily concerned with protected groups, as well as all agencies and educational institutions, are informed both verbally and in writing of _____ Affirmative Equal Opportunity Program. These sources are requested to assist _____ in recruiting and referring individuals on a nondiscriminatory basis.

     2. All advertisements are placed, depicted, and worded in a nondiscriminatory manner.

     3. _____ product and/or service advertising is nondiscriminatory.

4. _____ communicates to prospective employees the existence of its equal opportunity program and how they are affected by it.

5. _____ complies with all equal opportunity legal requirements, binding case decisions, and applicable regulations, orders, and instructions.

C.   EQUAL OPPORTUNITY POSTERS

_____ posts prominently all posters required by federal, state, or local laws and agencies concerning equal employment opportunity.

Additionally, _____ posts and disseminates its own Affirmative Equal Opportunity Policy Statement.

The following posters and notices are posted, as required by federal, state (_____), or local (_____) law, and _____ policy.

III.   Responsibility

A.   COMPANY

1. *Board Chairman and President of* _____ .

_____ , Board Chairman, President, _____ , has overall responsibility for _____ Affirmative Equal Opportunity Policy.

2. *Vice-President-Personnel Development.*

_____ , Vice-President-Personnel Development _____ , is specifically delegated responsibility for administration of _____ Affirmative Equal Opportunity Program. He/she is responsible for assuring that all necessary action be taken by all levels of management and subsidiaries to achieve _____ policy of equal opportunity.

3. *Vice-President-Legal.*

_____ , Vice-President-Legal reviews all legal compliance aspects of _____ Affirmative Equal Opportunity Program.

4. *Organization of* _____ *Personnel Department.*

The following represents the organizational chart of all personnel professions within _____ :

5. *Affirmative Equal Opportunity Program Subsidiary
    Responsibility.*

The following job positions and individuals are responsible for
implementing _____ Affirmative Equal Oppor-
tunity Program at the respectively listed subsidiaries companies:

_____

_____

_____

_____

_____

_____

_____

_____

_____

_____

_____

6. *Affirmative Equal Opportunity Duties.*

_____ personnel professionals responsible for
the affirmative equal opportunity program are also responsible
for the following:

a. Developing valid, written job qualifications and related selection pro-
    cedures to ensure equal opportunity;
b. Training interviewers;
c. Monitoring equal employment policies, practices, and procedures;
d. Updating procedures as is necessary to ensure legal compliance and
    fair practices;
e. Updating all manuals and policy statements;

f. Directing the coordination of training and development;
g. Directing the job evaluation process to assure nondiscrimination in pay and employment practices.

B.   AFFIRMATIVE EQUAL OPPORTUNITY PROGRAM RESPONSIBILITY FOR SUBDIVISIONS, SUBORDINATE OPERATIONS, DEPARTMENTS, INDIVIDUAL HOTELS, RESTAURANTS, OR PROPERTIES

The following job positions and individuals are responsible for implementing _____ Affirmative Equal Opportunity Program at the respectively listed subdivisions, subordinate operations, departments, and individual hotels, restaurants or properties:

_____

_____

_____

_____

_____

_____

_____

_____

_____

_____

_____

_____

_____

_____

_____

_____

_____

IV.   Work Force Analysis

The Work Force Analysis of _____ at the
_____
is based upon _____ personnel records as of
_____ ,
1979. On that date, _____ number of persons
were employed in _____ departments. The departmental work force analysis appears on the following page.

V.   Job Group Analysis

On or about _____ , 19 ___ , at the
_____
employed _____ persons in the total of
_____ individual job titles. These job titles
have been grouped for affirmative equal opportunity program
purposes, into _____ groups. The equal opportunity profiles of these job groups are set forth on the
following page.

VI.   Protected Group Availability Analysis

The _____
_____

WORK FORCE ANALYSIS

Department _____ Line of Progression _____ As of _____ 19__
(Date)

Job Title	SALARY/WAGE RANGE		EEO-1 Category	Total Employees	MALE						FEMALE						Total Minorities
	Minimum	Maximum			Total	White	Black	Oriental	Amer. Indian	Spanish Surname	Total	White	Black	Oriental	Amer. Indian	Spanish Surname	
Total – This Page																	
Grand Total – Last Page																	

Page__ of__

is located in the _____ and has an estimated
availability of individuals in protected groups set forth on the
following page. The Availability Factor Computation Method
is considered in determining the weight assigned to each factor
for each job group and is based upon a study of the actual
sources of employees hired or promoted into the job group.

However, _____ does not select in-
dividuals on a discriminatory basis, either for or against any protected group.

For the purpose of this analysis, _____
has assumed that the relevant labor market for the _____

_____

_____

at the _____

_____

includes the _____ SMSA and the following
counties:

_____

_____

_____

_____

_____

_____

_____

_____

does not necessarily believe that the eight availability factors
specified by various regulations are appropriate, nor does
_____ believe that the above-prescribed
geographic area is necessarily the correct labor market. Never-

theless, _____ is committed to making good
faith efforts to ensure nondiscrimination based upon the Availability Analysis. (See Availability Factor Computation Forms
on pages 224–225.)

VII. Protected Group Utilization Analysis

The _____
located in the _____
_____
_____

has compared the current level of protected group employment,
as set forth in the job group analysis, with the availability of
protected group employees as estimated in the Availability
Analysis. The result of this comparison reflects an attitude and
a practice of nondiscrimination by _____ .
Individuals are not adversely affected by employment practices
based upon a protected group at _____
_____ .

VIII. Goal and Timetables

The objectives of _____ Affirmative Equal
Opportunity Program shall be pursued by mobilization of available resources through good faith efforts. Goals have been established to provide a rational prediction of changes in utilization of
protected-group employees during a particular period of time.
    It is expressly prohibited that _____ Affirma-
tive Equal Opportunity Program be interpreted to select anyone
on account of his/her protected-group status. (See page 226.)

IX. Identification of Opportunities

The _____
located at _____

AVAILABILITY FACTOR COMPUTATION FORM

Form 3

Job Group _____

Job Group	Raw Statistics		Value Weight		Weighted Factor		Source of Statistics	Reason for Weighting Factor
	Min.	Fem.	Min.	Fem.	Min.	Fem.		
1. Percentage of minorities in population of labor area surrounding facility								
2. Percentage of minorities and women among unemployed in labor area surrounding facility								
3. Percentage of minorities and women in total workforce in immediate labor area								
4. Percentage of minorities and women among those having requisite skills in immediate labor area								
5. Percentage of minorities and women among those having requisite skills in reasonable recruitment area								
6. Percentage of minorities and women among those promotable or transferable within facility								
7. Percentage of minorities and women at institutions providing training in requisite skills								
8. Percentage of minorities and women among those at facility whom contractor can train in requisite skills								
9. Percentage of women among those seeking employment in labor or recruitment area								

AVAILABILITY FACTOR COMPUTATION FORM

Job Group	Raw Statistics		Value Weight		Weighted Factor		Source of Statistics
	Min.	Fem.	Min.	Fem.	Min.	Fem.	
1. Percentage of minorities in population of labor area surrounding facility							
2. Percentage of minorities and women among unemployed in labor area surrounding facility							
3. Percentage of minorities and women in total workforce in immediate labor area							
4. Percentage of minorities and women among those having requisite skills in immediate labor area							
5. Percentage of minorities and women among those having requisite skills in reasonable recruitment area							
6. Percentage of minorities and women among those promotable or transferable within facility							
7. Percentage of minorities and women at institutions providing training in requisite skills							
8. Percentage of minorities and women among those at facility whom contractor can train in requisite skills							
9. Percentage of women among those seeking employment in labor or recruitment area							
FINAL AVAILABILITY							

GOALS AND TIMETABLES

Job Group	Projected # of Opportunities (Growth & Attrition)	ANNUAL GOALS				ULTIMATE GOALS			
		Minorities		Females		Minorities		Females	
		Number	Percent	Number	Percent	Percent	By Year	Percent	By Year

has analyzed the composition of its work force, applicant flow, selection process, transfer and promotion practices, and training programs to identify problem areas. It has also reviewed the attitude of its work force and assured compliance with technical posting, notification, and document retention requirements.

There are several opportunities for increased amalgamation and utilization of a wide variety of protected-group employees.

X.   Program Activity

A.   INTRODUCTION

_____ views its affirmative equal opportunity program as a result-oriented program designed to enhance the opportunities of all employees. It recognizes that the ultimate success of this undertaking will be largely the result of *bona fide* efforts to eliminate the appearance of impropriety with respect to discrimination. There is executive support for this program. All employees have been informed of _____ commitment to equal employment opportunity. The following represents the substance of this program, including ongoing analysis.

B.   RECRUITMENT

_____ is actively seeking individuals and all protected groups for existing future employment. Local, state, and federal employment referral agencies are regularly contacted. Additionally, _____ Personnel Office maintains regular contact with all private employment and referral agencies and organizations. _____ Resource Directory lists the organization _____ regularly contacts or receives referrals from. _____ Affirmative Equal Opportunity Policy Statement is disseminated wherever it does business. _____ maintains a file of sources notified and acknowledgments received. _____ is ready, willing, and able to conduct briefing sessions on _____ premises with representatives from these recruiting sources. The _____ Employee Recruiting Program actively encourages the recruitment of individuals on a totally nondiscriminatory basis. All communications used in recruiting is nondiscriminatory.

C.   TESTS
_____ uses only validated tests of a nondiscriminatory nature, e.g., content valid skills tests of typing, dictation, transcription, and the like.

D.   EMPLOYMENT AND SELECTION
_____ periodically reviews the protected-group composition of applicants and employees to ensure equal opportunity exists in the employment and selection process.

All personnel professionals participating in hiring and selection are trained to ensure nondiscrimination is a fact in their job performance. _____ employment application form is objective and nondiscriminatory. It is included in the Appendix.

E.   PROMOTIONS
_____ had adopted a policy whereby employees are aware of job openings and may apply for job promotions.

The records of all protected-group employees are reviewed to ensure that qualified individuals are given equal consideration as opportunities for upgrading, promotion, and transfer occur. Where additional training and experience would be helpful for advancement, management counsels and assists all employees in this regard. In evaluating management employees for promotion, _____ specifically considers, among other factors, the individual's appreciation of its affirmative equal opportunity program.

F.   TRAINING
1.   Training for Employment.
_____ recognizes that the vast majority of applicants hired are qualified under regular selection criteria. Periodically, however, it becomes apparent that employees are not performing at the expected level of their qualifications. _____ maintains a nondiscriminatory policy designed to upgrade the skills of underqualified employees, if practicable.

2. *Training for Advancement.*
All protected-group employees are given equal access to all developmental training designed to enhance an employees' ability
to assume positions of greater responsibility. Records of employee attendance at developmental training courses are maintained according to the normal record retention policy.

G.   COMMUNITY ACTION
Various community groups are aware of _____
equal treatment of employees and prospective employees.

H.   FACILITIES
All work areas, rest areas, cafeterias, and recreational areas as
well as all other _____ facilities are maintained
on an objective, nondiscriminatory basis.

I.   SUBCONTRACTS
All _____ contracts include an equal employment opportunity clause where appropriate.

J. PROTECTED GROUPS
_____ complies with all legal and regulatory requirements concerning notices and communications relative
to protected-group status of employees and prospective employees.

XI.   Complaint Procedure

_____ maintains a nondiscriminatory policy
with respect to union and/or nonunion status of employees. Where
there is a collective bargaining agreement, _____
endeavors to negotiate and implement an equal opportunity
policy statement, affording employees an opportunity to file
grievances based upon violations of equal opportunity principles.
    Where there is no collective bargaining agreement, there is a
procedure for complaints in the area of equal opportunity.

XII.   Company Checkup Procedures

A.   INTRODUCTION
_____ has a systematic checkup procedure
monitored by the personnel department to evaluate the results
and progress of its affirmative equal opportunity program.

B.   INTERNAL REPORTS
    1. The following reports are generated and monitored
quarterly:

_____

_____

_____

_____

_____

_____

_____

    2. The following reports are generated and monitored
annually:

_____

_____

_____

_____

_____

_____

C.   INTERNAL COMPLIANCE REVIEWS

_____ Personnel Staff conducts compliance reviews at least annually, of all major subsidiaries and company subdivisions. These reviews enable the staff to identify local problems, summarize progress and performance, and make recommendations to the Vice-President-Personnel Development. _____ Compliance Reviewers monitor at least the following:

1. Composition of applicant and the hiring flow by protected groups;
2. Selection process for hiring, placement, transferring, and upgrading;
3. Attendance at developmental training courses by employees;
4. Proper display of all required posters and _____ policy statements;
5. Attitude of the work force;
6. Inclusion of EEO clause in purchase orders;
7. Notification to recruiting sources of EEO policy;
8. Dissemination of policy;
9. Progress of subdivisions towards goals and objectives; and
10. Resignations and dismissal by protected-group status.

XIII.   Compliance With Laws and Regulations

_____ has reviewed its recruitment and advertising policies, its job policies, practices, and procedures, and its wage structure to ensure compliance with all applicable Equal Opportunity Laws, regulations, and case decisions.

XIV.   Community Opportunities

_____ recognizes its roles as a corporate citizen in the community and is continuing its leadership through programs designed to strengthen the socioeconomic status of all protected-group employees. By participating in these programs, _____ management intends to serve as a catalyst in stimulating other leaders in commerce and industry to join forces in cooperative efforts to cope with

employment problems. _____ involvement
with the community includes the following:

_____

_____

_____

_____

_____

_____

_____

_____

XV.   CONCLUSION

_____ adopts this affirmative equal opportunity program as a confirmation of _____ long-
standing commitment to nondiscriminatory treatment of all
employees. _____ is sincerely desirous of
communicating this commitment to employees in an organized,
regular manner. This program is a documentation of
_____ systematic method of communicating
equal opportunity principles and objectives to employees. It
will be periodically reviewed, modified, and updated as necessary.

    Lastly, _____ commitment extends to all
subsidiaries, subdivisions, and subordinate properties within
_____.

Appendix

APPENDIX D

Sample Employee Handbooks and Chart

I am indebted to Carlson Companies, Hyatt Corporation, Omni International Hotels, Radisson Hotel Corporation, and Western International Hotels, Inc., for permission to reproduce materials in this Appendix and in Appendix F. These materials were specifically tailored to the factual situations and personnel policies of the companies, cities, states, and individuals involved. Therefore, it is *not* recommended that these forms be copied verbatim and applied indiscriminately. It *is* recommended that they be used as guides for drafting personnel documents tailored to your particular situation and personnel policies. Your lawyer should assist in drafting and reviewing all personnel documents. (Only selected pages of sample handbooks are reproduced here.)

HYATT HOTELS CORPORATION

Dear New Fellow Employee:

As an employee of Hyatt, each of us has an important role
in the continued success of our organization--and equally important,
each of us has an opportunity to develop ourselves personally and
professionally.

The purpose of this booklet is to let you know what you can
expect from us--and what will be expected of you.

Please keep this Handbook for your reference, and do not
hesitate to ask your supervisor or the Personnel Department about
the policies and benefits.

With sincere best wishes,

Pat Foley
President

ALL ABOUT
HYATT REGENCY ATLANTA
IN PEACHTREE CENTER

- One of the most famous, spectacular hotels in the world.
- Located in Peachtree Center and designed by John Portman and Associates of Atlanta.
- First hotel in the world boasting an open-atrium 23-story skylift lobby.
- 1000 rooms; 800 in the main building and 200 in the round bronze-tinted glass tower.
- 50 multi-room suites, some with fireplaces and complete bars.
- All rooms include color televisions, in-house movies, and conversation areas.
- 22nd floor "Club Level" for V.I.P. accommodations and service.
- Five restaurants: HUGO's, a gourmet dining room; POLARIS, a blue-domed restaurant-lounge atop the building revolving 360° in 41 minutes; KAFE KOBENHAVN, our coffee shop; CLOCK OF FIVES, specializing in great beef dishes and rotisserie-prepared duckling; and a cabaret night club located on the Terrace Level.
- Two lounges in the Main Lobby: the AMPERSAND, a cozy lounge with a relaxed atmosphere; and the PARASOL, sheltered by a suspended roof of sculptured iron and plexiglas.
- 28 meeting rooms, 13 created by sound-proof, portable walls.
- 17,500 square feet in Phoenix Ballroom, accommodating as many as 1800 persons.

GUARANTEE OF FAIR TREATMENT

HYATT's policy is to treat every employee, regardless of position, with dignity and respect and to be fair and just at all times. AS AN EQUAL OPPORTUNITY EMPLOYER, WE WILL ALWAYS ENDEAVOR TO SELECT THE BEST QUALIFIED INDIVIDUALS BASED ON JOB-RELATED QUALIFICATIONS, REGARDLESS OF RACE, COLOR, CREED, SEX, NATIONAL ORIGIN, AGE, OR HANDICAP.

HYATT will:
- Employ the best available personnel using the most appropriate and successful recruiting and screening techniques.
- Always maintain competitive wages and benefits.
- Provide training, development, and advanced opportunities.
- Make every effort to promote from within based on job-related qualifications.
- Provide and maintain safe, sanitary working conditions.

7   10

YOUR "TRY OUT" PERIOD

The first 60-working days you are employed with HYATT, we like to consider a "try out" period. It gives you an opportunity to find out if you will like it here, and us a chance to find out if your work, attitude, and attendance meet our standards of a good employee.

At any time during this period you may decide to resign without stating a reason or, should we feel your working habits are not meeting our standards, we may release you on the same basis without any bad effect on your employment record. We think it only fair that each of us have a period to adapt to our working relationship.

Since experience is the best teacher, your supervisor will give you ample opportunity to learn the correct way of performing your job by providing proper instructions.

Should you have difficulties or a problem, please talk with your supervisor or the Personnel Department.

YOU & YOUR SUPERVISOR

No one wants you to succeed in your job more than your supervisor. You were selected from among a number of candidates because your supervisor believed you to possess the abilities and personal qualities necessary for the job.

Within the first few months you are employed, your supervisor and others in our organization will invest in you one of their most valuable assets . . . time. Supervisors are in their jobs for the purpose of working with you to ensure that the hotel operates smoothly with as few problems as possible.

When you have a problem or question about your job duties, do not hesitate to ask your supervisor.

11

YOUR PROGRESS REPORT

At HYATT, we have a method we call "Performance Review", a procedure in which each supervisor evaluates the performance of every employee under his/her supervision, usually once at the end of the 60-working day probationary period and annually thereafter.

Based on such factors as the quality and quantity of your work, knowledge of your job, initiative, attendance, personal conduct record, and your attitude toward your job and other employees, this review gives us valuable information to use when considering employees for promotion, transfers, and future pay increases.

In addition, you will have an opportunity to have a personal discussion of your progress with your supervisor. He/she will point out how well you are carrying out your job and suggest how you can improve your on-the-job performance.

Should you have any questions about your progress between these reviews, ask your supervisor to talk with you in private. He/she will always try to help you in any way possible.

12

PROMOTION FROM WITHIN

It is the policy of HYATT to fill job vacancies by promoting qualified employees from within our company whenever reasonable. In selecting an employee to fill an up-graded job, the following qualifications will be carefully considered:

- Skill and ability
- Efficiency
- Physical qualifications
- Past disciplinary record
- Attendance and safety record
- Attitude

Should two or more qualified employees seek the same vacancy, the Personnel Director and the prospective supervisor will make the final determination.

TRANSFERS

The Personnel Department posts current job openings in Peachtree Downunder, our employee cafeteria. If you desire a transfer to one of these positions, you must contact the Personnel Department to complete a Request for Transfer form. To qualify for a department transfer, you must:

1. Have been employed in your present position for 6 months or longer.
2. Meet all job qualifications of the new position.
3. Have a good job performance record in your present department.

Should you wish to transfer to another HYATT property, the Personnel Department will investigate possible job openings and initiate the necessary paperwork. In order to apply for a transfer of this type, you must fulfill the above three qualifications as shown for transfers within the Hotel.

13

YOUR PERSONAL CONDUCT & HYATT POLICIES

You have the responsibility to us and to your fellow workers to conduct yourself according to certain rules of acceptable behavior. All businesses must establish rules so their employees may work amiably and fairly together.

HYATT policies were explained when you were hired to make sure you understood them. Your individual department regulations will be explained to you by your supervisor.

By following these rules and demonstrating good behavior and efficiency, you will remain a valued employee of HYATT for years to come. Failure to abide by these rules will require disciplinary action, including suspension and/or separation of your employment with HYATT.

DISCIPLINARY ACTION

In order for HYATT to maintain a desirable level of employee conduct and productivity, HYATT policies must be enforced. HYATT policy requires that employees not be dismissed or laid-off without just cause. However, should an employee violate a HYATT rule or policy, including those rules set forth by each department, disciplinary action may be necessary and the following steps will be taken:

1. A verbal warning will be given as an initial indication of lack of satisfaction with work performance, or for the first violation of an established HYATT rule or policy.
2. If the employee fails to correct his/her poor performance, or commits an additional violation of an established HYATT rule or policy, a written warning will be issued.
3. In general, 2 prior written warnings for similar offenses should be given before an employee is dismissed or suspended.
4. The purpose of a suspension is to give the employee the opportunity to think about whether he/she wants to follow HYATT rules or find another job. The suspension period will depend upon the seriousness of the offense.
5. When an employee continues to violate a HYATT rule or policy, or fails to improve his/her job performance, it may become necessary to dismiss him/her.

In the case of a severe rule violation, dismissal may be without prior warnings. HYATT policy requires an investigation prior to dismissal.

26

JUST CAUSES FOR DISMISSAL

Among the just causes for dismissal are the following:

- Possession, drinking, or being under the influence of alcoholic beverages or other intoxicants during working hours.
- Insubordination.
- Stealing (includes adding tips to guest checks).
- Fighting on premises.
- Violation of any HYATT rule or policy, or departmental regulation of which the employee has been notified.
- Insolence or lack of courtesy to supervisors, department heads, managers, fellow employees, or guests of HYATT.
- Failure to perform services required by employee's position.
- Lack of proper personal appearance, sanitation, and cleanliness.
- Inefficiency.
- Physical conditions endangering the health of the employee, fellow employee, or guests.
- Failure to report for work without notifying the supervisor, except in cases of established illness, which must be certified by a medical certificate when requested.
- Possession, selling, or being under the influence of drugs, narcotics, or related substances.
- Entering or leaving the Hotel by any exit other than the specified employee entrance, or entering the premises when not scheduled for work without prior authorization.
- Falsification of any Hotel records.
- Use of guest facilities without authorization.
- Taking food or utensils from any food outlet.
- Excessive tardiness.
- Wearing a HYATT uniform off Hotel premises.
- Leaving work area without authorization.
- Failure to report to work after the expiration of a Leave of Absence.
- Refusal to be searched or have personal packages examined by HYATT when entering or leaving Hotel premises.
- Possession of any weapons or dangerous materials.
- Gum chewing in public areas.
- Smoking in public areas, kitchens, or food preparation areas.
- Destruction or defacement of HYATT, guest, or employee property.

The above list is not all-inclusive, and HYATT shall have the right to dismiss any employee whose conduct is detrimental to the welfare of HYATT or its employees.

27

PAID VACATIONS

All full-time and regularly scheduled part-time employees who have at least one full year of seniority shall be entitled to a paid vacation on the following basis:

Years of Seniority (Continuous Service)	Vacation
1 year but less than 5 years	2 weeks
5 years or more	3 weeks

Employees working either full-time or part-time shall be paid vacation pay equal to the average straight time weekly pay received by such employee during the 12-month period during which such vacation is earned.

Employees who are discharged or who terminate their employment shall be entitled to pro-rated vacation pay earned and computed in accordance with method mentioned above.

Temporary layoffs or leaves of absence during the year shall not interrupt the continuity of seniority for the purpose of eligibility of vacation.

Employees shall be entitled to receive their vacation pay before leaving for vacation. Vacation requests should be submitted to your supervisor at least two weeks in advance. If you wish to receive your vacation pay in advance, you must also submit this request two weeks prior to your vacation period.

35

Each month, HYATT puts a sum of money into the Hospitality Employee's Medical Plan (HEMP) which is maintained by the Union. This plan has been set up for any employee working in a position covered by the collective bargaining agreement, whether or not they belong to the Union. The HEMP Fund is used to cover the first $100 deductible of the Hotel's Medical Plan. It has also been used to set up a dental plan. For application or further information regarding these benefits, contact the Union office.

DENTAL PLAN

After one year of service, HYATT provides a dental plan to all full-time and salaried employees. The following are the necessary requirements or restrictions for coverage under the dental plan:

1. The employee must be enrolled in the Medical Plan, either Plan A or Plan C.
2. Employees not governed by the collective bargaining agreement may cover dependents under the dental plan if the employee also covers such dependents under the Medical Plan.
3. Where there is a collective bargaining agreement, those employees subject to inclusion in such agreement are not eligible for this dental plan, whether or not they are active members of such collective bargaining agreements.

Those employees covered under the collective bargaining agreement are eligible to participate in a dental plan offered by the Union. Contact your Union representative for application and further information.

SOCIAL SECURITY BENEFITS

The payment of Federal Old Age Benefits and Medicare Benefits under the Social Security Act is made by you and HYATT. Normally you will be eligible to receive a monthly income from Social Security when you retire at age 62 to 65, or become totally and permanently disabled.

HYATT matches your contribution to Social Security and Medicare dollar for dollar and thereby pays ½ of the cost of your Old Age Retirement and Medicare Benefits under Social Security.

37

MEDICAL PLAN

Medical benefits may not seem important to you until you need to use them. You should, however, know about your employee medical coverage and what is available. We are happy to provide this protection for you and your family.

Upon request, every full-time employee becomes a participant in our Medical Plan after completing at least one full calendar month of service. This plan offers you protection through life insurance benefits, hospitalization, surgical benefits, accidental death and dismemberment, and major medical coverage. The cost of all this protection for you is paid entirely by HYATT. Without life insurance and accidental death and dismemberment protection, this same coverage is also available to your dependents at a reasonable cost, deducted from your paycheck upon your authorization.

HYATT also provides an optional Accidental Death and Dismemberment Insurance Plan for all full-time employees at a very reasonable cost. This additional coverage can be extended to substantial levels and even include members of your family. The cost for you and/or your family can be deducted from your paycheck upon your authorization.

So you and your family may have complete understanding and appreciation of the many benefits available under our group plan, please read the Medical Benefits booklet. (Plan C booklets are not distributed until the employee's medical benefits have gone into effect.) If you have misplaced your booklet or did not receive one, see the Personnel Department.

36

PROFIT SHARING PLAN

There is nothing mysterious about profit. We receive money for service to our customers. Most of it is used to pay wages and salaries to our employees and as payment for new equipment, maintenance, and many other necessary expenses. What is left is profit. Then a very large part of this profit is paid to the government in taxes. This includes city, county, state, and federal government.

In a healthy, free economy such as the one in our country, a good profit in a business is absolutely necessary. If the profit is small or does not exist at all, there is no real job security, no future. Without profit a company cannot meet competition. It cannot grow. It cannot provide steady work. It cannot survive for very long.

Therefore, we can easily see that profit is highly important to all of us. It's easy also to understand our goals under profit sharing — higher profits for HYATT mean greater financial security for you and our other HYATT employees.

Your pay check is only a part of your real income. HYATT contributes to the profit sharing plan and if you are a participant you would share in these contributions.

Why profit sharing?
Money for emergency
Financial security for your family
Build a reserve for your future

Who is eligible for profit sharing?
Each regular employee who has been with HYATT for at least 1 year and worked 1000 hours or more.

How does the plan operate?
You choose an amount to invest regularly by payroll deduction, a minimum of 3% (Required) to a maximum of 10%. This establishes your contribution account. HYATT contributes money to your 3% Required account each year, thereby establishing your HYATT contribution account.

Currently all funds are invested in non-fluctuating securities. You earn ownership of your HYATT contribution account at the rate of 10% for each full year as a participant in the plan.

You are 100% vested after 10 full years.

If you withdraw from the plan before 10 full years as a participant, you will receive the value of your contribution account(s) but you will forfeit a portion of your HYATT contribution account.

If you leave after only 5 full years in the plan, you would have earned 50% of the amount HYATT contributed for your benefit and 50% would be forfeited and redistributed to the other participants in the plan.

Your HYATT contribution account is automatically 100% vested at normal retirement, early retirement, death, permanent disability, or after 10 full years in the plan.

PAID SICK DAYS

Employees with at least 1 year of seniority on HYATT's active payroll (not on layoff or leave of absence) shall be granted sick pay for up to 6 days during the 12 months following each anniversary of his/her most recent date of employment, subject to a waiting period of 2 days at the beginning of each period of illness. Paid sick days shall be granted only for a bona fide illness where the employee is incapable of performing the duties of his/her job. Paid sick days shall not be cumulative. The rate of pay for each sick day shall be 8 times the employee's regular straight-time hourly rate. Provided, however, any employee with a perfect attendance record for the 3 consecutive previous years shall be exempt from the 2-day waiting period for that year in which he/she takes paid sick leave.

If you are absent for an extended period due to illness, you are expected to call your supervisor on a daily basis. Any employee absent for more than 7 days must be placed on an approved Sick Leave of Absence to protect his/her employment and patient rights.

When you are ready to return to work, call your supervisor. You must have a written note from your doctor stating that you are physically able to perform the duties of your job.

WORKER'S COMPENSATION INSURANCE

The cost of this insurance is paid entirely by HYATT and your eligibility begins on the day you begin work. If you are injured or become ill because of some on-the-job accident, you may receive weekly benefits starting on the 8th day of disability. If you are injured on the job, you must report to your supervisor immediately, both for treatment and to protect the benefits which may be paid under our Worker's Compensation Insurance. Report all accidents or injuries — no matter how small! Should you fail to notify your supervisor of an on-the-job accident and you later suffer complications from the accident, there may be reasonable doubt at the time of your claim and you may lose your compensation.

EDUCATIONAL ASSISTANCE

In an effort to encourage employees to advance within HYATT and within the industry, an Educational Assistance Program has been developed. HYATT's Educational Assistance Program will reimburse full-time employees, with 6 months or more continuous employment, after successful completion of job-related courses.

Before enrolling in any course, application should be made and submitted to the Personnel Office. Your application will then be forwarded to the General Manager for approval. The amount of reimbursement will depend upon the grade received and the sincere interest of the employee.

Remember, you must have prior approval from the General Manager before registering for a course under this program.

HYATTRAIN *HYATTRAIN*

HYATT has developed a training program open to all interested employees with the approval of their department head or General Manager. This program, known as HYATTRAIN, offers classes throughout the year. The class/lecture program and comprehensive examinations cover the major departments of the Hotel, providing individual courses of study, personal development, and improved communication. All HYATTRAIN participants are required to take a comprehensive exam upon completion of class sessions and discussions. However, the exams are not "graded" as such; they are simply scored. This allows the participant to measure him/herself against where he/she feels his/her skills and knowledge should place him/her. See the Personnel Department for more information.

DRY CLEANING SERVICES

HYATT offers personal dry cleaning services to our employees at a discount of up to 50%. Should you desire this service, take your articles to the Valet Department, located near the employee entrance, and complete all necessary forms. There is generally a minimum 4-day service time for employee dry cleaning.

WELCOME TO THE
Washington Plaza

"People Make The Difference"

EMPLOYEES' BENEFIT
MANUAL

WESTERN INTERNATIONAL HOTELS
Partners in travel with United Airlines

Harry Mullikin

WELCOME TO WESTERN INTERNATIONAL HOTELS!

In your new position, I know you will enjoy the friendly atmosphere, the spirit of cooperation, and the mutual respect you will find among all employees throughout the Company.

Western International Hotels has gained a reputation as one of the finest hotel management companies in the world — a reputation earned to a large extent through our emphasis on selecting, training and retaining highly competent and dedicated employees.

You were selected because we believe you have the potential and the desire to meet these high standards. At the same time, we have some obligations to you as employees . . .

  — to treat you fairly and with respect and dignity

  — to insure that your job responsibilities are clearly defined

  — to provide open two-way channels of communication and honest answers to your questions

  — to offer suitable recognition for your dedication and excellence of performance

We intend to meet these obligations.

Ours is a growth company, continually improving and expanding. I invite you to grow with us by taking advantage of the many opportunities open to you. As you progress, I know you will share with all of us the pride and satisfaction that is the part of being a member of the Western International Hotels family.

Sincerely,

Harry Mullikin

Harry Mullikin
President and Chief Executive Officer

WESTERN INTERNATIONAL HOTELS

Benefits
1. Free hotel rooms
2. Food & Beverage Discounts
3. Credit Union
4. Free Courses
5. Scholarships
6. Awards
7. Paid Vacation
8. Insurance
9. Childrens Christmas Party
10. Adult Christmas Party
11. Picnic
12. Casino Night

BENEFIT	ELIGIBILITY	PROVISIONS	COST TO YOU
1. VACATION	After one year of continuous service	Salaried: One through six years = 10 days Seven through fourteen years = 15 days Fifteen years or more = 20 days Hourly: Dependent upon Union contract	NONE — the hotel pays the cost
2. HOLIDAYS	As provided in Union contract for hourly employees	Paid straight time when not worked, double time if worked	NONE — the hotel pays the cost
3. UNIFORMS	On employment, if job requires	Provided, laundered, and maintained by the hotel. Clean uniforms provided when soiled one is turned in.	NONE — the hotel pays the cost
4. EMPLOYEE CAFETERIA	On employment	*Food and beverage items at a low cost *Complimentary coffee	Dependent upon item selected NONE — the hotel pays the cost
5. EDUCATION	On employment	*AH & MA COURSES —Course prepaid for you —Earn two hours of college credit —$25.00 bonus if grade of "A" or "B" is attained	NONE — if course is completed satisfactorily
	Employee or relatives of employee	*BRUCE PIERCE MEMORIAL SCHOLARSHIP —Application available from Personnel in March —Two $500 scholarships awarded by WIH per year	NONE — WIH pays the cost
6. COMPLIMENTARY ROOMS	After one year of service	A written request must be submitted to your department head at least 2 weeks in advance. You receive 5 days after one year of service; 10 days after two years; 15 days after ten years; 20 days after fifteen years; 25 days after twenty years and 30 days after 25 years.	NONE — the hotel pays the cost

BENEFIT	ELIGIBILITY	PROVISIONS	COST TO YOU
7. 25% FOOD & BEVERAGE DISCOUNT	After one year of service	You receive this benefit while using your complimentary room benefits	NONE — the hotel pays the cost
8. 50% ROOM DISCOUNT	On employment	There is space available at the hotel you wish to stay in and you show your hotel I. D.	NONE — the hotel pays the cost
9. CREDIT UNION	On employment	Automatic deductions from your paycheck. Excellent interest rate on your savings	NONE — the hotel pays the cost
10. MEDICAL, DENTAL & VISION INSURANCE	On the 1st of the month after employment	Salaried: After $200 deductible, 80% of the first $2000 eligible expenses, and 100% of all eligible expenses in one calendar year	NONE — the hotel pays the cost DEPENDENTS — if covered; hotel shares the cost
	Depending on Union contract	Hourly: Depending on Union contract	NONE — the hotel pays the cost
11. WORKER'S COMPENSATION	On employment	Pays your medical expenses and part of income should you be injured on the job	NONE — the hotel pays the cost
12. UNEMPLOYMENT COMPENSATION	On employment	Provides you with additional income in case you lose your job through no fault of your own	NONE — the hotel pays the cost
13. SOCIAL FUNCTIONS	On employment	Special functions, such as the Childrens Chistmas Party, are put on for your family	NONE — the hotel pays the cost
14. EMPLOYEE SERVICE AWARDS	After five years of service	Special awards and banquet after completing five, ten, etc., years of service	NONE — the hotel pays the cost
15. SPECIAL HOTEL AWARDS	After six months of service	The Washington Plaza appreciates outstanding performance, loyalty and dedication. You are given an opportunity to become "Employee of the Month" and the highest honor — winner of the Thurston Dupar Award	NONE — the hotel pays the cost

EMPLOYEES' COUNCIL

EMPLOYEES' COUNCIL — The Employees' Council is made up of representatives from the various departments of the hotel. The Council organizes social and sporting events, helps employees in need and is the liaison between management and the employees. All employees are welcome to attend the monthly meetings. Each has the right to exercise a vote.

-13-

EQUAL EMPLOYMENT OPPORTUNITY AND AFFIRMATIVE ACTION POLICY STATEMENT

I. Introduction and Purpose

This policy is the Washington Plaza Hotel's commitment to provide equal employment opportunity to each present and prospective employee. It is the goal of the Washington Plaza Hotel that all managers, supervisors and other employees become committed and motivated to effectively implement our Affirmative Action Program. The provisions of this policy are fully consistent with the overall objectives of this company.

II. Statement of Policy

It is the policy of the Washington Plaza Hotel to:

A. Recruit, hire, promote and pay for all job classifications without regard to race, color, age, sex, marital status, sexual orientation, creed, religion, political ideology, national origin, ancestry, or the presence of any sensory, mental or physical handicap (unless such handicap would prevent proper performance of the job) except where some characteristic listed above has been declared to be a bona fide occupational qualification for a specific job by the Washington State Human Rights Commission.

B. Base decisions of employment solely upon an individual's qualifications for the position being filled.

C. Base promotion decisions only on the individual's qualifications as related to the requirements of the position for which s/he is being considered.

D. Ensure that all other personnel actions such as compensation, benefits, transfers, layoffs, recall from layoffs, terminations, disciplinary actions, hotel-sponsored training, education tuition reimbursement, social and recreational programs will be administered on a non-discriminatory basis.

E. Set ambitious, attainable, affirmative action goals annually that will be achieved through:

(1) adherence to the spirit of the Equal Employment laws,

(2) aggressive efforts to promote employees from within our present workforce,

(3) providing our employees with the training that will qualify them for advancement, and

(4) maintaining constant awareness of affirmative action goals during the recruitment, selection and placement of qualified personnel.

F. Assign responsibility for setting and attaining affirmative action goals to each manager who has the authority to hire, transfer, promote or fire employees. Performance on the affirmative action program will be evaluated as is performance on other Hotel goals.

-17-

TRANSFERS – PROMOTIONS

After you have been here for six months, and find you would like to transfer into another area of the hotel, see your department head or the Personnel Director. The philosophy of "promotion from within" is an important one in Western International Hotels. This policy is as important to management as it is to you. Both you and they influence the success of that policy. There are several variables that effect whether you will be promoted.

They include:

1. Available openings;
2. Letting the Personnel office and your manager know that your are interested in another position;
3. Reminding your supervisor and the Personnel office of your continued interest;
4. The quality of work that you have been performing in your department;
5. Your dependability in terms of getting to work on time and on the days you are scheduled;
6. How well you get along with your co-workers, your supervisor, and the guests;
7. How well prepared you are to assume the responsibilities of the job;
8. How long you have been on your present job.

All of the above variables, except the first and last, are under your control. The Personnel Office staff will be happy to share their ideas about how you can use your ability to control those other variables, especially variables 6 and 7.

Remember, you have more influence on your success than anyone else.

PROMOTIONS FROM WITHIN

The Personnel Office is at your disposal if you are interested in being considered for a promotion or transfer in the future. As an Equal Opportunity Employer, we are concerned that all our employees, regardless of age, sex, race, religion, or national origin, have the opportunity to work up to their highest level of competence. If you would like to be considered for another position in the hotel please complete the following form and turn it into the Personnel Office.

CUT HERE

NAME_____

DEPARTMENT_____ POSITION_____

I would like to be considered for a _____ position in the _____ Department

DATE _____

-18-   _____
                                         (signature)

MILITARY POLICY – The military policy established by Western International Hotels is as follows:

1) If the employee wishes, s/he may use his vacation time for his military duty, or a leave of absence, regardless of the amount of vacation time actually due the employee. S/he will, however, be paid only for the amount of vacation actually due. Examples: If an employee had two weeks vacation coming, s/he would receive two weeks time off and two weeks pay. If an employee had one week of vacation coming, s/he would receive two weeks time off, one with pay and one week without pay.

2) If an employee does not want to take his/her vacation time for his/her military duty leave, s/he will be granted two weeks leave of absence without pay in addition to his/her regular vacation.

3) If an employee with two weeks vacation coming wishes to use only part of his/her vacation for his/her military duty leave, then he/she will be granted one week vacation with pay and one week without pay.

LEAVE OF ABSENCE POLICY FOR EMPLOYEES

1) An employee who is sick, temporarily disabled or pregnant is entitled to a leave of absence for the length of time s/he is physically unable to perform the duties of his/her current position.

2) Whether an employee is sick, disabled or pregnant, a slip from the doctor and/or company retained physician must be given to the department head, verifying the employee's inability to work.

3) "Inability to work" refers strictly to the physical disability of the employee and is not intended to cover home duties or postnatal care.

4) The employee is entitled to retain the same job with equivalent hours and pay as was held before the leave of absence. Or, if it is advantageous to both employee and employer, a similar job with at least the same pay as the previous job could be offered.

5) If an employee has been medically cleared to work and chooses not to return to his/her job at the designated time, the hotel can terminate the employee for "non-availability".

6) If the returning employee does not desire full time employment, seniority rights would no longer be in effect.

7) If an employee is physically unable to assume the full duties of his/her previous position, the hotel is only liable to assert a good faith effort to find a suitable position for the employee.

PERSONAL LEAVE OF ABSENCE

The Washington Plaza has a policy concerning personal leaves of absence. The maximum amount of time allowed is 30 days. If you need to have a personal leave of absence, your department head is the one who you should see. Whether or not he or she can grant a leave depends on the length of time you have been an employee and whether or not business will permit the absence of an employee from the department. Leaves of absence are not granted to accept other employment and all leaves must be approved by the General Manager.

-19-

SAFETY POLICY

SAFETY POLICY — It is the policy of the Washington Plaza Hotel to provide to each of its employees a safe and healthful place to work. Management also recognizes its responsibility to keep the hotel free from recognizable hazards which might cause death or serious physical harm. It is our intention to comply with the safety and health standards as set forth by the Occupational Safety and Health Act (OSHA).

The Hotel does, however, recognize that each employee has a responsibility to comply with these safety and health standards and all other rules and regulations issued to provide said safe and healthful conditions.

ACCIDENTS OR INJURIES — If a guest is involved in an accident or injury, notify your department head or assistant manager immediately.

If you are not directly involved in a particular accident, but you are a witness, be sure that you notify your department head.

EMPLOYEE INJURIES — Any injury incurred on hotel premises to yourself is to be reported immediately to your department head or the Personnel department. If there were any witnesses, be sure to get their names. In case of an injury, the employee should obtain an accident form from Personnel or a department head and report with it to the Virginia Mason Hospital. The Washington Plaza Hotel is a self-insured employer under worker's compensation. No matter how minor the injury may be, it must be reported so all necessary forms can be filled out.

THEFT — If a guest or employee is involved in a theft, notify your department head or assistant manager immediately.

If you, as an employee on the job, become involved in a theft, see your department head or assistant manager immediately.

If you are not directly involved in a particular theft, but are a witness, be sure to notify your department head immediately. NO MATTER HOW TRIVIAL OR HOW MAJOR THE ACCIDENT OR THEFT MAY BE, ALL EMPLOYEES MUST FOLLOW THE ABOVE PROCEDURES. THEFT BY AN EMPLOYEE IS CAUSE FOR IMMEDIATE DISMISSAL.

LEGAL OBLIGATIONS

DRUGS — Introduction, possession, or use of illegal drugs or narcotics on the hotel property, or reporting for work under the influence of same is cause for immediate dismissal. (This includes but is not limited to marijuana.)

WEAPONS — Carrying of concealed weapons, or violations of any criminal law, or conviction of a felony in any court of law will be cause for immediate dismissal.

ALCOHOL — Consumption of alcoholic beverages while on duty or reporting for duty under the influence of alcohol is strictly prohibited and cause for immediate dismissal.

DISHONESTY — Dishonesty, appropriation of hotel property or property of others is cause for immediate dismissal.

DISEASE — Knowingly reporting for duty with or harboring any infection or contagious disease is prohibited.

GAMBLING — Gambling in any form is prohibited.

DISPENSING LIQUOR — Selling or giving intoxicating liquors to minors or allowing such liquors to be consumed on the premises by minors is prohibited.

CONDUCT — Any conduct which violates the laws of common decency or morality is cause for immediate dismissal.

ABUSIVE LANGUAGE — Abusive language or profanity will not be tolerated and can be a cause for dismissal.

YOUR PAYCHECK — You will be paid on the 7th and 22nd of each month. A pay period starts on the first of the month and ends on the last day of the month. EXAMPLE: If you start on the 12th and work that day, you would receive a check on the 22nd which would pay you for the 12th, 13th, 14th and 15th, providing of course, you worked on those days. You will be paid for the actual days worked. Be sure your time card has been punched and your time turned into your department head for each day worked or you may not get paid for that day, as this is the only record we have of your time.

Deductions from your paycheck will be: F.I.C.A. (social security), income tax, and Worker's compensation.

Hourly personnel can obtain their paychecks at the timekeeper's office at 8 A.M. on payday. If it is not picked up within 5 days it is sent to the accounting department.

US SAVINGS BONDS — See the Personnel Office about our payroll deduction plan to purchase U.S. Savings Bonds.

FRONT MAGAZINE — As an employee of Western International Hotels you will receive each month a copy of "Front" magazine. This magazine will let you know what is happening at the other Western Hotels.

THE "CIRCULAR" — The Circular is the Washington Plaza's own newsletter, letting you know about the activities of your fellow employees and the various events going on at the Washington Plaza. If you have any news you would like to submit, articles are welcome anytime, and you may bring them to Personnel.

HEALTH, ACCIDENT & LIFE INSURANCE — Union Employees: Your health, accident and life insurance benefits are determined by the Union contract under which you work. Contact your Union for details. The Personnel office and the timekeeper have medical, dental and visual claim forms which can be picked up before an appointment.

Salaried Employees: At the time of hire you will receive a booklet explaining the coverage to which you are entitled. Medical and Dental claim forms are available in the Personnel Office.

For any questions concerning your benefits, contact the Personnel Office.

UNION POSITIONS

MEMBERSHIP — Union membership is mandatory for all employees working in a union position. If you are not already a union member, you will have 30 days to join the correct union local. Failure to pay dues after you are a member can result in your dismissal from the job in accordance with the union contract.

HEALTH CARDS — Before beginning the first day of work, all employees working as food or beverage handlers or in an area where food is prepared or served, are required to have a current health card on file. This card is obtained from the Public Safety Building on 4th Avenue between Cherry and James Streets. There is a $2.00 charge. You are to turn this card in to the Personnel Department. Your Health Card should be renewed every two years.

TIPS AND GRATUITIES — A change in the law on September 1, 1975, by the Internal Revenue Service, requires all employees to report, to the government, all income each employee receives from charge tips. The Washington Plaza reports all charge tips received by you to the Internal Revenue Service. You are required by law to report all cash and charge tips to your employer on form # 4070 on a semi-monthly basis. Copies of this form may be obtained from the Personnel Office.

UNIFORMS — All employees wearing a uniform are expected to treat your uniform with the same respect you do your own clothing. All uniforms are cleaned by the hotel. You must turn in your soiled uniform to Housekeeping in order to get a clean one. Uniforms are not to be worn outside the hotel.

GUESTS

GUEST PROPERTY — Protect the property of guests against loss, theft or damage. Frequently, guests or patrons of the hotel misplace or forget personal items. If such items are found, you are to turn them into the LOST & FOUND department immediately which is located in the Housekeeping department. If Housekeeping is closed, turn them over to the timekeeper. If not claimed within a reasonable period of time, they will become the property of the finder.

Failure to turn in lost articles could result in dismissal.

YOU AND THE GUEST — Everyone enjoys privacy. Do not give out information about a hotel guest. Be especially careful about divulging names or room numbers of one guest to another. As an employee, you are in a position to observe the personal lives of many people. It is mandatory that you refrain from discussing your observations either within or outside the hotel.

You are in a position of trust — do not betray it.

GUEST CONTACT — "PEOPLE MAKE THE DIFFERENCE". You represent the Washington Plaza Hotel. When a guest checks out he/she will remember not only the room but also the type of service he or she received.

Your attitude when dealing with our guests and your co-workers should always be one of friendliness and courtesy. Always have a smile, a "WELCOME TO THE WASHINGTON PLAZA", and a "GOOD BYE, HOPE YOU ENJOYED YOUR STAY".

By treating others as you would like to be treated when visiting a hotel, you will have little difficulty maintaining the proper attitude.

Socializing with or dating guests is strictly against hotel policy.

THE DOORMAN
Sez—

"SMILE — IT INCREASES YOUR FACE VALUE".

27.

EMPLOYEES' MANUAL AGREEMENT

Please read, sign and give to Personnel Director.

I hereby acknowledge having received the Employee Reference Manual and understand that I am to familiarize myself with its contents. I agree to abide by the rules and regulations as stated in this Manual, including the Standard of Dress Code and Appearance.

DATE: _____   SIGNED: _____

(Employee's Signature)

To: All Employees of the Washington Plaza Hotel.

The management of the Washington Plaza hereby specifies its policy not to discriminate against any employee or applicant for employment because of age, race, color, sex, creed, or national origin. This policy not to discriminate in employment includes, but is not limited to the following:

* Hiring, Placement, Upgrading, Transfer, or Promotion, Recruitment, Advertising or Solicitation for Employment;
* Training During Employment;
* Rates of Pay or Other Forms of Compensation;
* Selection for Training including Apprenticeship;
* Layoff or Termination

This notice is furnished you to be certain that all employees are aware of company policy in regard to non-discrimination in employment.

Signed: _____

Date: _____

33

FRINGE BENEFIT INSURANCE CHART

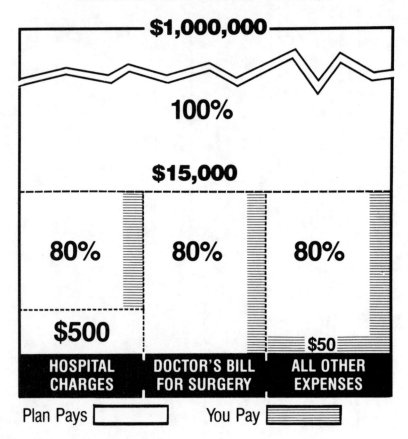

Source: Carlson Companies

APPENDIX E

Sample Equal Opportunity Law Test

CAVEAT: This test is merely an example of the kind of test which may be given supervisors. However, your attorney should draft any test for your property, and the test should be updated annually.

HOTEL
EQUAL OPPORTUNITY LAW TEST WITH ANSWERS

1. What is your hotel's general policy on equal opportunity as expressed on the application form?

This hotel is an equal opportunity employer and always strives to select the best qualified individual for the job, based upon job-related qualifications, and regardless of race, color, creed, sex, national origin, age, handicap, and any other protected groups under federal, state, or local laws.

2. True or false: Federal, state, and local Equal Opportunity Laws and regulations absolutely require your hotel to have a formal, written affirmative action plan.

False.

3. True or false: Homosexuals are not as yet protected by federal Equal Opportunity Laws.

True. However, various state and local Equal Opportunity and antidiscrimination laws do protect homosexuals. Check your local situation carefully.

4. True of false: The prohibition against religious discrimination established by Equal Opportunity Laws and cases protects atheists.*

True.

5. Which specific employment action fosters more charges of discrimination than all others?

The involuntary discharge of an employee.

6. List all types of possible unlawful discrimination raised in the following factual account:

On March 1, 1980, Gertrude Razyniwicz, a famous "dancer" at an infamous establishment in Gdansk, Poland (where the well-known Polish Institute of Marine Biology is, of course, located), applied for the position of cocktail waitress at the Hotel Waulo in Waulo, North Dakota. The Personnel Director, Malum Baroom (who is from Maseru, Lesotho), requested Gertrude to complete the application form and then to try on the uniform all cocktail waitresses were required to wear for the work in the hotel's exclusive restaurant/lounge.

This restaurant/lounge was located at the bottom of an old mine shaft twenty-seven floors down (on which the hotel was constructed) and was appropriately called the Bottom of the Waulo. The Bottom of the Waulo was world famous, since it was the source of the Hotel Waulo's greatest sales pitch, namely, that it was the deepest hotel in the world.

Additionally, the Bottom of the Waulo rotated like a giant screw and went three to four floors deeper into the ground every hour, reversing the process once the three-mile limit had been reached.

"Waulo Girls" (as they were often called) were required to do two things other than serve cocktails. They had to wear bottoms with very skimpy tops (since this was the Bottom of the Waulo); and once every shift, two Waulo Girls were required to engage in mud wrestling (or wallowing in the mud) in a ring in the center of the Bottom of the Waulo. This second requirement was imported to Waulo from Orlando, Florida—the mud-wallowing capital of midcentral Florida.

Anyway, Baroom required Gertrude to demonstrate these characteristics in order to determine whether she was the best-qualified for the job. Since Waulo Girls were required to wear skimpy tops, it was a necessary qualification that all Waulo Girls had "presentable" upper bodies which necessarily fostered a prurient interest in them on the part of the guest. Thus, the guest would buy more drinks, according to the Sales Department.

Gertrude's top was not tops in Baroom's judgment. So she was refused employment. Besides, she could not speak "American."

List the type(s) of discrimination you feel are present, if any.

NOTE: Obviously, this question is an extreme, humerous illustration of several key issues of discrimination. Satire is sometimes helpful to encourage interest.

The following types of discrimination are present in this factual situation:

a.   *The use of the term "Waulo Girls" is probably evidence of sex discrimination.*

b.   *The use of the word "girls" is probably evidence of age discrimination also.*

c.   *A policy of hiring only women as cocktail waitresses is probably also sex discrimination.*

d.   *Since there is no established "Playboy" image, it is no doubt also evidence of sex discrimination to hire women only because of alleged customer preference.*

e.   *It is probably national origin discrimination to refuse to hire an individual because she can not speak "American." Generally, the issue is whether the individual can communicate in order to adequately perform the job.*

f.   *While there is generally nothing wrong with examining prospective applicants in uniforms, again this could be evidence of sex discrimination, if only women were hired. Furthermore, it could be evidence of age discrimination if only young "girls" were hired.*

g.   *Equal Opportunity Law does not prohibit an employer from discriminating on the basis of "good looks"; unless such requirement would have the result of eliminating individuals in a protected group, e.g. sex or age discrimination.*

7.   List all types of possible unlawful discrimination raised in the following factual account:

On March 2, 1980, Strode Baunch, a third generation American Indian male and a Vietnam deserter recently pardoned by President Jimmy "the Grit" Carter after five years of self-imposed exile in a cave in the Pyrenees Mountains, applied for a job as an executive secretary to the General Manager of the hotel in Corbordello Square, a new $1 billion megastructure/complex just outside of the U.S. Marine Corps Supply Depot in Barstow, California.

The Personnel Director, Derek Yench, was not contacted, since the General Manager, Slurge Malloy, wanted to select his own secretary. However, Slurge did attempt to select the best-qualified individual based upon Slurge's experience and his required qualifications.

One of Slurge's qualifications was that his executive secretary give him a massage once a week. Obviously Slurge informed all applicants, including Storde, that there would be no hanky panky "required" during his weekly massages.

Strode was the only applicant of fifty interviewed who agreed to perform the weekly massages. Strode was happy to agree to do so, since, as he told Slurge, he had gender dysphoria and Klinefelter's syndrone and really wasn't sure whether he was a male or a female. Strode felt the weekly massages might afford him an opportunity to find his true sex. Slurge, of course, refused to hire Strode specifically, willfully, purposefully, and intentionally because he thought Strode "was a freak." Also, Slurge wanted a female secretary, since he could not believe Strode could perform all the necessary duties as adequately as a female.

What type(s) of discrimination might Strode charge?

NOTE: The question is obviously an extreme satire, again to encourage discussion of a very difficult and touchy subject.

The types of discrimination Strode might charge are as follows:

a. *Sex discrimination on the basis of his male sex. Strode should specifically charge that the hotel unlawfully refused to hire him because of his male sex.*
b. *Handicap discrimination in those states protecting mental and/or physical handicap and in any state where the hotel has a government contract or is determined to be a government contractor.*
c. *Strode should charge that the massage requirement is also evidence of sex discrimination.*

Obviously, the Personnel Director should be contacted in each situation, since the personnel professional can assist in avoiding expensive charges and lawsuits.

8. What rule (or admonition), above all others, should be followed in handling the release, discharge, or termination of employees?

Employees should never be summarily discharged but should be suspended pending investigation and then discharged only after the investigation.

9. What is the complete name of the federal agency which enforces and regulates federal Equal Opportunity Laws, and who selects its members?

United States Equal Employment Opportunity Commission and the commissioners are selected by the President, with the advice and consent of the Senate.

10. If the state or municipality in which your hotel is located has an Equal Opportunity or Fair Employment Practice Law and agency, is the federal agency allowed to investigate your policies, practices, and procedures before the local agency does?

Generally No. The EEOC must normally defer to the state or local Fair Employment Practice Agency before it investigates.

11. True or false: The federal Equal Opportunity Law Agency may not investigate your hotel unless a specific complaint has been filed.

True. The EEOC does not have the authority to conduct checks.

12. Once a lawsuit is filed in a U.S. District Court alleging that a particular hotel has discriminated against a protected group of employees in its employment practices, may the plaintiffs in that case (either private parties or the governmental agency) seek to expand the so-called class action to include all similarly situated or treated employees or former employees of all hotels and the corporation itself?

This is a possibility. There is precedent for the proposition that a class action on behalf of all individuals similarly situated may be maintained against an entire corporation which follows similar policies, practices, and procedures, where the plaintiffs in the initial lawsuit are representative of all those individuals who may be in the class. For example, a class action could be maintained against an entire corporation on behalf of all black former employees who were allegedly discharged on account of their race from hotels within a chain under similar circumstances. Accordingly, it is crucial that each hotel maintain the same standards and quality control regarding preventive law.

13. True or false: Title VII of the Civil Rights Act of 1964, as amended, prohibits job discrimination based on race, color, religion, sex, or national origin.

True.

14. True or false: The Age Discrimination in Employment Act of 1967, as amended, prohibits job discrimination based on age, but protection is limited to those who are at least forty years old and not more than seventy.

True. Note, however, some state laws do not have an upper age limitation, e.g., California.

15. True or false: There is nothing in Equal Opportunity Law that requires you to hire someone who is incapable of doing the job.

True.

16. True of false: Title VII of the Civil Rights Act of 1964, as amended, states that no employer has to give preferential treatment to any individual or group in order to meet a quota. As a matter of fact, Equal Opportunity Law requires that an individual NOT be hired because he/she is in (or not in) any protected group.

True.

17. True or false: Equal Opportunity Law allows pay differentials based upon a bona fide seniority system.

True.

18. True or false: An employer may refuse to hire an individual because he/she is not a U.S. Citizen.

False.

19. True or false: If a department head or supervisor is aware of discriminatory sexist remarks directed by men toward women employees (particularly by supervisory males against subordinate females) it is assumed that the General Manager is also aware of them.

True.

20. True or false: An employer must make reasonable attempts to accommodate the religious needs of his/her employees with regard to the Sabbath day.

True. On the other hand, if this employee cannot be replaced by an employee with substantially similar abilities and qualifications during this Sabbath day, the employer may require that the irreplacable employee work. The issue is whether the employer could prove there would be an undue hardship on the employer and that the accommodation of such employee would, therefore, be unreasonable.

21. True or false: A restaurateur may refuse to hire waitresses in his/her fine restaurant at night because it is assumed that the customer's preference is for waiters ("garcons").

False.

22. True or false: The sex of an employee is rarely a bona fide occupational qualification (BFOQ).

True. Sex is a BFOQ in the show business industry, where individuals may be hired for male and female roles specifically because of their authentic sex. However, in the hospitality and foodservice industry sex will rarely be a BFOQ. One example of where sex may be relevant would be the selection of a female security officer for the purpose of searching female employees, entering female locker rooms/restrooms, etc.

23. True or false: A hotel may refuse to hire a female because the lifting requirements make the job "too strenuous" for her.

False.

24. True or false: An employee may refuse to join a union on religious grounds and also may refuse to pay union dues and fees because of his/her religion.

True.

25. True or false: It is *not* a violation of Equal Opportunity Law to require prospective employees to have a high school diploma and pass certain aptitude tests prior to being considered.

False.

26. True or false: Typing tests and simple mathematical tests for individuals required to add and subtract are generally lawful if applied to the relevant job.

True.

27. True or false: Equal Opportunity Law generally requires that an employer keep all records on file of any employee who has filed a charge or a lawsuit against the hotel.

True. Whenever a case is pending against an employer, all relevant records in connection with that case should be maintained until the case is finally resolved.

28. True of false: It is generally lawful to consider a felony conviction within the last five years of prospective applicants and employees.

True, unless a rule against hiring convicted felons has an adverse impact on minorities AND is not job-related.

29. True or false: The Personnel Director should not be contacted prior to dismissing an employee for a serious violation of company rules, such as fighting on the job.

False. The Personnel Director or some individual responsible for the personnel function should always be contacted prior to the termination or separation of employees, regardless of the situation.

30. True or false: When an employee commits a serious violation of company policy, he/she should be summarily discharged.

False. Regardless of the offense, employees should be suspended pending an investigation prior to being finally discharged. No employee should be summarily discharged. All facts relevant to the incident should be obtained prior to discharging an employee.

APPENDIX F

**Forms—Application, Personnel Action,
and Attitude Survey**

CAVEAT: It is *not* recommended that the forms in this Appendix be reproduced indiscriminately. It *is* recommended that they be used as guides for the preparation of personnel documents which should be drafted and reviewed by your attorney. (The forms are reproduced here by permission.)

(PLEASE PRINT OR TYPE)

APPROVED BY GAO B—180541 (RO511) Expires 1-31-81	CHARGE OF DISCRIMINATION IMPORTANT: This form is affected by the Privacy Act of 1974; see Privacy Act Statement on reverse before completing it.	CHARGE NUMBER(S) (AGENCY USE ONLY) ☐ STATE/LOCAL AGENCY ☐ EEOC

Equal Employment Opportunity Commission and
_____ (State or Local Agency)

NAME (Indicate Mr., Ms. or Mrs.)	HOME TELEPHONE NUMBER (Include area code)
STREET ADDRESS	
CITY, STATE, AND ZIP CODE	COUNTY

NAMED IS THE EMPLOYER, LABOR ORGANIZATION, EMPLOYMENT AGENCY, APPRENTICESHIP COMMITTEE, STATE OR LOCAL GOVERNMENT AGENCY WHO DISCRIMINATED AGAINST ME. (If more than one list below).

NAME	TELEPHONE NUMBER (Include area code)
STREET ADDRESS CITY, STATE, AND ZIP CODE	

NAME	TELEPHONE NUMBER (Include area code)
STREET ADDRESS CITY, STATE, AND ZIP CODE	

CAUSE OF DISCRIMINATION BASED ON MY (Check appropriate box(es))

☐ RACE   ☐ COLOR   ☐ SEX   ☐ RELIGION   ☐ NATIONAL ORIGIN   ☐ OTHER (Specify)

DATE MOST RECENT OR CONTINUING DISCRIMINATION TOOK PLACE *(Month, day, and year)*

THE PARTICULARS ARE:

I will advise the agencies if I change my address or telephone number and I will cooperate fully with them in the processing of my charge in accordance with their procedures.	NOTARY — (When necessary to meet State and Local Requirements) I swear or affirm that I have read the above charge and that it is true to the best of my knowledge, information and belief. SIGNATURE OF COMPLAINANT
I declare under penalty of perjury that the foregoing is true and correct.	SUBSCRIBED AND SWORN TO BEFORE ME THIS DATE (Day, month, and year)
DATE: CHARGING PARTY (Signature)	

EEOC FORM 5B JAN. 78   PREVIOUS EDITIONS OF ALL EEOC FORM 5'S ARE OBSOLETE AND MUST NOT BE USED

CHARGE FILE COPY

NOTICE OF NON-RETALIATION REQUIREMENT

Section 704(a) of the Civil Rights Act of 1964, as amended, states:

It shall be an unlawful employment practice for an employer to discriminate against any of his employees or applicants for employment, for an employment agency to discriminate against any individual, or for a labor organization to discriminate against any member thereof or applicant for membership because he has opposed any practice made an unlawful employment practice by this title, or because he has made a charge, testified, assisted, or participated in any manner in an investigation, proceeding, or hearing under this title.

Persons filing charges of employment discrimination are advised of this Non-Retaliation Requirement and are instructed to notify the Equal Employment Opportunity Commission if any attempt at retaliation is made.

PRIVACY ACT STATEMENT

(This form is covered by the Privacy Act of 1974, Public Law 93-579 Authority for requesting and uses of the personal data are given below.)

1. FORM NUMBER/TITLE/DATE
   EEOC Form 5B, Charge of Discrimination, Jan. 78.

2. AUTHORITY
   42 USC 2000e 5(b)

3. PRINCIPAL PURPOSE(S) The purpose of the charge, whether recorded initially on Form 5B or abstracted from a letter, is to invoke the Commission's jurisdiction.

4. ROUTINE USES. This form is used to determine the existence of facts which substantiate the Commission's jurisdiction to investigate, determine, conciliate and litigate charges of unlawful employment practices. It is also used to record information sufficient to maintain contact with the Charging Party and to direct the Commission's investigatory activity. A copy of the charge will be served upon the person against whom the charge is made.

5. WHETHER DISCLOSURE IS MANDATORY OR VOLUNTARY AND EFFECT ON INDIVIDUAL FOR NOT PROVIDING INFORMATION. Charges must be in writing, signed under penalty of perjury, setting forth the facts which give rise to the charge of employment discrimination and be signed by or on behalf of a person claiming to be aggrieved. However, use of EEOC Form 5B is not mandatory. Technical defects or omissions may be cured by amendment.

HYATT HOTELS CORPORATION
9701 WEST HIGGINS ROAD
ROSEMONT, ILLINOIS 60018

EMPLOYEE ATTITUDE SURVEY

The purpose of this questionnaire is to give you a chance to state your views about your job and the Company.

PLEASE DO NOT SIGN YOUR NAME — this survey is completely confidential. Please answer every question. This is not a test; there are no "right" or "wrong" answers. Just check the box that comes closest to describing how you feel about each question. In a few places, you'll be asked to write in answers in your own words.

Be frank — write exactly what you feel. Then we'll know how well or poorly we've been doing, or where improvements may be needed. Thanks for your help.

FIRST — some questions about you — not for the purpose of identification, but merely so we can compare the answers given by different groups of our people.

THE NAME OF MY HOTEL IS:

| | | | |

(Place the three-number code of your hotel above.)

4. My job classification can be described as falling into one of three categories:
(Please check one.)

_____ Department Head and Above
_____ Food and Beverage
         (Kitchen Staff, Bar/Lounge, Restaurants and Coffee Shop employees)
_____ Rooms Department and Related Areas
         (Bell Service, Front Desk, Reservations, PBX, Personnel, Accounting, Clerical, Maintenance, Security, Housekeeping, and Garage employees)
_____ Sales, Catering and Convention Services

5. My Employee status is: (Please check one.)

_____ Full Time - Regularly work over 30 hours
_____ Park Time - Regularly work less than 30 hours

6. I have worked at Hyatt for: (Please check one.)

_____ Less than 1 year
_____ Over 1 year but less than 5 years
_____ Over 5 years

Survey Questions

7. How well do you like your present work?
    (Please check one.)   J1
    >   Very well   _____ (a)
    >   Fairly well   _____ (b)
    >   Not too well   _____ (c)
    >   Not at all   _____ (d)

8. Does your Supervisor correct your work in a helpful manner?
    (Please check one.)   S1
    >   Always   _____ (a)
    >   Most of the time   _____ (b)
    >   Sometimes too critical & not constructive   _____ (c)
    >   Always critical, in a degrading manner   _____ (d)

9. Does your supervisor pass on instructions and informaton
    to you promptly? (Please check one.)   C1
    >   Immediately   _____ (a)
    >   In ample time   _____ (b)
    >   Sometimes late   _____ (c)
    >   Usually late   _____ (d)

10. Please comment below on any suggestions you may have for
    the overall improvement of your hotel, as concerns both
    yourself and the hotel guests:
    (Please check the line at right if you make a comment.)   _____ GN

    _____

    _____

    _____

    _____

    _____

11. Do you receive praise when it is deserved?
    (Please check one.)   W1
    >   Always   _____ (a)
    >   Most of the time   _____ (b)
    >   Generally not   _____ (c)
    >   Rarely   _____ (d)

12. When you started your present job, how well did your supervisor
    or sponsor explain your job to you? (Please check one.)   T1
    >   Very well   _____ (a)
    >   Adequately   _____ (b)
    >   Not very well   _____ (c)
    >   Not at all   _____ (d)

13. Are you paid a fair amount for the work you do? (Total
    compensation) (Please check one.)   P1
    >   Generous   _____ (a)
    >   Adequate   _____ (b)
    >   Below par   _____ (c)
    >   Unreasonably low   _____ (d)

Survey Questions

14. Do you have any comments about your job or the Company?
(Please check the line at right if you make a comment.) _____ JN

_____

_____

_____

15. When openings occur in your department, are the best qualified
people chosen for promotion? (Please check one.) A1
Always _____ (a)
Usually _____ (b)
Generally not _____ (c)
Rarely _____ (d)

16. Hyatt Profit Sharing Plan. (Please check one.) B1
I'm a member. _____ (a)
When eligible, I will join. _____ (b)
I'm eligible, but haven't been asked to join. _____ (c)
I'm eligible, but I'm not planning to join. _____ (d)

17. If you have discussed your progress with your supervisor, do
you feel the discussion has helped you develop to be a better
employee? (Please check one.) R1
Yes, very helpful _____ (a)
Has helped some in my self-improvement _____ (b)
Has helped little in my self-improvement _____ (c)
Has not helped at all in my self-improvement _____ (d)

18. Do you have comments to make concerning your supervisor?
(Please check the line at right if you make a comment.) _____ SN

_____

_____

_____

19. The word that most describes the cleanliness of your depart-
ment or work area. (Please check one.) E1
Very satisfactory _____ (a)
Satisfactory _____ (b)
Unsatisfactory _____ (c)
Very unsatisfactory _____ (d)

20. How would you rate Hyatt as a company to work for?
(Please check one.) J2
Excellent _____ (a)
Above Average _____ (b)
Below Average _____ (c)
Poor _____ (d)

21. Does your Supervisor criticize within the hearing of others?
(Please check one.) S2
Never _____ (a)
Rarely _____ (b)
Sometimes _____ (c)
Frequently _____ (d)

Survey Questions

22. Do you have any comments to make concerning Hyatt's interest
    in the welfare of its employees? (Please check the box at right
    if you make a comment.)   _____ WN

    _____

    _____

    _____

23. Do you receive conflicting instructions from your supervisor
    and others? (Please check one.)   C2
        Never   _____ (a)
        Rarely   _____ (b)
        Sometimes   _____ (c)
        Frequently   _____ (d)

24. Do you receive credit for your suggestions? (Please check one.)   W2
        Always   _____ (a)
        Most of the time   _____ (b)
        Generally not   _____ (c)
        Rarely   _____ (d)

25. I have received salary increases without asking for them.
    (Please check one.)   P2
        Frequently   _____ (a)
        Occasionally   _____ (b)
        Seldom   _____ (c)
        Never   _____ (d)

26. Do you have any comments to make about the training opportu-
    nities available in your hotel? (Please check the line at right
    if you make a comment.)   _____ TN

    _____

    _____

    _____

    _____

27. Does the Department Manager do enough to help people prepare
    themselves for advancement? (Please check one.)   A2
        Very helpful   _____ (a)
        Enough is done   _____ (b)
        Not enough is done   _____ (c)
        I don't know   _____ (d)

28. How was the Profit Sharing Plan explained to you when you
    became eligible for it? (Please check one.)   B2
        Very well   _____ (a)
        Fairly well   _____ (b)
        Not so well   _____ (c)
        Not at all   _____ (d)

Survey Questions   **Page 5**

29. When was the last time you discussed your progress with a
supervisor? (Please check one.)   R2
        Within the past 6 months   _____ (a)
        Within the past 6-12 months   _____ (b)
        Over 1 year ago   _____ (c)
        Over 2 years ago   _____ (d)

30. Do you have any comments about the pay policy of your hotel?
(Please check the line at right if you make a comment.)   _____ PN

_____

_____

_____

31. The word that best describes the cleanliness of the restrooms
employees use. (Please check one.)   E2
        Very satisfactory   _____ (a)
        Satisfactory   _____ (b)
        Unsatisfactory   _____ (c)
        Very unsatisfactory   _____ (d)

32. My General Manager addresses me by name. (Please check one.)   M1
        Frequently   _____ (a)
        Occasionally   _____ (b)
        Seldom   _____ (c)
        Never   _____ (d)

33. When you ask your supervisor a question, do you generally
get a satisfactory answer? (Please check one.)   S3
        Always   _____ (a)
        Most of the time   _____ (b)
        Generally not   _____ (c)
        Rarely   _____ (d)

34. Do you have any comments to make concerning your supervisor's
appraisals? (Please check the line at right if you make a comment.)   _____ RN

_____

_____

_____

35. How well informed do you generally feel about the Hyatt
Corporate office? (Please check one.)   C3
        Extremely well informed   _____ (a)
        Fairly well informed   _____ (b)
        Not too well informed   _____ (c)
        Not at all informed   _____ (d)

36. How interested do you think Hyatt Management is in the welfare
of its employees? (Please check one.)   W3
        Very interested   _____ (a)
        Interested   _____ (b)
        Not very interested   _____ (c)
        Not interested at all   _____ (d)

Survey Questions

37. How long ago did you receive your last pay increase?
    (Please check one.)   P3
                    Within the last year   _____ (a)
                    Within the past 1-2 years   _____ (b)
                    Within the past 2-5 years   _____ (c)
                    Never   _____ (d)

38. My overall feeling about my General Manager is:
    (Please check the line at right if you make a comment.)   _____ MN

    _____

    _____

    _____

39. If you receive a Profit Sharing Annual Statement, has any member
    of Management ever explained it to you? (Please check one.)   B3
                    Explained to me fully   _____ (a)
                    Adequately explained   _____ (b)
                    Partially explained   _____ (c)
                    Never explained   _____ (d)

40. The word that best describes the ventilation in your work area:
    (Please check one.)   E3
                    Very satisfactory   _____ (a)
                    Satisfactory   _____ (b)
                    Unsatisfactory   _____ (c)
                    Very unsatisfactory   _____ (d)

41. I have had the opportunity to talk with my General Manager:
    (Please check one.)   M2
                    Frequently   _____ (a)
                    Occasionally   _____ (b)
                    Seldom   _____ (c)
                    Never   _____ (d)

42. Do you feel free to discuss problems with your supervisor?
    (Please check one.)   S4
                    Definitely   _____ (a)
                    Generally   _____ (b)
                    Generally not   _____ (c)
                    Definitely not   _____ (d)

43. Do you feel that employees are treated fairly in your
    department? (Please check one.)   W4
                    Always   _____ (a)
                    Most of the time   _____ (b)
                    Generally not   _____ (c)
                    Rarely   _____ (d)

44. The word that best describes the lighting in your work area:
    (Please check one.)   E4
                    Very satisfactory   _____ (a)
                    Satisfactory   _____ (b)
                    Unsatisfactory   _____ (c)
                    Very unsatisfactory   _____ (d)

Survey Questions

45. My General Manager visits and observes my work place:
(Please check one.)   M3
        Frequently   _____ (a)
        Occasionally   _____ (b)
        Seldom   _____ (c)
        Never   _____ (d)

46. Does your supervisor consider your personal feelings?
(Please check one.)   S5
        Always   _____ (a)
        Usually   _____ (b)
        Generally not   _____ (c)
        Rarely   _____ (d)

47. I have attended general employee meetings conducted by my
General Manager: (Please check one.)   M4
        Within the last 6 months   _____ (a)
        Within the past 6-12 months   _____ (b)
        Within the past 1-2 years   _____ (c)
        Never   _____ (d)

48. My overall feeling about my Executive Assistant Manager-Rooms is:
(Please check the line at right if you make a comment.)   _____ MN1

_____

_____

_____

49. My overall feeling about my Food and Beverage Director is:
(Please check the line at right if you make a comment.)   _____ MN2

_____

_____

_____

50. My overall feeling about my Executive Chef is:
(Please check the line at right if you make a comment.)   _____ MN3

_____

_____

_____

51. My overall feeling about my Sales Director is:
(Please check the line at right if you make a comment.)   _____ MN4

_____

_____

_____

Survey Questions   **Page 8**

52. My overall feeling about my Controller is:
    (Please check the line at right if you make a comment.)   _____ MN5

    _____

    _____

    _____

53. My overall feeling about my Chief Engineer is:
    (Please check the line at right if you make a comment.)   _____ MN6

    _____

    _____

    _____

54. My overall feeling about my Personnel Director is:
    (Please check the line at right if you make a comment.)   _____ MN7

    _____

    _____

    _____

55. Feel free to comment on your overall feelings about any other
    Department Head in the hotel. (Please check the line at right if
    you make a comment.)   _____ MN8

    Title of Department Head: _____

    Comments: _____

    _____

    _____

    _____

EMPLOYMENT APPLICATION

Carlson Companies are equal opportunity employers. and always endeavor to employ the best qualified individual for the job based upon job-related qualifications and regardless of race. color. creed. sex. national origin. age. handicap or other protected group.

PERSONAL

Date _____

Name _____
       Last   First   Middle Initial

Social Security No. _____

Present address _____
     No   Street   City   State   Zip

How many years have you lived at this address? _____   Telephone No. (   ) _____

Position applied for _____   Earnings expected $ _____

Are you willing to relocate?   Yes ☐   No ☐   Geographical area preferred _____

Do you want to work   ☐ Full-time or   ☐ Part-time.   Specify days and hours if part-time _____

Have you worked for us before? _____   If yes, when? _____

Under what name? _____

How did you learn of this position? _____

_____

If hired, on what date will you be available to start work? _____

If hired, do you have a reliable means of transportation to get to work? _____

Have you ever been refused a fidelity bond?   Yes ☐   No ☐

Are you at least eighteen (18) years of age?   ☐ Yes   ☐ No

Are you a United States Citizen?   ☐ Yes   ☐ No

Have you ever been convicted of a felony within the last five (5) years?   ☐ Yes   ☐ No

Person to be notified in case of accident or emergency
Name _____
Address _____ Phone Number _____

EDUCATION AND TRAINING: *Note: Carlson Companies do not require specific educational levels for employment.*

NAME OF SCHOOL AND LOCATION	CIRCLE LAST YEAR COMPLETED	DID YOU GRADUATE	DEGREE RECEIVED	LAST YEAR ATT'D.	MAJOR SUBJECTS STUDIED	ADVISOR
HIGH SCHOOL NAME ADDRESS	1 2 3 4	YES NO □ □			☐ GENERAL ☐ COMMERCIAL ☐ COLL PREP. ☐ _____	
COLLEGE NAME ADDRESS	1 2 3 4	□ □			MAJOR MINOR	
GRADUATE SCHOOL NAME ADDRESS	1 2 3 4	□ □			MAJOR MINOR	
BUSINESS COLLEGE NAME ADDRESS	1 2 3 4	□ □			MAJOR MINOR	
TRADE SCHOOL NAME ADDRESS	1 2 3 4	□ □			MAJOR MINOR	

LIST YOUR SPECIFIC JOB SKILLS AND MACHINES OR EQUIPMENT YOU CAN OPERATE

MILITARY SERVICE RECORD - United States Only

Have you ever served in the armed forces? ☐ Yes ☐ No If yes, what branch?_____

Dates of duty: From_____ To _____ Rank at Discharge _____

What were your duties in the service (include special training and duty station)?_____

_____

PERSONAL REFERENCES (Exclude Former Employers or Relatives)

Name and Occupation	Address	Phone Number
1.		
2.		
3.		

PRIOR WORK HISTORY (LIST IN ORDER, LAST OR PRESENT EMPLOYER FIRST
ATTACH ADDITIONAL SHEET IF NECESSARY)

DATES		NAME AND ADDRESS	RATE OF PAY		SUPERVISOR'S NAME	REASON FOR
From	To	OF EMPLOYER	Start	Finish	AND TITLE	LEAVING

YOUR TITLE _____ DESCRIBE IN DETAIL THE WORK YOU DID _____
_____
_____

DATES		NAME AND ADDRESS	RATE OF PAY		SUPERVISOR'S NAME	REASON FOR
From	To	OF EMPLOYER	Start	Finish	AND TITLE	LEAVING

YOUR TITLE _____ DESCRIBE IN DETAIL THE WORK YOU DID _____
_____
_____

DATES		NAME AND ADDRESS	RATE OF PAY		SUPERVISOR'S NAME	REASON FOR
From	To	OF EMPLOYER	Start	Finish	AND TITLE	LEAVING

YOUR TITLE _____ DESCRIBE IN DETAIL THE WORK YOU DID _____
_____
_____

DATES		NAME AND ADDRESS	RATE OF PAY		SUPERVISOR'S NAME	REASON FOR
From	To.	OF EMPLOYER	Start	Finish	AND TITLE	LEAVING

YOUR TITLE _____ DESCRIBE IN DETAIL THE WORK YOU DID _____
_____
_____

May we contact the employers listed above? _____ If not, indicate below which one(s) you do not wish us

to contact _____

SUMMARY

Occasionally the form of an application blank makes it difficult for an individual to adequately summarize his her complete background. To assist in finding the proper position for you, use the space below to summarize any additional information necessary to describe your full qualifications.

Thank you for completing this application form and for your interest in employment with us. We would like to assure you that your opportunity for employment will be based only on your ability and on no other consideration.

PLEASE READ CAREFULLY
APPLICANT'S CERTIFICATION AND AGREEMENT

I certify that the facts set forth in this Employment Application are true and complete to the best of my knowledge. I understand that if I am employed, falsified statements on this application shall be considered sufficient cause for dismissal. You are hereby authorized to make any investigation of my personal history and financial and credit record through any investigative or credit agencies or bureaus of your choice. However, I will be advised if an investigative report is obtained, and my financial and credit record will not be used as a basis for not employing me.

Date _____ Signature of Applicant _____

DO NOT WRITE BELOW THIS LINE

INTERVIEW ▢ YES ▢ NO Date_____ Hour_____

Result of Interview:_____

Date of offer_____ Starting Date _____ Starting Rate _____Shift ____

Job Title _____ Dept. _____

Interviewed by_____Employed by _____

Approved by _____

124-150(6/78)

O M N I
INTERNATIONAL HOTELS, INC.

POSITION DESIRED

1. _____
2. _____
3. _____

Employment Application

APPLICATIONS WILL BE KEPT IN OUR ACTIVE FILES FOR SIX MONTHS

OMNI INTERNATIONAL HOTELS, INC. is an equal opportunity employer and selects the best qualified applicant for the job based upon job related qualifications, without regard to an applicant's race, color, creed, sex, national origin, age or handicap.

In order that your application may be properly evaluated it is essential that all of the following questions be answered carefully and completely. If you need more space for your answers, please attach a separate sheet. Feel free to add any additional information which will help us in placing you where you are best qualified.

Name _____
Last

First

Middle

Date _____

F—PSNL—2(6/78)

OMNI INTERNATIONAL HOTELS, INC

APPLICATION FOR EMPLOYMENT

PERSONAL

Print Name:	Last	First	Middle	Maiden	Social Sec. No.

Present Address:	Street	City	State	Zip	Telephone

Have you ever used another name? _____ If so, list other names: _____

Have you ever used another Social Security number? _____ If so, list other numbers: _____

Have you ever been refused bonding? _____ Are you willing to be bonded? _____

Are you at least 18 years old? _____ When did you last draw Workmen's Compensation? _____

When did you last draw Unemployment Compensation? _____

Notify in emergency: _____
Name   Address   Telephone

Give the telephone number and name of someone who can always contact you: _____

Do you have any physical, mental, or other limitations? _____ If so, please explain _____

Are you legally authorized to work in the United States? _____ Visa number: _____

Have you ever been convicted of a felony? _____ If so, please explain _____

JOB INTEREST

POSITION DESIRED	WAGES OR SALARY DESIRED $	Per	HR. WK. MO.

WHAT OTHER POSITIONS ARE YOU QUALIFIED FOR?   DATE AVAILABLE

WHAT INTERESTED YOU IN OMNI INTERNATIONAL HOTELS?

List Names and Departments of Relatives Employed By OMNI

Have you ever been employed by OMNI International Hotels before? If Yes, Where & When?   Have you ever applied for work at OMNI? If Yes, Where & When?

TRAINING

CIRCLE HIGHEST GRADE COMPLETED:	GRADE SCHOOL 1 2 3 4 5 6 7 8	HIGH SCHOOL 9 10 11 12	COLLEGE 1 2 3 4	GRAD. SCHOOL 1 2 3 4
	NAME	LOCATION	Yr. Graduated	Class Standing
GRADE SCHOOL				
HIGH SCHOOL		COURSE-DEGREE		
COLLEGE				
GRADUATE SCHOOL				
Apprentice, Business or Vocational School				

OTHER TRAINING OR SKILLS (Hotel or Office Machines Operated, Special Courses, etc.)   SECRETARIAL: Typing _____ wpm   SHORTHAND/SPEEDWRITING _____ wpm

WHAT FOREIGN LANGUAGES DO YOU SPEAK FLUENTLY?   READ   WRITE

ACTIVITIES

List High School and College activities in which you were active (e.g., social and honorary societies, class organization, athletics, etc.). Also list offices held ....

To what community, social, and professional organizations do you now belong. Also list offices held. ....

What hobbies or recreational activities do you enjoy? ....

What books, magazines, journals, etc. do you read frequently? ....

LIST MOST RECENT EMPLOYER FIRST. WE WILL CHECK REFERENCES.

EMPLOYMENT DATA:

Present Employer (or Most Recent)	Dates Worked		Duties & Responsibilities	Reason for Leaving	
	From Mo. Yr.	To Mo. Yr.			
COMPANY					
ADDRESS	POSITION TITLE				
CITY					
STATE ZIP	(AREA CODE) PHONE			SALARY	HOURS
May we contact this employer? _____	Supervisor's Name and Title:				

PREVIOUS EMPLOYER	Dates Worked		Duties & Responsibilities	Reason for Leaving	
	From Mo. Yr.	To Mo. Yr.			
COMPANY					
ADDRESS	POSITION TITLE				
CITY					
STATE ZIP	(AREA CODE) PHONE			SALARY	HOURS
May we contact this employer? _____	Supervisor's Name and Title:				

PREVIOUS EMPLOYER	Dates Worked		Duties & Responsibilities	Reason for Leaving	
	From Mo. Yr.	To Mo. Yr.			
COMPANY					
ADDRESS	POSITION TITLE				
CITY					
STATE ZIP	(AREA CODE) PHONE			SALARY	HOURS
May we contact this employer? _____	Supervisor's Name and Title:				

PREVIOUS EMPLOYER	Dates Worked		Duties & Responsibilities	Reason for Leaving	
	From Mo. Yr.	To Mo. Yr.			
COMPANY					
ADDRESS	POSITION TITLE				
CITY					
STATE ZIP	(AREA CODE) PHONE			SALARY	HOURS
May we contact this employer? _____	Supervisor's Name and Title:				

ADDITIONAL EXPERIENCE	State what you did in any periods nor already covered including part-time, temporary or self employment. Additional sheets may be attached if necessary
Dates	

MEDICAL HISTORY

When did you last see a physician? _____ For what reason? _____

Number of days you have been absent from work in the last year due to illness: _____

Do you have, or have you ever had, any communicable diseases? (catching diseases) _____

_____

MILITARY

BRANCH OF U.S. SERVICE	DATE ENTERED	DATE DISCHARGED	FINAL RANK	SERVICE NO.
SERVICE SCHOOLS OR SPECIAL EXPERIENCE				TYPE DISCHARGE

WORK INFORMATION

Do you want part-time or full-time work? _____ Will you work overtime? _____

Do you want permanent or temporary work? _____ Method of transportation to work _____

Do you want to work days or evenings? _____ Approximate miles to work _____

I cannot work (give days): _____ I cannot work the following shifts: 7–3 ☐   3–11 ☐   11–7 ☐

Uniform information: Height _____   Weight _____   Uniform Size _____

IMPORTANT: READ CAREFULLY. I understand and agree that any agreement entered into between Omni International Hotels, Inc. acting as agent for the owner and me is predicted upon the truthfulness and accuracy of the statements contained herein and, unless otherwise stated in written agreement, employment is terminable at the will of the Omni International Hotel. In making this application for employment I also understand that an investigative report may be made where information is obtained through interviews with former employers, or others with whom I am acquainted. I understand that I have the right to make a written request within a reasonable period of time to receive additional detailed information about the nature and scope of this investigative report. Furthermore, I agree that upon termination of my employment any accounts which I owe Omni International Hotel may, at the discretion of Omni International Hotel, be withheld from my final salary or wages.

PRE-EMPLOYMENT POLICE RECORD CHECK

AUTHORIZATION

I, do hereby authorize the Omni International Hotel to request the CRIME INFORMATION CENTER, any information available on their records.

I understand that the information requested may be used in considering my application for employment.

I have read and understand the above AUTHORIZATION for Pre-employment Police Record Check.

Please Sign Here _____
                                                    SIGNATURE

Date Completed _____

— FOR OMNI USE —

POSITION	DEPT.	HIRED BY: _____
RATE:	PER	(Dept. Head Signature & Date)
DATE TO START		

PERSONNEL COMMENTS:. . . . .

. . . .

. . . . Signed: _____ Date: _____

DEPARTMENT HEAD COMMENTS: . . . .

. . . .

. . . .

. . . .

. . . . Signed: _____ Date: _____

HYATT CORPORATION AN EQUAL OPPORTUNITY EMPLOYER
EXECUTIVE OFFICES: 9701 WEST HIGGINS ROAD, ROSEMONT, ILLINOIS 60018 • PHONE (312) 399-2100

NAME OF PROPERTY _____

Print or Type

NAME			POSITION DESIRED	
STREET ADDRESS			SALARY DESIRED	DATE AVAILABLE FOR WORK
CITY	STATE	ZIP	SOCIAL SECURITY NUMBER	
PHONE • HOME	WORK		ARE THERE ANY DAYS OF THE WEEK THAT YOU WILL NOT BE ABLE TO WORK? REASON:	

IF YOU HAVE WORKED FOR HYATT BEFORE, STATE WHERE, WHEN, FINAL POSITION, REASON LEFT:

WORK EXPERIENCE

List your previous experience beginning with your most recent position.

1
EMPLOYER	
ADDRESS	PHONE
STARTING POSITION	STARTING SALARY
LAST POSITION	FINAL SALARY
DATES EMPLOYED FROM TO	IMMEDIATE SUPERVISOR
DUTIES	
REASON FOR LEAVING	

2
EMPLOYER	
ADDRESS	PHONE
STARTING POSITION	STARTING SALARY
LAST POSITION	FINAL SALARY
DATES EMPLOYED FROM TO	IMMEDIATE SUPERVISOR
DUTIES	
REASON FOR LEAVING	

3
EMPLOYER	
ADDRESS	PHONE
STARTING POSITION	STARTING SALARY
LAST POSITION	FINAL SALARY
DATES EMPLOYED FROM TO	IMMEDIATE SUPERVISOR
DUTIES	
REASON FOR LEAVING	

4
EMPLOYER	
ADDRESS	PHONE
STARTING POSITION	STARTING SALARY
LAST POSITION	FINAL SALARY
DATES EMPLOYED FROM TO	IMMEDIATE SUPERVISOR
DUTIES	
REASON FOR LEAVING	

O *Please circle the name of any employer or supervisor whom you do not want contacted at this time.*

EDUCATION

SCHOOL	LOCATION	DATES	GRADUATED	MAJOR
HIGH SCHOOL				
COLLEGE				
ADDITIONAL TRAINING				

WHICH LANGUAGES OTHER THAN ENGLISH DO YOU SPEAK FLUENTLY?

IF JOB RELATED: TYPING SPEED _____ WPM   OTHER BUSINESS MACHINES OPERATED _____
STENO SPEED _____ WPM

REFERRED TO
RESULTS
DATE INTERVIEWED   INTERVIEWED BY

WALLER PRESS REV. 1-78

WHO REFERRED YOU TO HYATT? (IF A SPECIFIC AGENCY OR ORGANIZATION, PLEASE GIVE FULL NAME):

LIST NAMES AND POSITIONS OF ANY RELATIVES EMPLOYED IN THIS PROPERTY OR WITH HYATT:

WHY ARE YOU INTERLSTED IN WORKING FOR HYATT, AND WHAT ARE YOUR CAREER OBJECTIVES?

CITIZENSHIP

ARE YOU A U.S. CITIZEN? ☐ YES ☐ NO   IF NO, ALIEN REGISTRATION CARD NO. _____

DO YOU HAVE THE LEGAL RIGHT TO WORK IN THIS COUNTRY? ☐ YES ☐ NO   HAVE YOU EVER BEEN CONVICTED OF A FELONY? ☐ YES ☐ NO

IF YES, STATE DETAILS AND DATES: _____

MILITARY SERVICE

HAVE YOU EVER SERVED IN THE UNITED STATES ARMED FORCES? ☐ YES ☐ NO   WHICH BRANCH? _____

FROM _____ TO _____ RESERVE STATUS _____

INDICATE ANY SPECIAL TRAINING RECEIVED:

MEDICAL HISTORY

ARE YOU AT LEAST 18 YEARS OF AGE? ☐ YES ☐ NO
ARE YOU AT LEAST 21 YEARS OF AGE? ☐ YES ☐ NO

NUMBER OF DAYS YOU HAVE BEEN ABSENT FROM WORK IN LAST YEAR DUE TO ILLNESS

WHEN DID YOU LAST SEE A PHYSICIAN?   FOR WHAT REASON?

DO YOU HAVE ANY PHYSICAL DEFICIENCIES WHICH PRECLUDE YOUR PERFORMING CERTAIN KINDS OF WORK? ☐ YES ☐ NO   IF YES, DESCRIBE

SUCH DEFICIENCIES AND SPECIFIC WORK LIMITATIONS:_____

PERSON TO NOTIFY IN CASE OF EMERGENCY: NAME _____

STREET ADDRESS _____ CITY _____ STATE _____ PHONE NO. _____

BUSINESS REFERENCES

PLEASE LIST 3 OR 4 BUSINESS REFERENCES:

NAME	POSITION & COMPANY	CURRENT ADDRESS	TELEPHONE

PLEASE READ THE FOLLOWING AND SIGN YOUR NAME BELOW . . .

I declare my answers to the questions on this application are true and give this Company the right to investigate all references and information given. I agree that any false statement or misrepresentation on this application will be cause for refusal to hire or for immediate dismissal. I agree that my employment may be terminated by this Company at any time without liability for wages or salary except such as may have been earned at the date of such termination. If requested by the management at any time, I agree to submit to search of my person or of any locker that may be assigned to me, and I hereby waive all claims for damages on account of such examination. I authorize any physician or hospital to release any information which may be necessary to determine my ability to perform the duties of a job I am being considered for prior to employment or in the future during my employment with Hyatt.

Hyatt is an equal opportunity employer, and always selects the best qualified individual for the job based upon job-related qualifications, regardless of race, color, creed, sex, national origin, age, or handicap.

DATE _____ SIGNATURE _____

PERSONNEL ACTION FORM

Carlson Companies Inc.

| SUBMIT COPIES 1, 2, 3, 4 | RETAIN COPY 5 |

OFFICE USE ONLY

IMPORTANT — THIS SECTION MUST BE COMPLETED FOR ALL TYPES OF ACTION

EMPLOYEE'S NAME

DATE OF REQUEST   /   /

SOCIAL SECURITY NO. [ ][ ][ ] — [ ][ ] — [ ][ ][ ][ ]

CURRENT LEVEL

EMPLOYMENT DATE   /   /

CURRENT TITLE

CURRENT DEPARTMENT

CURRENT STATUS ☐ FT. ☐ PERM. ☐ PT. ☐ TEMP.

REASON(S) FOR ACTION (Please Check)
- TRANSFER ☐ COMPLETE SECTION 1
- EARNINGS CHANGE ☐ COMPLETE SECTION 2
- STATUS CHANGE ☐ COMPLETE SECTION 3
- LEAVE OF ABSENCE ☐ COMPLETE SECTION 4
- TERMINATION ☐ COMPLETE SECTION 5
- ADDITION ☐ COMPLETE SECTION 6

SECTION 1   TRANSFER

- PROMOTION ☐
- JOB UPGRADE ☐
- LATERAL ☐
- DEMOTION ☐

NEW TITLE

NEW LEVEL

NEW DEPARTMENT

DEPT. NUMBER

EFFECTIVE DATE   /   /

REPLACING

SECTION 2   EARNINGS CHANGE

(DO NOT COMMUNICATE CHANGE TO EMPLOYEE UNTIL APPROVED COPY IS RETURNED)

- MERIT ☐
- PROMOTION ☐
- STRUCTURE CHANGE ☐
- DEMOTION ☐

FROM $ TO $ PER

AMOUNT OF CHANGE $ PERCENT OF CHANGE   %

EFFECTIVE DATE   /   /   W&S APPROVAL   /   /

DATE OF MOST RECENT PERFORMANCE REVIEW   /   /

LAST CHANGE $ EFFECTIVE   /   /   %

OFFICE USE ONLY	PERIOD	HOURLY 1	HOURLY 2

SECTION 3   STATUS CHANGE

FROM			TO	
EXEMPT	NON-EXEMPT (TIME CLOCK)		EXEMPT	NON-EXEMPT (TIME CLOCK)
☐	☐	REGULAR FULL-TIME	☐	☐
☐	☐	REGULAR PART-TIME	☐	☐
☐	☐	TEMPORARY FULL-TIME	☐	☐
☐	☐	TEMPORARY PART-TIME	☐	☐

FROM _____ HOURS PER WEEK TO _____ HRS. PER WEEK

SECTION 5   TERMINATION

☐ RESIGNED   ☐ RELEASED

REASON:

LAST DAY WORKED   /   /   REHIRE

	ATTACHED	NOT APPLICABLE	CHARGES DUE
INVENTORY RECORD	☐	☐	☐
DEPARTMENT CHECK OFF LIST	☐	☐	☐

VACATION HOURS DUE	SEPARATION HOURS DUE	CHARGES DUE $

TERMINATION HANDLED BY   PERSONNEL

EMPLOYEE'S SIGNATURE

EMPLOYEE'S PERMANENT MAILING ADDRESS

SECTION 4   LEAVE OF ABSENCE

FROM   /   /   TO   /   /

EXTEND TO   /   /

REASON:

RETURNED TO WORK   /   /

SECTION 6   ADDITION

☐ REPLACEMENT NEEDED   ☐ NEW POSITION   ☐ PROPERLY APPROVED POSITION DESCRIPTION IS ATTACHED

DATE NEEDED   /   /   REPLACING

SPECIAL REQUIREMENTS:

APPROVALS

COMMENTS:

1. _____ (IMMEDIATE SUPERVISOR)

2. _____ (2ND LEVEL SUPERVISOR)

3. _____

4. _____ (PERSONNEL)

124-014 (8-73)

| SUBMIT COPIES 1, 2, 3, 4 | RETAIN COPY 5 |

NOTICE TO GUESTS

WELCOME TO THE **XYZ HOTEL.** YOUR SAFETY IS MOST IMPORTANT TO US. PLEASE TAKE ADVANTAGE OF THE FOLLOWING:

1) SAFETY DEPOSIT VAULTS
Available at no charge at front desk. State law **relieves hotel from liability** unless deposit boxes are used.

2) DOUBLE LOCKS AND CHAINS
Please lock deadbolt and fasten chain prior to retiring. Please use peephole before answering door.

3) FIRE ESCAPES
Please familiarize yourself with diagram below. If you detect fire or smoke.

XYZ HOTEL, INC.

MANAGEMENT RESERVES THE RIGHT:

TO TERMINATE THE OCCUPANCY OF GUESTS FOR OBJECTIONABLE CONDUCT.

TO CHARGE FOR DAMAGES CAUSED BY GUESTS.

TO REFUSE SERVICE OF ALCOHOLIC BEVERAGES TO GUESTS WHO ARE INTOXICATED. PLEASE DO NOT DRINK TO EXCESS.

RESCUE	CPR:
	MOUTH TO MOUTH:
HEIMLICH:	

CHECK OUT:
GUESTS MUST HAVE KEYS TO CHECK OUT.
CHECK OUT TIME: **12:00 NOON**

GUEST COMMENTS ARE WELCOMED. PLEASE FILL OUT CARD PROVIDED.

4) PET RULES:

5) SWIMMING POOL RULES:

6) PERSONAL CHECK POLICY:

7) ICE AND VENDING MACHINES:
Located behind elevators on each floor.

8) NON-ALLERGENIC PILLOWS
Available on request at front desk.

9) PARKING GARAGE RULES:

10) FOREIGN LANGUAGE ASSISTANCE:

11) NO-SMOKING FLOORS ARE:

STATE LAWS	SUMMARY
101-1	
101-2(d)	
101-77-17	
5.50	
22.22	

IN EMERGENCY, DIAL "O"

Tell Operator your Room No. and state that it is an **EMERGENCY.** If time permits, state details.

*MAXIMUM ROOM OCCUPANCY*_____

WE HOPE YOU ENJOY YOUR STAY AND WILL RETURN SOON!

ROOM RATES	A._____ B._____ C._____

ELEVATORS

7701	7771
7702	7772
7703 ★	7773
7704	7774

7700		7770	STAIRS
ATRIUM		ATRIUM	
7705 STAIRS		7775 ▲ STAIRS	

★ YOUR ROOM
▲ NEAREST FIRE EXIT
IN CASE OF FIRE, DO **NOT** USE ELEVATORS— USE STAIRS NEAREST ROOM WHEN ALARM BELL RINGS.
PLEASE **DO NOT SMOKE** WHILE IN BED OR IF DROWSY.

About the Author

A prominent labor lawyer, author, and lecturer, with the law firm of Stokes, Lazarus & Stokes, Arch Stokes received the Doctor of Law Degree from Emory University where he was managing editor of the *Law Journal* and chairman of the Southern Law Review Conference.

As a trial lawyer, judge, and labor lawyer in the Marine Corps, Mr. Stokes tried many cases and negotiated contracts.

He is an authority on Labor and Employee Relations Laws as they affect hospitality, foodservice, and public assembly facilities, institutions, and associations. Having worked since his youth in various jobs in hotels, restaurants, and hospitals, Arch Stokes is familiar with the practical, as well as the legal problems involved.

He represents management in labor litigation, collective bargaining negotiations, discrimination lawsuits, wage and hour cases, union campaigns, and job safety and health cases.

Mr. Stokes is a member of the Labor Relations Law and Litigation Sections of the American Bar Association, and is listed in various *WHO'S WHO* books. He is also in Union Internationale des Avocats and Confrérie de la Chaine des Rotisseurs.